M000271819

PÂTISSERIE AT HOME

PÂTISSERIE AT HOME

MÉLANIE DUPUIS
PÂTISSERIE & INSTRUCTIONS

PHOTOGRAPHY BY PIERRE JAVELLE
ILLUSTRATIONS BY YANNIS VAROUTSIKOS
SCIENTIFIC EXPLANATIONS BY ANNE CAZOR
STYLING BY ORATHAY SOUKSISAVANH

HARPER
DESIGN
An Imprint of HarperCollinsPublishers

CONTENTS

HOW TO USE THIS BOOK

BASE RECIPES

Discover all the basic pâtisserie recipes, categorized
as pastries, creams, frostings, decorations and sauces.
For each base: a diagram and explanations regarding
the special characteristics of the mixture.

PASTRIES

Put the base recipes to work to construct cakes and desserts.
For each recipe: cross-references to the base recipes, a diagram
to understand the composition of the gâteau and step-by-step
photos to create the different elements and their assembly.

ILLUSTRATED GLOSSARY

To enrich your knowledge regarding the usage of products and
to explain the main techniques with illustrations.

CHAPTER 1
BASE RECIPES FOR PÂTISSERIE

SWEET
PIE CRUST

Understand

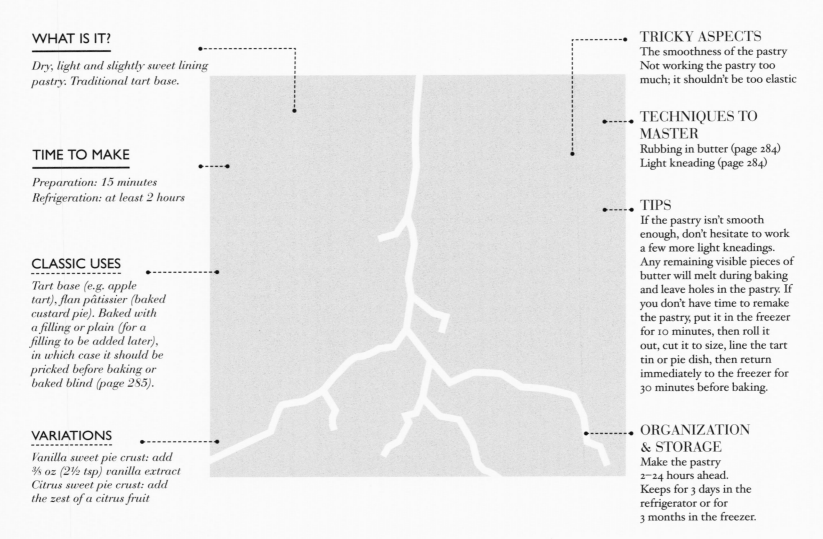

WHAT IS IT?

Dry, light and slightly sweet lining pastry. Traditional tart base.

TIME TO MAKE

Preparation: 15 minutes
Refrigeration: at least 2 hours

CLASSIC USES

Tart base (e.g. apple tart), flan pâtissier (baked custard pie). Baked with a filling or plain (for a filling to be added later), in which case it should be pricked before baking or baked blind (page 285).

VARIATIONS

Vanilla sweet pie crust: add ⅜ oz (2½ tsp) vanilla extract
Citrus sweet pie crust: add the zest of a citrus fruit

TRICKY ASPECTS

The smoothness of the pastry
Not working the pastry too much; it shouldn't be too elastic

TECHNIQUES TO MASTER

Rubbing in butter (page 284)
Light kneading (page 284)

TIPS

If the pastry isn't smooth enough, don't hesitate to work a few more light kneadings. Any remaining visible pieces of butter will melt during baking and leave holes in the pastry. If you don't have time to remake the pastry, put it in the freezer for 10 minutes, then roll it out, cut it to size, line the tart tin or pie dish, then return immediately to the freezer for 30 minutes before baking.

ORGANIZATION & STORAGE

Make the pastry 2–24 hours ahead. Keeps for 3 days in the refrigerator or for 3 months in the freezer.

HOW CAN THE PASTRY BIND TOGETHER BUT BE CRUMBLY AT THE SAME TIME?

Shortcrust pastry doesn't contain whole eggs, but the kneading coats the flour grains in fat; this means they don't stick together, which prevents the pastry having a uniform hard layer after baking. During cooking, the starch grains in the flour swell while the butter melts and joins all the grains together. The butter therefore serves as a sort of glue, and it's this binding that creates the crumbly texture.

TO MAKE 1 × 9½ IN ROUND BASE OR 8 × 3¼ IN ROUND BASES

7 oz (about 1.6 cups) all-purpose flour
3½ oz (7 tbsp) cold butter, cut into small cubes
1¾ oz (3½ tbsp) water
1/32 oz salt (⅓ tbsp)
⅞ oz (2 tbsp) superfine sugar
½ oz egg yolk (about 1 yolk)

1 Make a mound of the flour with a well in the middle and place the butter in the well.

2 Rub the butter into the flour using your fingers (page 284) until the mixture resembles breadcrumbs.

3 Add the water, salt, sugar and egg yolk. Mix into a dough using your fingers.

4 Knead lightly (page 284) by flattening the dough twice using the heel of your hand. Check the smoothness and knead again if necessary; there must be no visible butter remaining.

5 Press flat, wrap in plastic wrap and refrigerate for at least 2 hours, ideally overnight.

SUGAR CRUST
PASTRY

Understand

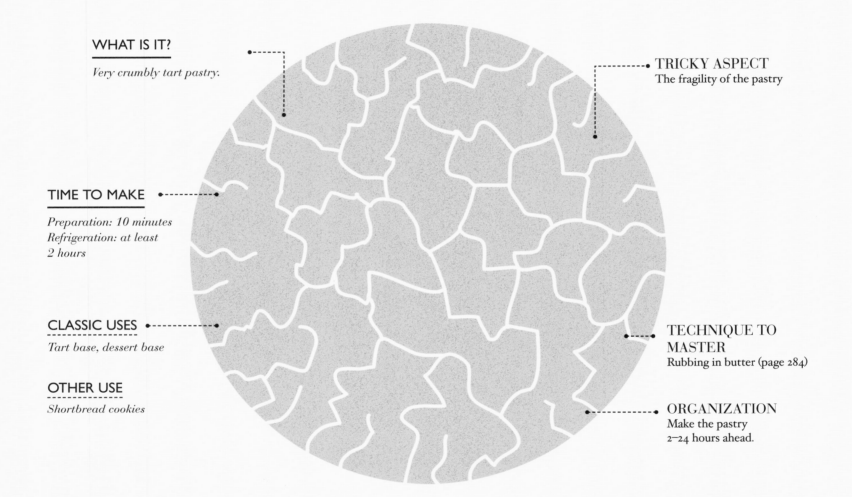

WHAT IS IT?
Very crumbly tart pastry.

TIME TO MAKE
Preparation: 10 minutes
Refrigeration: at least
2 hours

CLASSIC USES
Tart base, dessert base

OTHER USE
Shortbread cookies

TRICKY ASPECT
The fragility of the pastry

TECHNIQUE TO MASTER
Rubbing in butter (page 284)

ORGANIZATION
Make the pastry
2–24 hours ahead.

WHY IS THE PASTRY CRUMBLY AND SANDY?

The pastry is crumbly because rubbing in the butter stops too many linkages forming between the ingredients. With this technique, no network of gluten forms and the pastry doesn't become too elastic. In addition, the sugar doesn't dissolve in the fat, which means a certain quantity of sugar remains as crystals. This adds to the sandy texture of the pastry.

TO MAKE 1 × 9½ IN ROUND BASE OR 8 × 3¼ IN ROUND BASES

7 oz (about 1.6 cups) all-purpose flour
1⁄32 oz salt (⅓ tbsp)
2½ oz (5 tbsp) cold butter, cut into small cubes
2½ oz (about .6 cup) confectioners' sugar
1¾ oz egg (1 egg)

1 Mix the flour and salt, then add the butter. Rub the butter into the flour (page 284) until the mixture resembles breadcrumbs, rubbing the whole mixture between your hands without crushing it.

2 Add the confectioners' sugar and the egg. Mix using a spatula until the dough has a uniform consistency.

3 Press flat, wrap in plastic wrap and refrigerate for at least 2 hours, ideally overnight.

SWEET CRUST
PASTRY

Understand

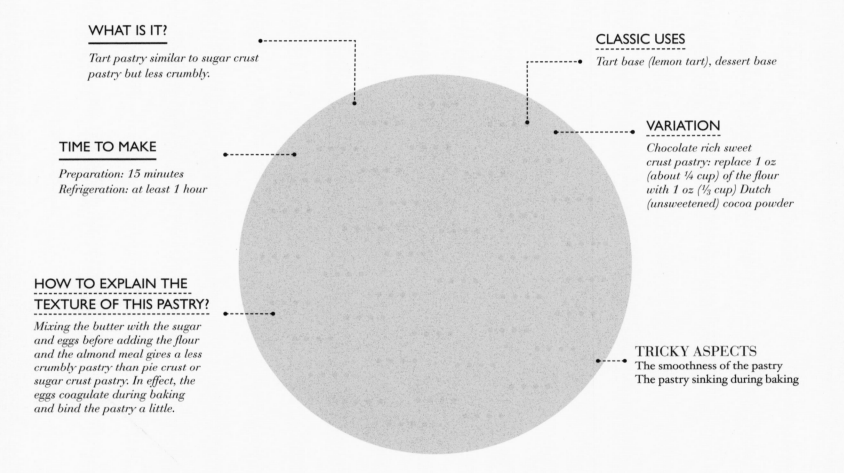

WHAT IS IT?
Tart pastry similar to sugar crust pastry but less crumbly.

TIME TO MAKE
Preparation: 15 minutes
Refrigeration: at least 1 hour

HOW TO EXPLAIN THE TEXTURE OF THIS PASTRY?
Mixing the butter with the sugar and eggs before adding the flour and the almond meal gives a less crumbly pastry than pie crust or sugar crust pastry. In effect, the eggs coagulate during baking and bind the pastry a little.

CLASSIC USES
Tart base (lemon tart), dessert base

VARIATION
Chocolate rich sweet crust pastry: replace 1 oz (about ¼ cup) of the flour with 1 oz (⅓ cup) Dutch (unsweetened) cocoa powder

TRICKY ASPECTS
The smoothness of the pastry
The pastry sinking during baking

TECHNIQUES TO MASTER
Softening butter (page 276)
Creaming butter and sugar (page 276)
Light kneading (page 284)

TIPS
If the pastry isn't smooth enough, don't hesitate to knead it for a few more turns. Any remaining visible pieces of butter will melt during baking and leave holes in the pastry.

ORGANIZATION
Make the pastry 1–24 hours ahead.

TO MAKE 1 × 9½ IN ROUND BASE OR 8 × 3¼ IN ROUND BASES

5 oz (10 tbsp) butter, softened
3½ oz (about .8 cup) confectioners' sugar
1¾ oz egg (1 egg)
1/32 oz (1/8 tsp) fine salt
9 oz (2 cups) all-purpose flour
7/8 oz (about ¼ cup) almond meal

1 Cream the butter and confectioners' sugar (page 276) using a spatula.

2 Mix in the egg and the salt.

3 Add the flour and almond meal. Mix using the spatula.

4 Knead lightly (page 284) by flattening the dough once or twice using the heel of your hand. Press flat, wrap in plastic wrap and refrigerate for at least 1 hour, ideally overnight.

PUFF
PASTRY

Understand

WHAT IS IT?

A fine and crusty pastry, rich in fat, made by inserting layers of butter in a base pastry called "détrempe," then folding repeatedly to create flakiness during baking.

TIME TO MAKE

Preparation: 1 hour 10 minutes (détrempe 10 minutes, two turns 20 minutes, two turns 20 minutes, two turns 20 minutes)
Cooking: 20–40 minutes
Refrigeration: 2–3 days

TRICKY ASPECT

Turning the pastry: the butter must not stick out, and the folds must be exactly square so that the pastry has the same number of turns all over.

TECHNIQUE TO MASTER

Making a simple turn

SPECIAL EQUIPMENT

Straight rolling pin

HOW DOES THE FLAKINESS HAPPEN?

The principle of puff pastry is to enclose the butter in the layers of pastry, so that during baking the water that evaporates from the pastry is trapped by the layer of butter and the steam makes the pastry puff up.

WHY DOES THE DÉTREMPE NEED TO BE RESTED?

When the water is mixed with the flour, the starch grains swell up. The added butter interposes itself between the swollen starch grains, and the wheat proteins form a network of gluten. During the resting period, the gluten network, greatly stretched from working the pastry, shrinks back and gives the pastry a less firm texture.

WHY DO WE ADD WHITE VINEGAR?

White vinegar is an antioxidant that stops the pastry going gray.

TIPS

Be careful not to overwork the pastry. Stop as soon as the mixture is smooth, because too much elasticity means the pastry will shrink too much when it is stretched. Always cut the pastry neatly; don't roll it into a ball. Make no more than six turns. Beyond that, the layers of pastry and butter will start to mix. When that happens, you'll be closer to shortcrust pastry than puff pastry. To remember how many turns you've made, mark the pastry with your fingertips.

CLASSIC USES

Tart base, turnover, Epiphany cake, mille-feuilles (Napoleon), pithiviers. It can be filled or cooked plain in slabs (mille-feuilles).

OTHER USE

Palmiers

DERIVATIONS

Inverse puff pastry: in controlled conditions (64°F), you can make inverse puff pastry by reversing the layers, i.e. by surrounding the détrempe in the butter. You end up with more layers of butter than pastry, and the result is even crispier. Croissant dough: a yeast pastry where the butter is incorporated in the same way as for puff pastry.

ORGANIZATION & STORAGE

Détrempe – incorporating butter +
two turns – two turns – two turns
Separate into portions, wrap
in plastic wrap and freeze
for up to 3 months.

TO MAKE 2 LB 3 OZ PASTRY

1 DÉTREMPE

1 lb 2 oz (about 4 cups) all-purpose flour
7¾ oz (about 1 cup) water
¾ oz (1½ tbsp) white vinegar
⅜ oz (1¼ tbsp) salt
2 oz (4 tbsp) butter, melted

2 LAYERING

10½ oz (1⅓ cups) butter

Making puff pastry

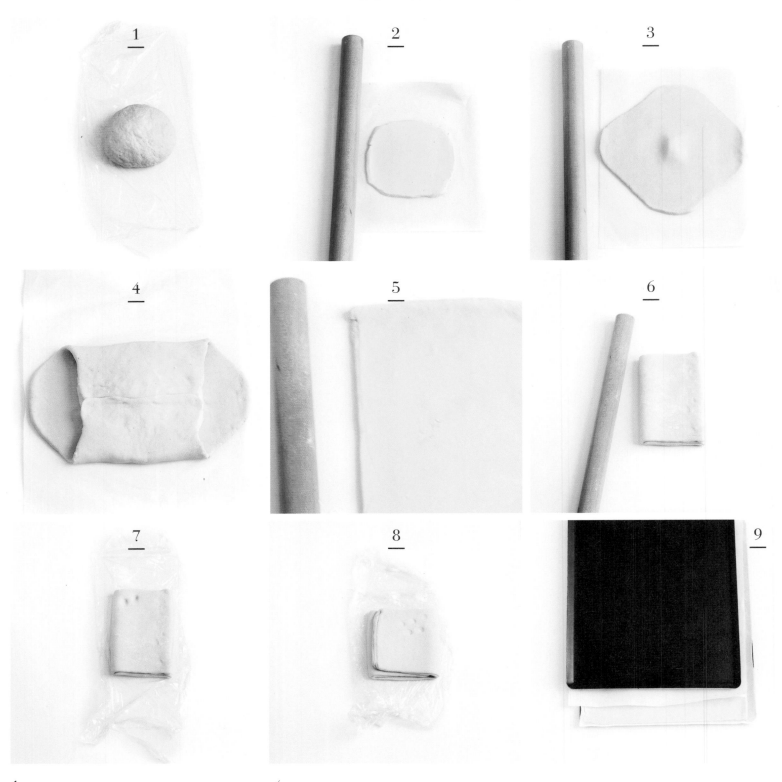

1   Make a mound with the flour on the work surface, make a well in the middle, then place the remaining détrempe ingredients in the well. Using the tips of your fingers, gradually incorporate the flour until you have a smooth dough. Wrap in plastic wrap and let the détrempe rest in the refrigerator for 2 hours: this allows the pastry to become more supple.

2   Place the 10½ oz butter between two layers of baking paper and tap on it with a rolling pin to make a block about 6 in square and ⅜ in thick. Leave the block in a cool place.

3   After 2 hours, bring the détrempe and the butter to room temperature. Wait 30 minutes before working with them. On a flour-dusted work surface, roll out the détrempe to a 14 in square. Make sure the pastry is slightly thicker in the middle of the square, like a hill, to avoid the butter coming out the bottom.

4   Place the butter in the middle of the détrempe, at a 45 degree angle. Cover the butter by folding the four corners of the détrempe toward the center. The thickness should be the same all over.

5   Make the first turn as follows. Roll out the détrempe evenly to make a rectangle. Always roll straight in front and away from you.

6   Fold this "pâton" in three, like a wallet: fold the bottom third toward the top, then turn the top third down over it. Turn the pastry 90 degrees counterclockwise. The first turn is complete.

7   If the butter hasn't pierced the détrempe, you can start the second turn. Otherwise, leave it in a cool place for 2–3 hours. Roll it out again, always rolling straight in front of you. Refold the pâton like a wallet, then turn it 90 degrees

counterclockwise. Let it rest in the refrigerator after the second turn, ideally overnight.

8   Do two more turns, then leave it to rest again for 3–4 hours. Do one or two more turns at the most before using.

9   Preheat the oven to 360°F and line a cookie sheet with baking paper. Roll out the pastry to ¹⁄₁₂ in thickness. Place on the prepared cookie sheet and cover with another sheet of baking paper, then with another cookie sheet, so that the layering develops uniformly. Place in the oven. After 15 minutes, check every 5 minutes to see if the pastry is cooked. The pastry and the edges must be uniformly golden. Transfer to a wire rack to cool.

BRIOCHE
DOUGH

Understand

WHAT IS IT?

Rich and runny yeast pastry with soft inner dough.

TIME TO MAKE

Preparation: 1 hour
Proofing: 1 hour 30 minutes to 2 hours
Refrigeration: 2–24 hours

EQUIPMENT

Electric mixer with dough hook attachment

TRICKY ASPECT
Kneading the dough

TECHNIQUE TO MASTER
Knocking back dough (page 284)

WHAT CAN MAKE A BRIOCHE RUBBERY?

The dough has been worked too long and the network of gluten is too well developed. This creates an elasticity that is undesirable in a brioche.

WHY DOES THE DOUGH NEED TO BE KNOCKED BACK?

After the first proofing, the yeast has consumed all the sugar and the nearby water. By knocking back the dough, you modify the environment around the yeast cells and make them act differently. They restart their development and reproduction thanks to the nutrients that are now accessible again.

WHY IS THE FIRST PROOFING DONE IN THE REFRIGERATOR?

The cold slows down the proofing and so prevents the dough rising too strongly, which would not allow the structure of the gluten network to develop properly at the same time.

WHAT HAPPENS IF THE PASTRY RISES TOO MUCH?

When the brioche goes into the oven, the heat dilates the carbon dioxide bubbles, inflates the bubbles of air trapped during kneading, and evaporates the water to make steam. These three phenomena will make any air pockets grow even more. If the dough has already risen too much beforehand, the gluten network might not bear the stretching and the gases will escape from the dough. This would make the brioche sink.

CLASSIC USES

Flavored brioches of various kinds

OTHER USES

"Chinese" brioche, St Genix brioche, panettone, Tropézienne tart, kugelhopf

VARIATIONS

Vanilla brioche: add ½ oz (3⅓ tsp) vanilla extract to the dough. Orange-scented brioche: add the zest of 1 orange to the dough.

TIPS
If the dough is too sticky, you can dust it lightly with flour or place it in the refrigerator. If some of the butter melts at the moment it is incorporated and the dough warms up during kneading, you can leave it in the refrigerator for 2 hours, then remove and add the remaining butter.

TO MAKE 2 LB DOUGH

¾ oz fresh baker's yeast, crumbled
14 oz (about 3.2 cups) all-purpose flour
⅜ oz (1¼ tbsp) salt
1⅜ oz (about 3 tbsp) superfine sugar
9 oz egg (5 eggs)
7 oz (14 tbsp) butter, cut into small cubes

1   Place all the ingredients in the refrigerator at least 1 hour in advance. In the bowl of an electric mixer with the dough hook attached, place, in order, the yeast, flour, salt, sugar and egg. Switch on the mixer at a quarter of its full speed. Keep mixing until the dough sticks to the sides. It will become elastic but must not warm up.

2   Gradually add the butter, kneading with the dough hook, until it is completely incorporated.

3   Turn off the mixer, transfer the dough to a large stainless-steel bowl dusted with flour. Sprinkle a little flour on top of the dough, so that it doesn't dry out and form a crust. Cover with a dish towel or plastic wrap, without letting it touch the dough. Place in the refrigerator for 1 hour 30 minutes to 2 hours.

BABA DOUGH

Understand

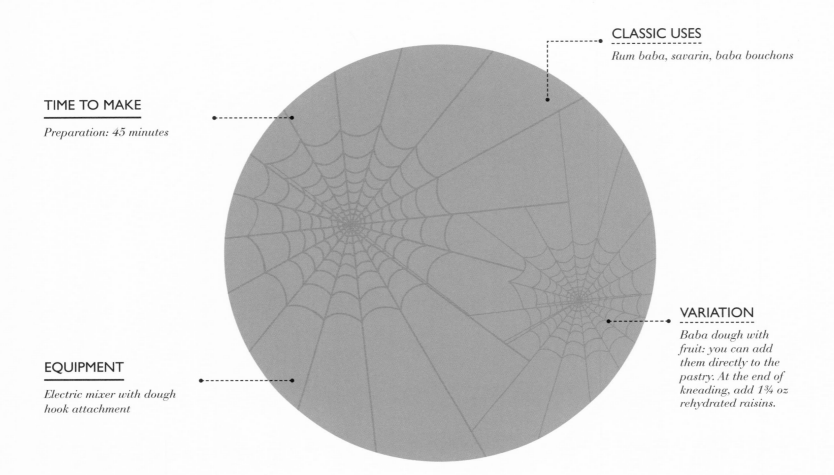

CLASSIC USES

Rum baba, savarin, baba bouchons

TIME TO MAKE

Preparation: 45 minutes

EQUIPMENT

Electric mixer with dough hook attachment

VARIATION

Baba dough with fruit: you can add them directly to the pastry. At the end of kneading, add 1¾ oz rehydrated raisins.

WHY CAN YOU STRETCH THE DOUGH INTO A "SPIDERWEB?"

The flour is made up of starch grains and proteins (gluten). When you knead the flour with the other ingredients, such as milk, in this recipe, the proteins form an elastic network that makes the dough stretchable like a spiderweb.

WHY DO WE NEED TO PUT ALL THE INGREDIENTS IN THE REFRIGERATOR?

It is necessary to beat the ingredients long enough to make the dough elastic, but it must not warm up too much or it would harm the yeast and the structure of the dough. Starting with cold ingredients ensures the dough doesn't warm up too much.

TRICKY ASPECT
The long kneading time (30–45 minutes)

TIP
Refrigerate all the ingredients at least 1 hour before making the pastry; they must be well chilled to prevent the dough warming up too quickly.

TO MAKE 10 × 1¾ OZ RUM BABAS OR 1 LARGE BABA

½ oz fresh baker's yeast, crumbled
9 oz (about 2 cups) all-purpose flour
³⁄₁₆ oz (2 tsp) salt
½ oz (3½ tsp) superfine sugar
5 oz (about ⅔ cup) milk
3½ oz egg (2 eggs)
2⅝ oz (5¼ tbsp) cold butter, cut into small cubes

1   Place all the ingredients in the refrigerator at least 1 hour in advance. In the bowl of an electric mixer with the dough hook attached, place, in order, the yeast, flour, salt, sugar, milk and egg.

2   Switch on the mixer at a quarter of its full speed and let it run until the dough sticks to the sides and slaps against it (30–45 minutes). It will become elastic and look like a spiderweb without tearing. The dough must not warm up.

3   Gradually add the butter until it is completely incorporated. Turn off the mixer. Use the dough immediately.

CROISSANT
DOUGH

Understand

WHAT IS IT?

Yeast dough with butter incorporated in the same way as for puff pastry.

EQUIPMENT

Straight rolling pin

TIME TO MAKE

Preparation: 2 hours
Refrigeration: 12 hours

WHAT IS SPECIAL ABOUT CROISSANT DOUGH?

The croissant is the result of a mixture of two techniques: yeast dough and layering with butter. The yeast dough brings lightness, the layering crustiness.

CLASSIC USES

Croissants, pains au chocolat, pains aux raisins

TRICKY ASPECT
Turning the dough evenly

TECHNIQUES TO MASTER
Knocking back dough (page 284)
Making a simple turn (page 18)

TIP
You can make the détrempe in an electric mixer with the dough hook attached.

ORGANIZATION
Making the détrempe – resting – turning – shaping – proofing

**TO MAKE I LB 3 OZ
DOUGH**

1 DÉTREMPE

⅝ oz fresh baker's yeast
2¼ oz (4½ tbsp) water
2¼ oz (4½ tbsp) milk
9 oz (about 2 cups) all-purpose flour
½ oz egg, beaten
½ oz (1⅔ tbsp) salt
⅞ oz (2 tbsp) superfine sugar

2 LAYERING

4⅜ oz (8¾ tbsp) dry butter
(page 276) or butter

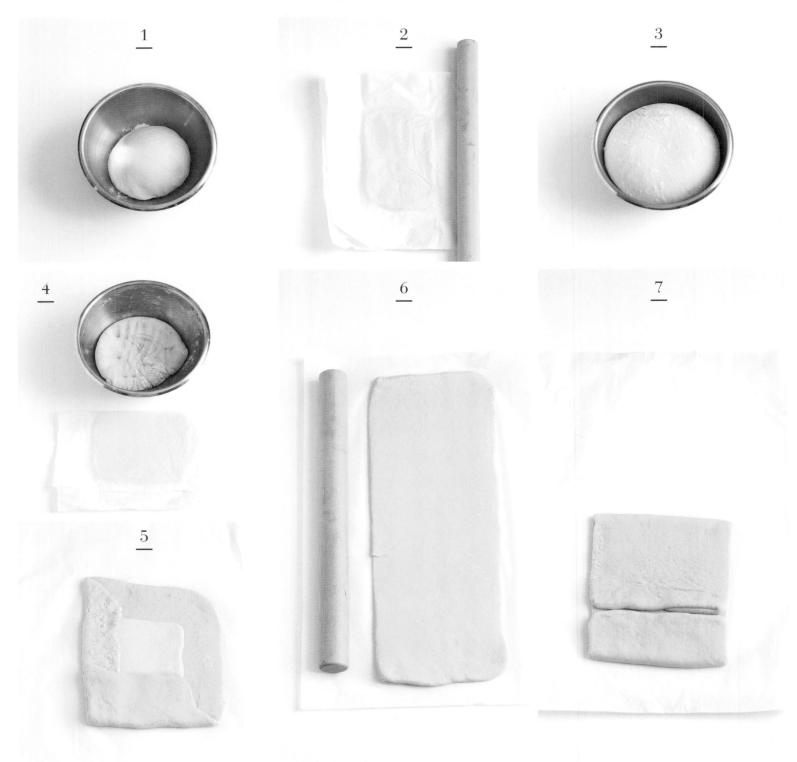

1   Dissolve the yeast in a mixture of the water and milk. Form the flour into a mound with a well in the middle, then place the yeast mixture, egg, salt and sugar in the well. Using the tips of your fingers, gradually incorporate the flour until you have a smooth dough. Be careful not to work the dough too much. Place in a large stainless-steel bowl. Cover with plastic wrap, with the plastic touching the dough and also over the bowl. Leave to prove in the refrigerator overnight.

2   Place the 4⅜ oz (8⅜ tbsp) butter between two sheets of baking paper and tap on it with a rolling pin to make a block about 10 in square. Leave to rest in the refrigerator overnight.

3   The next day, remove the détrempe from the refrigerator; it should have doubled in volume.

4   Knock back the dough (page 284) and remove the butter from the refrigerator. Wait 30 minutes before working with them.

5   On a flour-dusted work surface, roll out the détrempe with a rolling pin. Form it into a 16 in square. Place the butter in the middle, then cover it by folding the four corners of the dough toward the middle. The thickness should be the same all over.

6   Roll out the détrempe evenly into a rectangle ¼ in thick. Always roll straight in front and away from you.

7   Make three simple turns. Keep in the refrigerator until you are ready to use.

Croissant dough

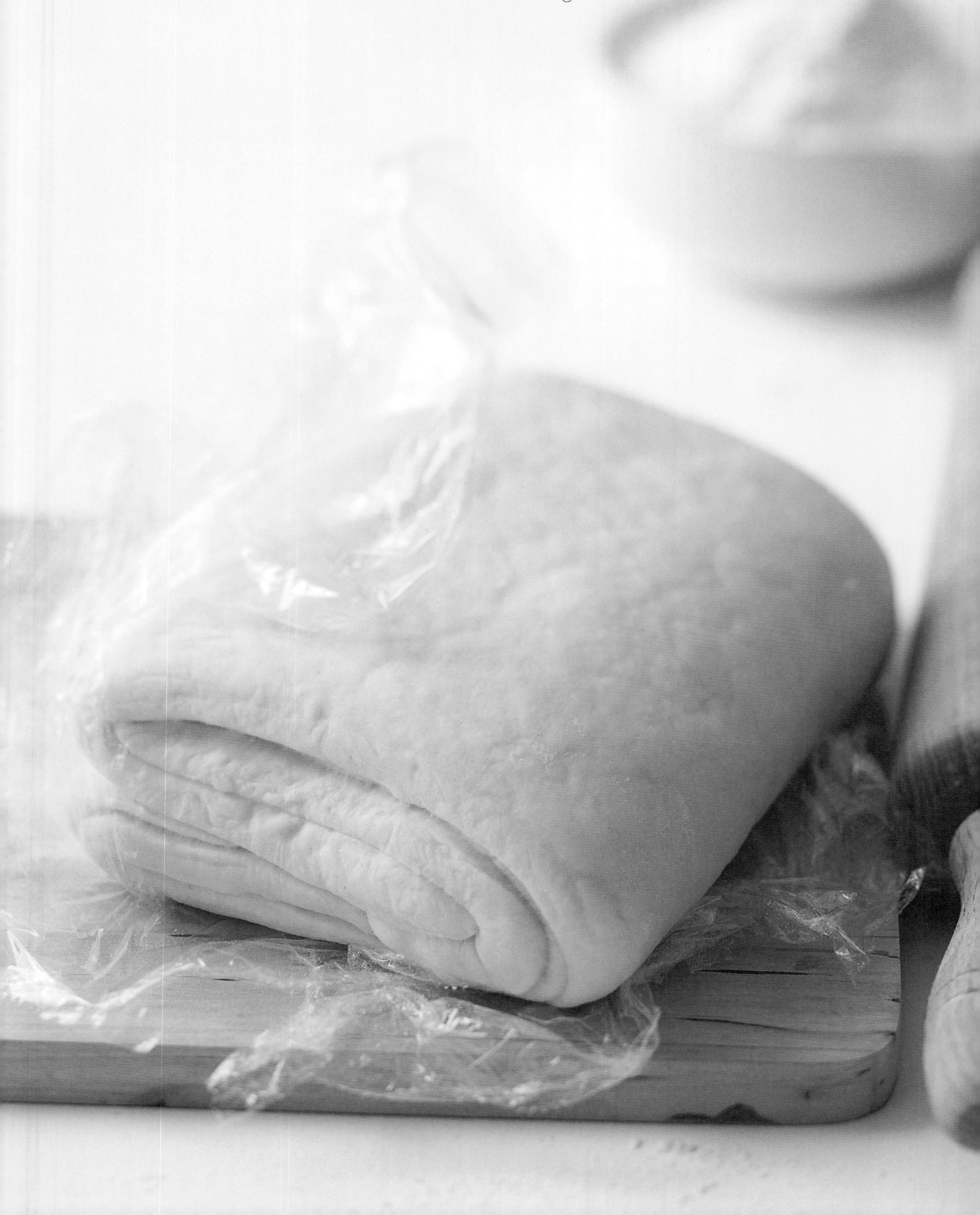

CHOUX PASTRY

Understand

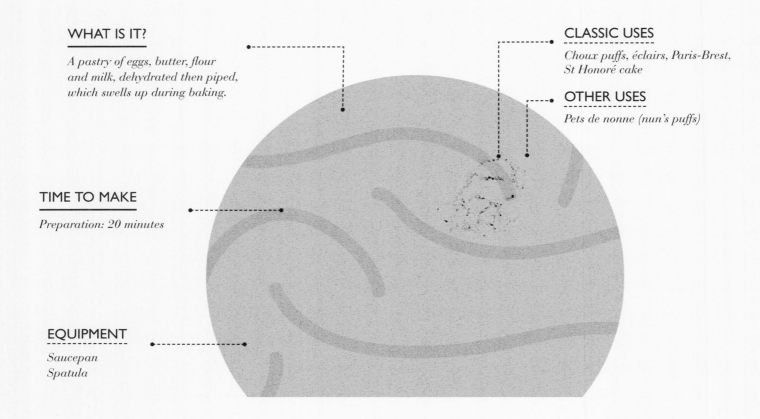

WHAT IS IT?
A pastry of eggs, butter, flour and milk, dehydrated then piped, which swells up during baking.

TIME TO MAKE
Preparation: 20 minutes

EQUIPMENT
Saucepan
Spatula

CLASSIC USES
Choux puffs, éclairs, Paris-Brest, St Honoré cake

OTHER USES
Pets de nonne (nun's puffs)

WHY IS EVACUATING THE STEAM DURING COOKING NECESSARY?
To continue cooking in a dry atmosphere and achieve the raised temperatures necessary for the pastry to color.

WHAT MAKES CHOUX PASTRY RISE?
During baking, the water remaining in the pastry evaporates, passing from liquid to gas. This steam is responsible for the swelling of the pastry. The network of gluten, developed during the preparation of the pastry, will congeal and allow the cooked choux to retain their swollen shape.

TIPS
Avoid piping the pastry onto a silicone mat; the air won't circulate properly and that will make a hole in the bottom. Dry the dough well to ensure the egg is well absorbed and the pastry is as well developed as possible. To ensure the cooked choux has a perfect structure, add the egg when the "panade" (first mixture) is still warm.

TRICKY ASPECT
Controlling the quantity of egg: the weight of liquid (water + milk) must be equal to that of the eggs (for 7 oz liquid, measure out 7 oz egg); if there is more, beat the eggs, weigh them and keep the surplus for the glaze.

TECHNIQUE TO MASTER
Making a panade and drying out (page 282)

TO MAKE 14 OZ PASTRY

3½ oz (7 tbsp) milk
3½ oz (7 tbsp) water
1/16 oz (2/3 tsp) salt
1/16 oz (½ tsp) superfine sugar
3 oz (6 tbsp) butter
3½ oz (about .8 cup) all-purpose flour
7 oz egg (4 eggs)

1   Preheat the oven to 450°F. Put the milk, water, salt, sugar and butter in a saucepan. Bring the mixture to the boil; the butter must be completely melted.

2   When the mixture begins to boil up towards the top of the pan, remove the saucepan from the heat, then pour in the flour in one go and mix using a spatula. This first mixture is called the "panade" (page 282).

3   When the panade is very smooth, flatten it in the bottom of the saucepan and return it to the heat without mixing. As soon as you hear crackling, shake the saucepan and look at the bottom: an evenly thin film on the bottom of the pan indicates that the pastry is sufficiently dry.

4   Remove from the heat and mix with the spatula until most of the steam has evaporated. Add the first egg. When it is completely incorporated, add the second, and so on until the pastry is very smooth. Use immediately, or keep in a cool place until use (3 hours at the most).

GENOESE SPONGE

Understand

WHAT IS IT?

Very light and supple dessert base, often soaked in syrup.

TIME TO MAKE

Preparation: 30 minutes
Cooking: 15–25 minutes

EQUIPMENT

9½ in round cake tin 2 in high, or 12 in × 16 in cookie sheet
Candy thermometer

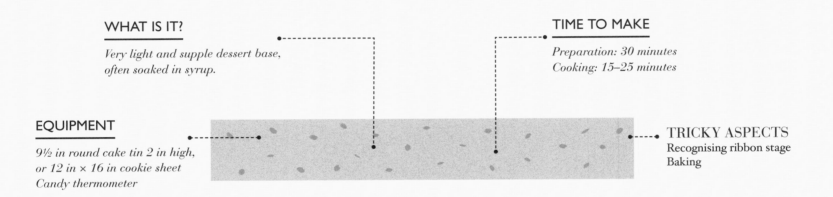

TRICKY ASPECTS

Recognising ribbon stage
Baking

CLASSIC USES

Dessert base (fraisier cake, mocha cake, Black Forest cake, rolled dessert such as a yule log)

TECHNIQUE TO MASTER

Preparing a water bath
(page 270)

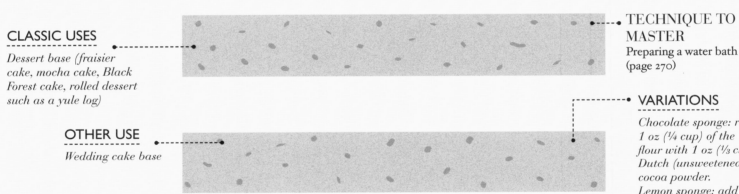

OTHER USE

Wedding cake base

VARIATIONS

Chocolate sponge: replace 1 oz (¼ cup) of the flour with 1 oz (⅓ cup) Dutch (unsweetened) cocoa powder.
Lemon sponge: add the zest of 1 lemon to the dough. Vanilla sponge: add the seeds scraped from 1 vanilla bean to the dough.

WHY MUST THE EGGS AND SUGAR BE HEATED OVER A WATER BATH?

This more gentle mode of cooking reduces the risk of the egg proteins coagulating too much, and therefore of lumps forming.

WHY MUST THE BOWL NOT TOUCH THE WATER IN THE WATER BATH?

To avoid the cooking temperature becoming too high. The water vapor transfers its heat rather than the water itself; this way, the thermal transfer is gentler.

TIP

Touch with a finger to test if the sponge is cooked: if your finger makes a lasting dent, the sponge is not completely cooked. If the dent bounces back, take the tin out of the oven and remove the sponge from the tin straightaway to stop it cooking.

TO MAKE 1 SPONGE (1 ROUND OF 9½ IN OR 1 SLAB OF 12 IN ×16 IN)

7 oz egg (4 eggs)
4⅜ oz (about .6 cup) superfine sugar
4⅜ oz (1 cup) all-purpose flour, sifted

1   Preheat the oven to 360°F. Grease the cake tin and line the sides and base with baking paper.

2   Prepare a water bath (page 270). Put the egg and the sugar in the bowl.

3   When the water is simmering, place the bowl over the saucepan; the stainless-steel bowl must not touch the water. Whisk the mixture, trying to incorporate as much air as possible, until it reaches a temperature of 120°F.

4   Remove the bowl from the water bath and continue whisking until the mixture has cooled. If the batter is well made, the mixture should be at ribbon stage (page 279). Fold in the flour using a silicone spatula.

5   Immediately pour the mixture into the prepared mold, spreading it out with the spatula as necessary. Bake for 15–25 minutes, depending on the thickness of the sponge.

ALMOND
SPONGE

Understand

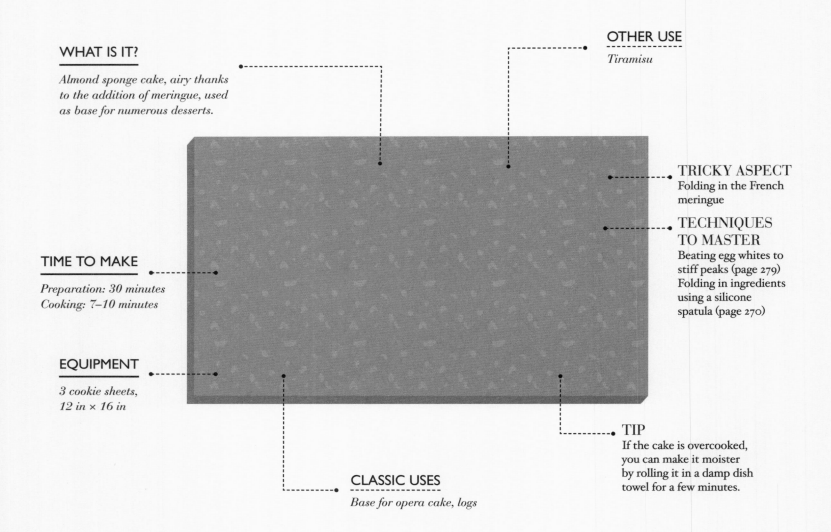

WHAT IS IT?

*Almond sponge cake, airy thanks
to the addition of meringue, used
as base for numerous desserts.*

OTHER USE

Tiramisu

TRICKY ASPECT
Folding in the French
meringue

**TECHNIQUES
TO MASTER**
Beating egg whites to
stiff peaks (page 279)
Folding in ingredients
using a silicone
spatula (page 270)

TIME TO MAKE

*Preparation: 30 minutes
Cooking: 7–10 minutes*

EQUIPMENT

*3 cookie sheets,
12 in × 16 in*

TIP
If the cake is overcooked,
you can make it moister
by rolling it in a damp dish
towel for a few minutes.

CLASSIC USES

Base for opera cake, logs

HOW DOES THE CAKE STAY MOIST?

*The presence of the sugar and the method of baking help retain moisture.
The sugar captures water (we call it hygroscopic). The rapid baking
prevents too much evaporation and allows the retention of moisture.*

WHY DOES THE DOUGH INCREASE IN VOLUME?

*Whipping the eggs forms a foam of the proteins they contain.
This gives volume to the dough.*

VARIATIONS

*For a pistachio sponge, add ½–1 oz
(1–2 tbsp) pistachio paste at the beginning.
For a citrus sponge, add the zest of
2 pieces of citrus to the mixture.
For a chocolate sponge, add 1 oz (⅓ cup)
Dutch (unsweetened) cocoa powder.*

ORGANIZATION
Base – meringue – cake – spreading – baking

TO MAKE 3 SLABS, 12 IN × 16 IN

1 SPONGE BASE

7 oz (1⅔ cups) confectioners' sugar
7 oz (about 2.1 cups) almond meal
10½ oz egg (6 eggs)
1 oz (about ¼ cup) all-purpose flour, sifted

2 MERINGUE BASE

7 oz egg white (about 7 whites),
    at room temperature
1 oz (2¼ tbsp) superfine sugar

1 Preheat the oven to 375°F. Using an electric mixer, whip together the confectioners' sugar, almond meal and 7 oz of the egg (4 eggs). The mixture should double in volume. Add the remaining egg and whip for another 5 minutes.

2 To make the meringue, gently beat the egg white until soft peaks form. Increase the speed of the mixer and add a quarter of the sugar. When the mixture thickens, add another quarter of the sugar. When ridges start forming on the surface, add the remaining sugar to draw the meringue together into stiff peaks. Beat for 2 minutes, then switch off.

3 Using a silicone spatula (page 270), fold one-third of the meringue into the first mixture, followed by the flour. When the mixture is smooth, gently fold in the remaining meringue.

4 Divide the mixture between three cookie sheets lined with baking paper (about 10½ oz per sheet) and place in the oven immediately. Bake for 7–10 minutes; the cake must remain moist.

35

LADYFINGERS

Understand

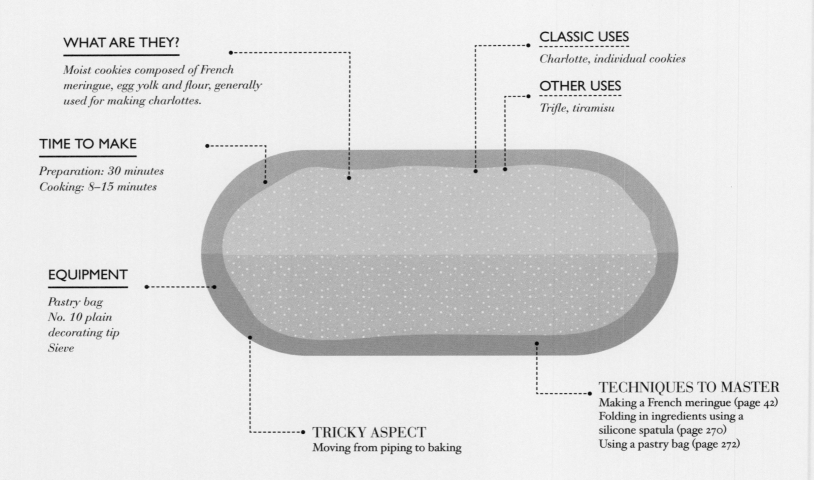

WHAT ARE THEY?

Moist cookies composed of French meringue, egg yolk and flour, generally used for making charlottes.

TIME TO MAKE

Preparation: 30 minutes
Cooking: 8–15 minutes

EQUIPMENT

Pastry bag
No. 10 plain decorating tip
Sieve

CLASSIC USES

Charlotte, individual cookies

OTHER USES

Trifle, tiramisu

TECHNIQUES TO MASTER
Making a French meringue (page 42)
Folding in ingredients using a silicone spatula (page 270)
Using a pastry bag (page 272)

TRICKY ASPECT
Moving from piping to baking

WHAT MECHANISMS OCCUR DURING PREPARATION?

The French meringue provides air. The air bubbles are trapped in the cookie during cooking by the coagulation of the egg proteins, but equally by the gelatinization of the starch (swelling of the starch) from the vital addition of the flour.

ORGANIZATION
& STORAGE
French meringue – mixture – piping – baking
Keeps for 1 day in the refrigerator and for 3 months in the freezer.

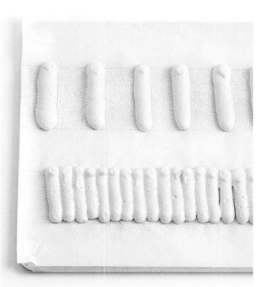

TO MAKE 30 COOKIES

or 2 discs (9½ in diameter) or
2 "cartridge belts" (continuous 16 in strips of ladyfinger)

1 THE BASE

3½ oz (about .8 cup) all-purpose flour
⅞ oz (2½ tbsp) potato starch
2¾ oz egg yolk (about 4 yolks), beaten

2 FRENCH MERINGUE

5¼ oz egg white (about 5 whites)
4⅜ oz (about .6 cup) superfine sugar

3 DUSTING

1 oz (¼ cup) confectioners' sugar

1 Preheat the over to 360°. Sift the flour with the potato starch using a sieve or a sufficiently fine strainer.

2 Make a very firm French meringue (page 42). Using a silicone spatula, fold in the egg yolk, then the flour and potato starch mixture.

3 Line a cookie sheet with baking paper. To make individual cookies, pipe (page 272) well-spaced sausages 2½ in long. To make a "cartridge belt," pipe sausages of a uniform 2½ in length, right next to each other, on the sheet. To make a disc, pipe an even spiral from the center outward (page 272). Dust twice with confectioners' sugar 5 minutes apart. Bake for 8–15 minutes, depending on the shape. When you lift the baking paper you should be able to detach the ladyfinger.

ALMOND
MERINGUE BASE

Understand

WHAT IS IT?

Crisp meringue made from egg white and nut meal, used as a dessert base.

CLASSIC USE

Succès

TIME TO MAKE

Preparation: 30 minutes
Cooking: 15–25 minutes

VARIATIONS

Replace the walnut meal with the same quantity of almond meal or hazelnut meal.

EQUIPMENT

12 in × 16 in cookie sheet (or 2 round tins of 8 in diameter)
Pastry bag
No. 10 plain decorating tip

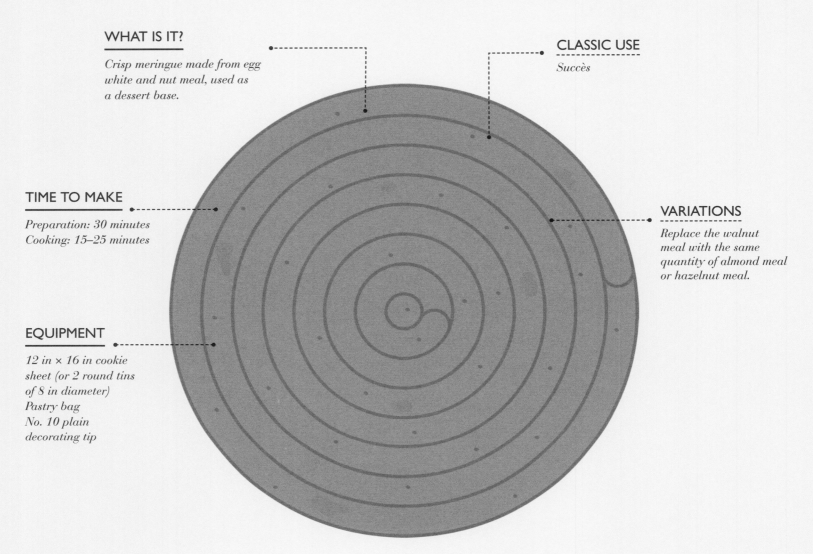

WHERE DOES THE CRUMBLY TEXTURE OF THIS BASE COME FROM?

It is explained by the absence of whole egg and the low flour content of the base. The proteins of the egg whites in the meringue base are more or less the only elements that play a role in the way the finished product holds together.

TECHNIQUES TO MASTER
Folding in ingredients using a silicone spatula (page 270)
Using a pastry bag (page 272)

ORGANIZATION
French meringue – base – piping – baking

TO MAKE A 12 IN × 16 IN SLAB

(or 2 discs of 8 in diameter)

1 NUT BASE

1⅜ oz (about ⅓ cup) all-purpose flour
4⅛ oz (about 1¼ cups) walnut meal
4½ oz (about ⅔ cup) superfine sugar

2 FRENCH MERINGUE

6¾ oz egg white (about 6 whites)
2½ oz (about ⅓ cup) superfine sugar

1   Preheat the oven to 360°F. Sift all the dry base ingredients.

2   Make a French meringue (page 42). Fold in the sifted dry ingredients using a silicone spatula.

3   To make discs: draw two circles of 8 in diameter on a sheet of baking paper. Use the mixture to fill a pastry bag fitted with a no. 10 tip. Pipe snail-shell circles starting in the center (page 273). For a slab, use a frosting spatula to spread the mixture out on a cookie sheet lined with baking paper.

4   Bake for 15–25 minutes. When you lift the baking paper, the bottom of the meringue should be lightly colored.

39

FLOURLESS CHOCOLATE
CAKE

Understand

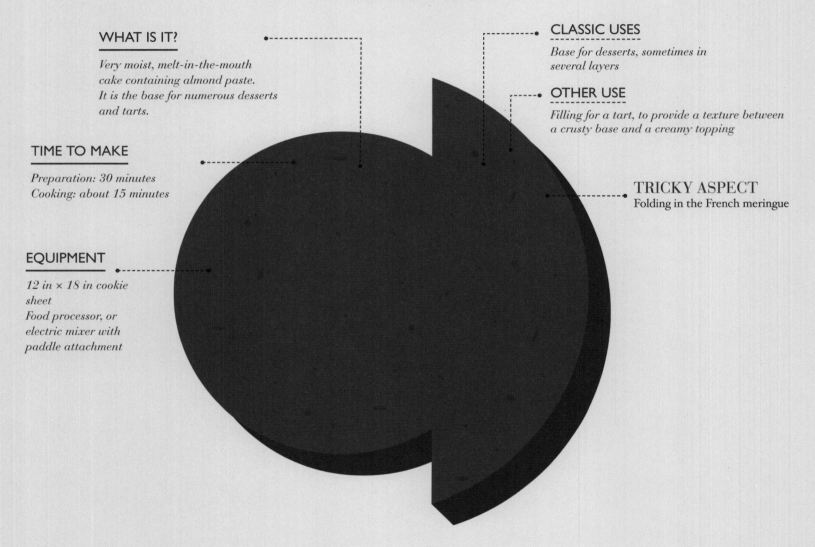

WHAT IS IT?

Very moist, melt-in-the-mouth cake containing almond paste. It is the base for numerous desserts and tarts.

TIME TO MAKE

*Preparation: 30 minutes
Cooking: about 15 minutes*

EQUIPMENT

*12 in × 18 in cookie sheet
Food processor, or electric mixer with paddle attachment*

CLASSIC USES

Base for desserts, sometimes in several layers

OTHER USE

Filling for a tart, to provide a texture between a crusty base and a creamy topping

TRICKY ASPECT
Folding in the French meringue

HOW CAN YOU MAKE A CAKE WITHOUT FLOUR?

In a cake, the flour provides the structure after cooking thanks to the gelatinization (swelling) of the starch. To make a lighter base while still guaranteeing a good structure, the tip is to replace the flour with almond paste: it will mimic the effect of the gelatinization. On the other hand, by avoiding the addition of flour, you avoid the presence of gluten, which is an allergen for some people.

TECHNIQUES TO MASTER
Preparing a water bath (page 270)
Making a French meringue (page 42)
Folding in ingredients using a silicone spatula (page 270)

ORGANIZATION
Melted chocolate – cake base mixture – French meringue – baking

TO MAKE A 12 IN × 16 IN SLAB

1 CHOCOLATE CAKE BASE

1⅜ oz (2¾ tbsp) butter
5 oz chocolate (66% cacao)
2½ oz (⅓ cup) almond paste
1 oz egg yolk (about 1½ yolks)

2 FRENCH MERINGUE

5⅝ oz egg white (about 5 whites)
2 oz (4½ tbsp) superfine sugar

1 Preheat the oven to 360°F. Prepare a water bath (page 270) and gently melt together the butter and the chocolate.

2 Put the almond paste in the bowl of a food processor with the blade attached or in the bowl of an electric mixer with the paddle attached. Turn on the machine at average speed, gradually adding the egg yolk. Scrape down the sides from time to time using a spatula.

3 Once the mixture is smooth, add the melted butter and chocolate at low speed. Pour into a large stainless-steel bowl.

4 Make a French meringue (page 42). Put one-third of the meringue in the chocolate mixture and whip vigorously.

5 Add the remaining meringue and fold in delicately using a silicone spatula (page 270).

6 Once the mixture is smooth, line a cookie sheet with baking paper and spread the dough out on it. Bake for 12 minutes. When it comes out of the oven, remove the baking paper and leave the cake on the work surface so it doesn't dry out.

FRENCH
MERINGUE

Understand

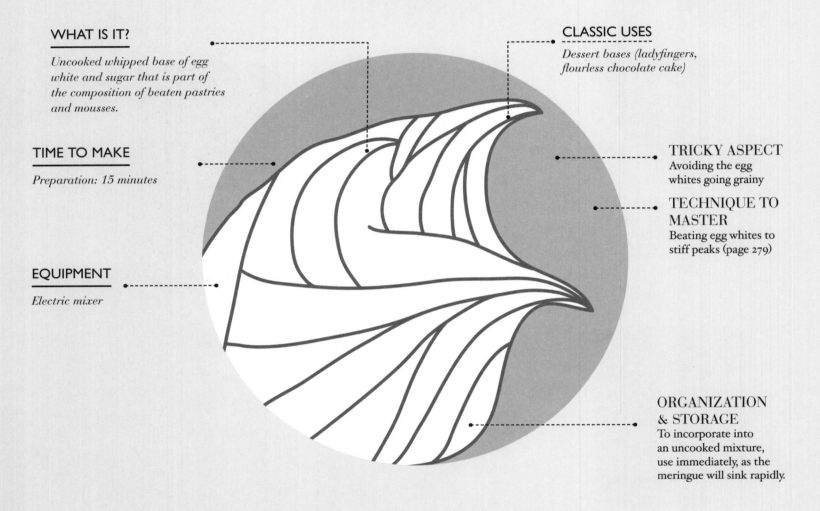

WHAT IS IT?

Uncooked whipped base of egg white and sugar that is part of the composition of beaten pastries and mousses.

TIME TO MAKE

Preparation: 15 minutes

EQUIPMENT

Electric mixer

CLASSIC USES

Dessert bases (ladyfingers, flourless chocolate cake)

TRICKY ASPECT
Avoiding the egg whites going grainy

TECHNIQUE TO MASTER
Beating egg whites to stiff peaks (page 279)

ORGANIZATION & STORAGE
To incorporate into an uncooked mixture, use immediately, as the meringue will sink rapidly.

WHAT CREATES THE FROTHY, MOUSSE-LIKE TEXTURE?

A mousse is a dispersion of gas bubbles in a liquid. When the egg white is beaten to stiff peaks, its proteins are unfolded by the action of the whisk and come between the water and the air. The sugar added to make the meringue increases the viscosity of the liquid, slowing down any sinkage and reducing the size of the bubbles.

WHY IS THERE A RISK OF THE EGG WHITES BECOMING GRAINY?

The egg whites go grainy if they are over-beaten. When the whites are beaten, the proteins unfold, favoring the incorporation and stabilization of air bubbles. If the whites are over-beaten, the proteins will end up meeting and forming bonds; the mousse thus takes on a curdled appearance.

WHY USE THE EGGS AT ROOM TEMPERATURE AND WHY USE OLDER EGGS?

This is not absolutely necessary, but it does allow the egg whites to form stiff peaks more easily, as more of the proteins are already unfolded and thus stabilize the air bubbles more rapidly.

TO MAKE 9¾ OZ MERINGUE

5¼ oz egg white (5 whites)
4⅜ oz (about .6 cup) superfine sugar

1 Put the egg white and a quarter of the sugar in the bowl of an electric mixer with the whisk attached.

2 Turn the mixer on at a quarter of its full speed: the mixture should become foamy.

3 Increase the mixer to half its full speed. Once you see little waves forming on the surface of the egg white, add a quarter of the sugar.

4 Increase the mixer to three-quarters of its full speed then, once the egg white clumps around the whisk, add the remainder of the sugar and turn the speed to maximum. Beat for 2 minutes. The meringue will form stiff peaks when you pull the whisk out.

ITALIAN
MERINGUE

Understand

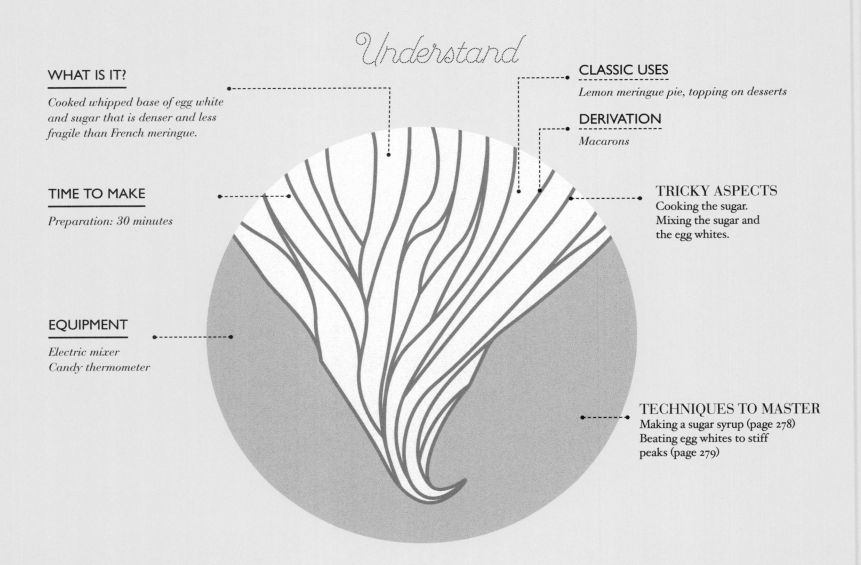

WHAT IS IT?

Cooked whipped base of egg white and sugar that is denser and less fragile than French meringue.

TIME TO MAKE

Preparation: 30 minutes

EQUIPMENT

Electric mixer
Candy thermometer

CLASSIC USES

Lemon meringue pie, topping on desserts

DERIVATION

Macarons

TRICKY ASPECTS
Cooking the sugar.
Mixing the sugar and
the egg whites.

TECHNIQUES TO MASTER
Making a sugar syrup (page 278)
Beating egg whites to stiff
peaks (page 279)

WHY HEAT THE SUGAR TO 250°F?

When the syrup is heated to 250°F, it becomes well dispersed in the beaten egg white. The heat makes the mousse swell up while also evaporating some of the water content, and the syrup is sufficiently viscous to hold the mousse together. Cooked sugar therefore produces a better result than uncooked sugar.

WHAT IS SPECIAL ABOUT ITALIAN MERINGUE?

It is a cooked meringue. It is better adapted than other meringues to topping tarts and cakes because it can be added directly to cooked pastries. This avoids the overcooking that often occurs when a meringue is baked at the same time as the cake.

ORGANIZATION
Syrup – whipping the egg white –
incorporating the syrup into the
whites – whipping until cool

TO MAKE 14 OZ MERINGUE

2¾ oz (about ⅓ cup) water
9 oz (about 1¼ cups) superfine sugar
3½ oz egg white (about 3 whites)

1   Pour the water into a very clean saucepan. Delicately add the sugar to the water, avoiding splashes.

2   Put the saucepan on the heat. Keep an eye on the cooking with the aid of a thermometer – it must not touch the sides or the bottom of the pan.

3   When the syrup reaches 237°F, beat the egg white with the mixer at full speed.

4   When the syrup reaches 249°F, remove the saucepan from the heat. When there are no more bubbles, pour the syrup in a thin stream into the egg white while beating, then continue to beat until the mixture has cooled.

SWISS MERINGUE

Understand

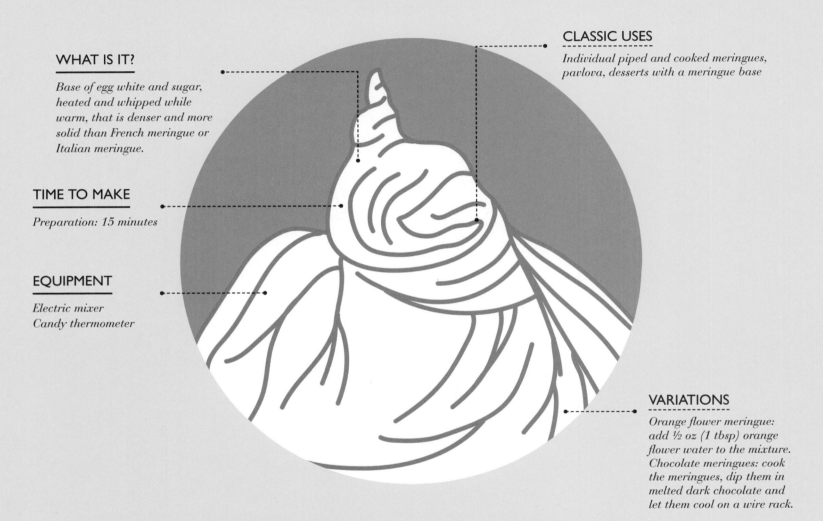

WHAT IS IT?

Base of egg white and sugar, heated and whipped while warm, that is denser and more solid than French meringue or Italian meringue.

TIME TO MAKE

Preparation: 15 minutes

EQUIPMENT

*Electric mixer
Candy thermometer*

CLASSIC USES

Individual piped and cooked meringues, pavlova, desserts with a meringue base

VARIATIONS

Orange flower meringue: add ½ oz (1 tbsp) orange flower water to the mixture. Chocolate meringues: cook the meringues, dip them in melted dark chocolate and let them cool on a wire rack.

WHY WHIP THE EGG WHITES OVER A WATER BATH?

Whipping the egg whites over a water bath at 120°F allows the unfolding of the egg proteins, which means they capture more air and form smaller air bubbles. This is why Swiss meringue is denser and holds together better than other meringues.

TRICKY ASPECT
Cooking and whisking simultaneously

TECHNIQUES TO MASTER
Preparing a water bath (page 270)
Beating egg whites to stiff
peaks (page 279)

TO MAKE 10½ OZ MERINGUE

3½ oz egg white (about 3 whites)
3½ oz (about ½ cup) superfine sugar
3½ oz (1 cup) confectioners' sugar, sifted

1 Prepare a water bath (page 270). Put the egg white and superfine sugar in the water bath; the water must be simmering. Whisk the egg white and sugar, trying to incorporate as much air as possible, to thicken them. Keep an eye on the temperature and stop whisking when it reaches 120°F.

2 Remove the bowl from the water bath and continue whipping until cooled. The meringue will become thick.

3 Fold in the confectioners' sugar using a silicone spatula.

CARAMEL

Understand

WHAT IS IT?

Caramel is obtained by melting sugar crystals and evaporating water.

STORAGE

Use rapidly, as caramel hardens quickly. It can be reheated several times, but the color will gradually darken.

EQUIPMENT

Saucepan
Pastry brush
Candy thermometer

TRICKY ASPECTS

Stopping the cooking at the right moment
Avoiding crystallization

VARIANT

Dry caramel, made without water

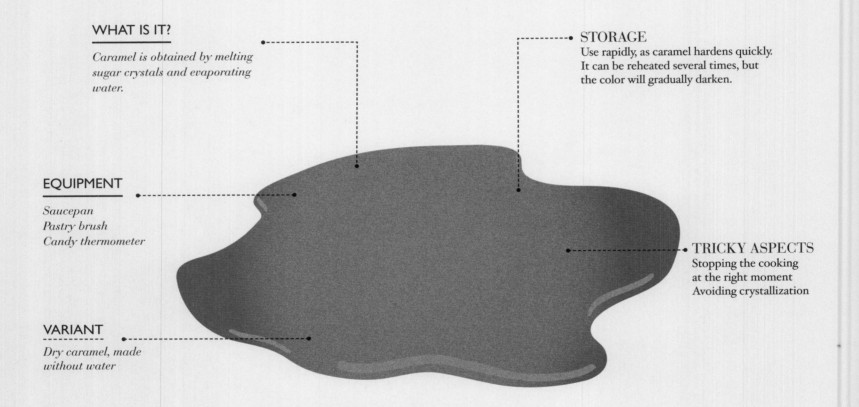

WHAT IS THE DIFFERENCE BETWEEN A CLASSIC CARAMEL AND A DRY CARAMEL?

Classic caramel (made with sugar and water) is used to make sugar decorations and the frosting for choux puffs. Dry caramel (made without water) is used in certain caramel flavorings (e.g. caramel mousse). Its taste is more pronounced.

HOW IS TEMPERATURE A GOOD INDICATOR OF HOW COOKED IT IS?

When sugar is cooked, the water evaporates and the temperature rises. The temperature is therefore a good indicator of the concentration of sugar in the syrup.

WHAT MAKES THE SUGAR CLUMP TOGETHER?

Sugar forms a mass when it crystallizes; during cooking, some crystals are formed, which triggers the crystallization of the whole mass. This occurs if the sugar is not well dissolved, and when crystals formed on the side of the pan fall back into the mixture.

TO MAKE 1 LB 9 OZ CARAMEL

4⅜ oz (.55 cup) water
1 lb 2 oz (2.55 cups) superfine sugar
3½ oz (⅓ cup) glucose syrup

1   Clean the saucepan thoroughly (for a copper saucepan, rub with steel wool using a mixture of rock salt and white vinegar). Prepare a large bowl of iced water and place it beside the cooktop. Add the water to the saucepan first, then the sugar, taking care to leave the sides of the saucepan clean.

2   Bring to the boil, then pour in the glucose syrup. Using a moist pastry brush, clean the sides of the saucepan and continue to cook until the mixture reaches 330°F. Whatever you do, don't stir the syrup. Once the temperature is reached, stand the saucepan in the bowl of iced water to stop the caramel cooking.

DRY CARAMEL

Put the sugar in the saucepan. Heat over medium-high heat. As soon as the sugar starts to dissolve and transform into caramel, stir with a whisk.

NOUGATINE

Understand

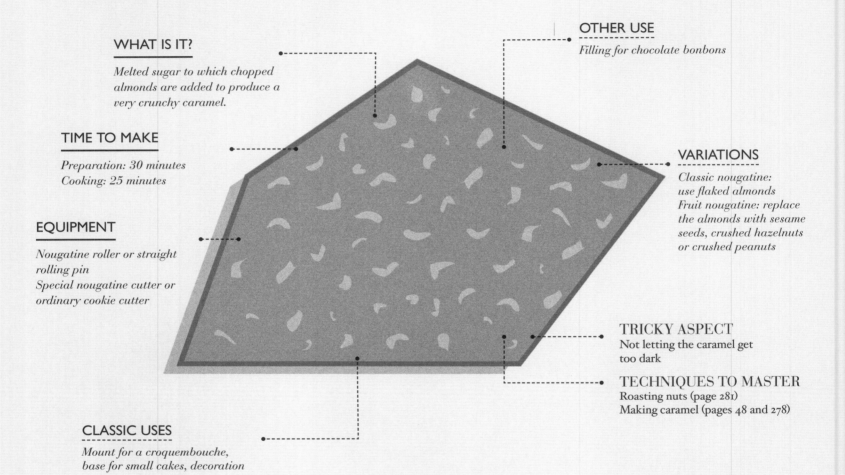

WHAT IS IT?

Melted sugar to which chopped almonds are added to produce a very crunchy caramel.

TIME TO MAKE

Preparation: 30 minutes
Cooking: 25 minutes

EQUIPMENT

Nougatine roller or straight rolling pin
Special nougatine cutter or ordinary cookie cutter

CLASSIC USES

Mount for a croquembouche, base for small cakes, decoration

OTHER USE

Filling for chocolate bonbons

VARIATIONS

Classic nougatine: use flaked almonds
Fruit nougatine: replace the almonds with sesame seeds, crushed hazelnuts or crushed peanuts

TRICKY ASPECT

Not letting the caramel get too dark

TECHNIQUES TO MASTER

Roasting nuts (page 281)
Making caramel (pages 48 and 278)

WHY USE GLUCOSE SYRUP RATHER THAN SUGAR?

The glucose syrup doesn't crystallize, unlike sucrose (sugar). This is why it is used so much in confectionery, particularly for making nougatine.

TIPS

If nougatine is not used immediately or if it has become too hard to be manipulated, place in a 280°F oven and keep an eye on it. To avoid the nougatine sticking to utensils and the work surface, oil them lightly.

ORGANIZATION & STORAGE

Roasting the nuts – caramel – stretching – baking – cutting
Keep in a dry, not-too-cool place.

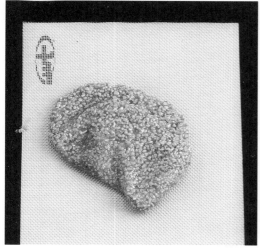

TO MAKE 1 LB 2 OZ NOUGATINE

9 oz (2⅓ cups) chopped almonds
10½ oz fondant
9 oz (about .8 cup) glucose syrup

1 Preheat the oven to 360°F. Line a cookie sheet with baking paper or a silicone mat. Lightly roast (page 281) the almonds in the oven for 15–20 minutes: they should be golden.

2 In a large, very clean saucepan, heat the fondant with the glucose syrup, mixing them from time to time with a spatula. When the caramel is clear, add the almonds and stir them in.

3 Once the mixture has reached the desired color (2–5 minutes), turn out onto the cookie sheet. To ensure an even temperature, draw the edges of the nougatine toward the center several times using a dough scraper. Set aside in a 280°F oven, keeping an eye on it, or turn out onto an oiled work surface and use immediately.

PASTRY
CREM

Understand

WHAT IS IT?

Custard-like cream prepared cold, based on milk and egg yolk, with a thick texture, traditionally flavored with vanilla.

TIME TO MAKE

Preparation: 15 minutes
Cooking: 45 seconds per cup of milk
Cooling: 1 hour

EQUIPMENT

Saucepan

CLASSIC USES

To fill cream puffs, éclairs, religieuses, mille-feuilles

DERIVATIONS

German buttercream (crème mousseline)
Diplomat cream (crème diplomate)
Frangipane cream (crème frangipane)
Chiboust cream (crème Chiboust)

TRICKY ASPECT
Cooking

TECHNIQUE TO MASTER
Blanching egg yolks (page 279)

STORAGE
Keeps for 3 days in the refrigerator.

TIPS
We use cornstarch rather than flour or custard powder to obtain a lighter cream. Restore the consistency before use: whip the cream vigorously to make it smooth and give it a supple consistency.

WHY BLANCH THE EGG YOLKS AND SUGAR?

The blanching of the egg yolks with the sugar allows the mixture to become smooth. The sugar plays a "protective" role for the proteins during heating. If it is mixed well with the egg yolk proteins, the risk of lumps forming is decreased.

WHY CAN A "SKIN" FORM ON THE SURFACE OF THE CREAM AFTER COOLING?

This is due to the coagulation of the proteins during heating (like the skin that forms when milk is heated) and to dehydration at the surface.

WHAT IS THE DIFFERENCE BETWEEN A PASTRY CREAM MADE WITH FLOUR AND ONE MADE WITH CORNSTARCH?

Changing the thickening agent changes the source of starch and therefore the texture of the cream. The different starches have different properties. To make two pastry creams with the same texture, you would use less cornstarch than you would flour (wheat starch). A pastry cream made with cornstarch will be lighter than a pastry cream made with an equivalent quantity of flour.

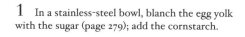

TO MAKE 1 LB 12 OZ CREAM

3½ oz egg yolk (about 6 yolks)
4¼ oz (.6 cup) superfine sugar
1¾ oz (about .4 cup) cornstarch
1 lb 2 oz (2¼ cups) milk
1 vanilla bean
1¾ oz (3½ tbsp) butter

1   In a stainless-steel bowl, blanch the egg yolk with the sugar (page 279); add the cornstarch.

2   Pour the milk into a saucepan with the seeds scraped from a vanilla bean and the bean itself. Bring the milk to the boil, remove the vanilla bean, pour half the milk over the egg yolk, sugar and cornstarch mixture and whisk. Return to the saucepan and heat rapidly while whisking energetically.

3   When the mixture thickens, continue to whisk. From the time it starts to boil, count 90 seconds per cup of milk.

4   Remove from the heat and add the butter.

5   Pour into a cookie sheet to cool rapidly and cover with plastic wrap, with the plastic touching the surface of the cream. Always whip the cream vigorously before using, to smooth it out.

FRENCH
BUTTER CREAM

Understand

WHAT IS IT?

A smooth, melt-in-your-mouth cream, based on butter creamed with sugar, combined with a bombe mixture. Like pastry cream, it is a component of many classics.

TIME TO MAKE

Preparation: 30 minutes
Cooking: 10 minutes

EQUIPMENT

Electric mixer or food processor
Candy thermometer

CLASSIC USES

Filling for logs, opera cakes, mocha cakes and religieuses

OTHER USE

Cupcake topping

VARIATIONS

Some recipes cream the butter with Italian meringue; the result is slightly lighter.
Vanilla buttercream: add 3/16 oz (1¼ tsp) vanilla extract at the end.
Coffee buttercream: add 1 oz (2 tbsp) coffee extract at the end.
Chocolate buttercream: add 2¾ oz (about .9 cup) Dutch (unsweetened) cocoa powder at the end.

TRICKY ASPECTS
Making the sugar syrup
Incorporating the butter

TECHNIQUES TO MASTER
Softening butter (page 276)
Making a sugar syrup (page 278)

WHAT IS THE ACTION OF THE 240°F SUGAR ON THE EGGS?

Cooking the sugar to 240°F allows the evaporation of a certain quantity of the water in the syrup. When they come into contact with the hot syrup, some of the egg proteins are denatured, in other words modified in their composition. These transformations are manifested in a thickening of the egg and sugar mixture.

TIPS
Take the butter out of the refrigerator 3 hours in advance (1 hour in summer) so it softens. The butter and eggs must be at the same temperature at the moment they are mixed. If the cream becomes grainy, place it in a container in the refrigerator until the edges harden, then whip it up in the electric mixer while warming it a little with a kitchen blowtorch.

ORGANIZATION & STORAGE
Removing the butter from the refrigerator – whipping up the eggs – syrup – incorporating the butter Ideally, use immediately. Otherwise, it will keep in the refrigerator for 3 days and the freezer for 3 months in an airtight container wrapped in plastic wrap.

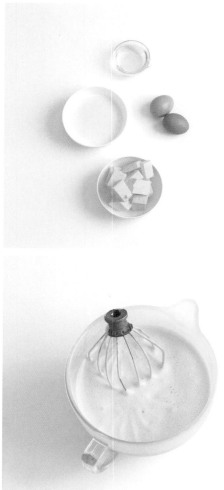

TO MAKE 1 LB CREAM

3½ oz egg (2 eggs)
1⅜ oz (2¾ tbsp) water
4½ oz (about ⅔ cup) superfine sugar
7 oz (14 tbsp) butter, softened

1   Beat the egg in an electric mixer.
It should triple in volume.

2   Pour the water into a small saucepan
and cover with the sugar. Make a syrup (page
278). Heat to 240°F, then stop cooking.

3   Pour the syrup into the egg in a thin stream,
beating the whole time. The mixture should be
thick and creamy.

4   Once completely cooled, add the butter,
little by little, beating the whole time. Flavor
the cream if desired.

GERMAN
BUTTER CREAM

Understand

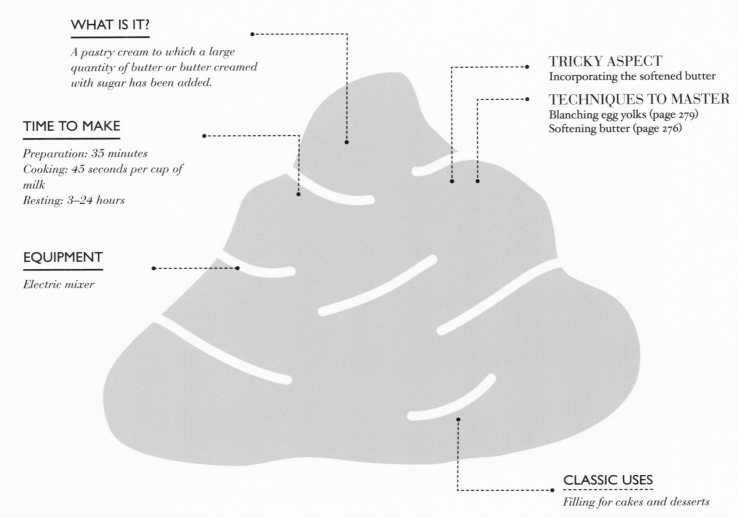

WHAT IS IT?

A pastry cream to which a large quantity of butter or butter creamed with sugar has been added.

TIME TO MAKE

Preparation: 35 minutes
Cooking: 45 seconds per cup of milk
Resting: 3–24 hours

EQUIPMENT

Electric mixer

TRICKY ASPECT
Incorporating the softened butter

TECHNIQUES TO MASTER
Blanching egg yolks (page 279)
Softening butter (page 276)

CLASSIC USES
Filling for cakes and desserts

WHAT GIVES THE CREAM ITS GREAT STRUCTURE?
This cream is made from a pastry cream into which, after cooling, softened butter is added. When cooled, this butter will stiffen the texture of the cream.

ORGANIZATION & STORAGE
Pastry cream – incorporating butter
Keeps for 3 days in the refrigerator.

TO MAKE 2 LB 3 OZ CREAM

1 PASTRY CREAM

3½ oz egg yolk (about 6 yolks)
4¼ oz (.6 cup) superfine sugar
1¾ oz (about .4 cup) cornstarch
1 lb 2 oz (2¼ cups) milk
4⅜ oz (8¾ tbsp) butter

2 BUTTER

4⅜ oz (8¾ tbsp) butter, softened

1 Make the pastry cream (page 52).

2 Turn out into a bowl, cover with plastic wrap, with the plastic touching the surface of the cream then, once cool, place in the refrigerator.

3 Once the cream has cooled completely, whisk it for 3–5 minutes. While still beating, add the softened butter until the mixture is smooth. Use immediately.

BOMBE
MIXTURE

Understand

WHAT IS IT?

A preparation based on eggs and sugar syrup that aerates and brings lightness to desserts.

TIME TO MAKE

Preparation: 20 minutes

EQUIPMENT

*Candy thermometer
Electric mixer*

CLASSIC USES

*Bombe glacé,
chocolate mousse,
fruit mousse*

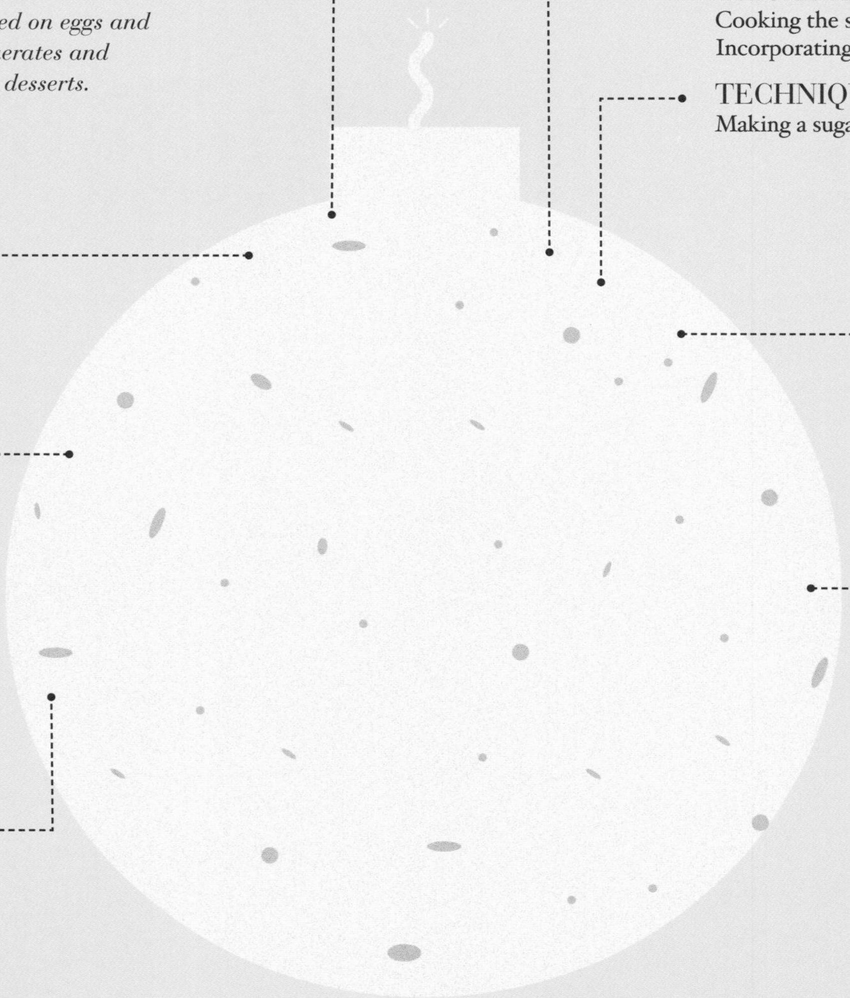

TRICKY ASPECTS

Cooking the sugar syrup
Incorporating the sugar syrup

TECHNIQUE TO MASTER

Making a sugar syrup (page 278)

ORGANIZATION & STORAGE

Whipping up the eggs – making the sugar syrup – incorporating
Use immediately.

WHAT IS SPECIAL ABOUT THIS MIXTURE?

It is an egg mousse stabilized by the coagulation of certain egg proteins when the hot syrup is added to the beaten base.

TO MAKE 9 OZ BOMBE MIXTURE

3½ oz egg (2 eggs)
1⅜ oz (2¾ tbsp) water
4½ oz (about ⅔ cup) superfine sugar

1 Put the egg in the bowl of an electric mixer and beat it at full speed. It should triple in volume.

2 In a small saucepan, make a sugar syrup (page 278) with the water and the sugar. Continue to cook until it reaches 240°F.

3 Remove from the heat. When there are no more bubbles, pour in a thin stream into the egg while beating vigorously, then continue beating until cool. Use immediately.

ENGLISH EGG CUSTARD OR
CRÈME ANGLAISE

Understand

WHAT IS IT?

A pouring cream, made by the controlled coagulation of egg yolks and traditionally flavored with vanilla.

TIME TO MAKE

Preparation: 30 minutes

EQUIPMENT

Candy thermometer

CLASSIC USES

Floating islands, accompanying sauce, base for ice cream

DERIVATIONS

Bavarois, creamy ganache

VARIATIONS

For a caramel crème anglaise, make a dry caramel with 2 oz (4½ tbsp) of the sugar (use the remaining ¾ oz (1⅔ tbsp) to blanch the egg yolk), deglaze with the milk, then follow the usual recipe. For a very fragrant custard, infuse 1 star anise, 10 cardamom seeds and 1 cinnamon stick in the milk, then follow the usual recipe.

WHY IS IT PARTICULARLY NECESSARY TO KEEP AN EYE ON THE TEMPERATURE OF THIS CUSTARD?

During cooking, the egg proteins coagulate, which produces the thickness of the mixture. If the temperature passes 185°F, too many of the proteins coagulate and the mixture ends up thick and not pourable.

TIP
If the custard starts to coagulate, transfer it to another clean bowl, then blend and strain.

TRICKY ASPECT
Cooking

TECHNIQUES TO MASTER
Blanching egg yolks (page 279)
Straining (page 270)

STORAGE
Keeps for 3 days in the refrigerator.

TO MAKE 1 LB 7 OZ CUSTARD

3½ oz egg yolk (about 6 yolks)
2¾ oz (about .4 cup) superfine sugar
1 vanilla bean, scraped
1 lb 2 oz (2¼ cups) milk

1   Blanch the egg yolk with the sugar using a whisk (page 279).

2   Put the vanilla bean and scraped seeds in a saucepan with the milk. Bring to the boil.

3   When the milk rises to the top of the pan, pour half over the egg yolk and sugar mixture. Whisk gently. Once the mixture is smooth, pour it back into the saucepan.

4   Return to medium heat, stirring constantly with a spatula, until the mixture reaches 185°F at the most. Strain (page 270), then set aside in the refrigerator.

CHANTILLY CREAM

Understand

WHAT IS IT?

Sweetened whipped cream containing at least 30 percent fat, possibly flavored but with no other additive.

TIME TO MAKE

Refrigeration:
30 minutes
Preparation:
15 minutes

EQUIPMENT

Electric mixer with whisk attachment, or hand mixer

CLASSIC USES

Fillings, accompaniment

VARIATIONS

Praline chantilly cream: add 1 oz praline.
Pistachio chantilly cream: add ⅜ oz (¾ tbsp) pistachio paste.
Mascarpone chantilly cream (thicker and firmer than classic chantilly cream): add 1 tablespoon mascarpone.

TIP

Have the cream and utensils very cold, to stabilize the fat content.

ORGANIZATION & STORAGE

Cooling the utensils – whipping Keeps for 3 days in the refrigerator; if it starts to sink, whip it again a little.

WHY IS THERE A MINIMUM PERCENTAGE FOR FAT CONTENT?

The fat contained in the cream crystallizes around the air bubbles incorporated during whipping. If the fat content is insufficient, there won't be enough crystals to stabilize the air bubbles and therefore to stabilize the chantilly cream.

WHY DOES THE CREAM WHIP UP BETTER IF IT IS COLD?

The coldness is necessary for the formation of the fat crystals, without which the chantilly cream won't be stabilized.

WHY USE A COLD STAINLESS-STEEL BOWL IN PREFERENCE?

Stainless steel facilitates thermal exchange. Using a cold stainless-steel bowl favors the formation of fat crystals and thus means the cream will set well. If the ambient temperature is high, whip the cream in a stainless-steel bowl sitting in an ice bath.

WHAT HAPPENS IF THE CREAM IS OVERWHIPPED?

You make butter. The emulsion destabilizes, and the water and fat separate.

AT WHAT POINT SHOULD THE SUGAR BE ADDED AND WHY?

To avoid the chantilly cream destabilizing when the sugar is incorporated, it is preferable to add it at the beginning. That way, it will be dissolved in the cream.

TO MAKE 1 LB 3 OZ CREAM

1 lb 2 oz (2¼ cups) whipping cream
    (at least 30% fat)
2¾ oz (about ⅔ cup) confectioners' sugar

1 Refrigerate the utensils and the cream (utensils for 30 minutes, cream for 2 hours). Put the cream and sugar in the bowl of an electric mixer.

2 Whisk gently to mix the sugar into the cream.

3 Whisk at full speed to whip the cream to stiff peaks: it should not be at all shiny. Use immediately or set aside in the refrigerator.

ALMOND
CREAM

Understand

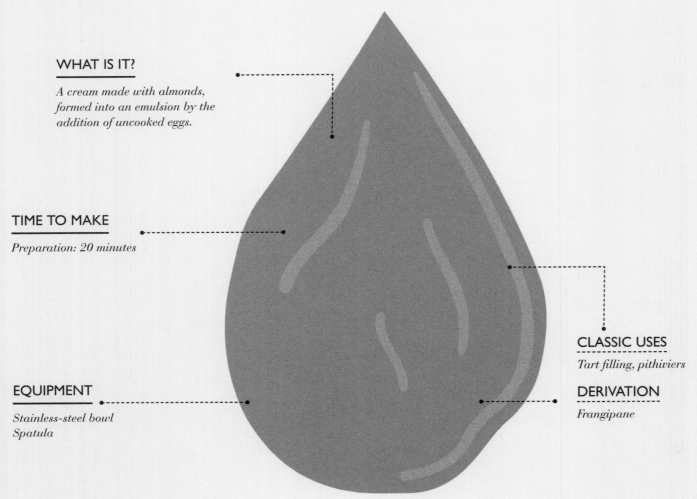

WHAT IS IT?

A cream made with almonds, formed into an emulsion by the addition of uncooked eggs.

TIME TO MAKE

Preparation: 20 minutes

EQUIPMENT

*Stainless-steel bowl
Spatula*

CLASSIC USES

Tart filling, pithiviers

DERIVATION

Frangipane

**WHY DOES IT SWELL UP
WHEN COOKED?**

During cooking, the air bubbles incorporated while mixing will dilate and make the cream swell up, giving it a foamy appearance.

TRICKY ASPECT
Mixing well

TECHNIQUE TO MASTER
Creaming butter and sugar (page 276)

TIP
If you keep the cream in the refrigerator, be sure to take it out before you want to use it, to give it time to take on the consistency of softened butter.

STORAGE
Keeps for 2 days in the refrigerator.

TO MAKE 14 OZ CREAM

3½ oz (7 tbsp) butter
3½ oz (½ cup) superfine sugar
3½ oz (about 1 cup) almond meal
3½ oz egg (2 eggs)
¾ oz (2¾ tbsp) all-purpose flour

1 Make sure you take the butter out of the refrigerator in advance, so that it is well softened. Put the butter and sugar in a stainless-steel bowl and mix until light and fluffy (cream) using a spatula.

2 Add the almond meal, egg and flour. Fold in using the spatula, taking care not to incorporate too much air. Use straightaway or set aside in the refrigerator.

CHIBOUST
CREAM

Understand

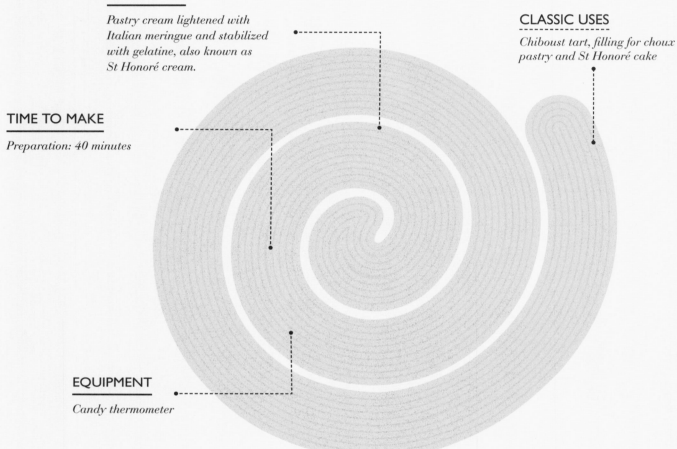

WHAT IS IT?

Pastry cream lightened with Italian meringue and stabilized with gelatine, also known as St Honoré cream.

TIME TO MAKE

Preparation: 40 minutes

CLASSIC USES

Chiboust tart, filling for choux pastry and St Honoré cake

EQUIPMENT

Candy thermometer

WHAT EFFECT DOES THE ADDITION OF MERINGUE HAVE?

The incorporation of the meringue base considerably lightens the pastry cream.

TRICKY ASPECT
Cooking the pastry cream

TECHNIQUES TO MASTER
Hydrating gelatine (page 270)
Incorporating with a whisk then
a silicone spatula (page 270)

ORGANIZATION
& STORAGE
Pastry cream – cooling – Italian meringue –
combining the two mixtures
Keeps for 3 days in the refrigerator.

**TO MAKE 1 LB 5 OZ
CHIBOUST CREAM**

1 PASTRY CREAM

¼ oz leaf gelatine
1¾ oz egg yolk (about 3 yolks)
2 oz (4½ tbsp) superfine sugar
⅞ oz (about 3 tbsp) cornstarch
9 oz (1 cup 2 tbsp) milk
⅞ oz (1¾ tbsp) butter

2 ITALIAN MERINGUE

1⅜ oz (2¾ tbsp) water
4⅜ oz (about .6 cup) superfine sugar
1¾ oz egg white (about 1½ whites)

1 Hydrate the gelatine. Make the pastry cream (page 52); at the end of cooking, add the drained gelatine, then set aside to cool to 90°F.

2 Make the Italian meringue (page 44). Whisk the pastry cream, then whisk in one-third of the meringue.

3 Gently fold in the remaining meringue using a silicone spatula. Use immediately.

DIPLOMAT
CREAM

Understand

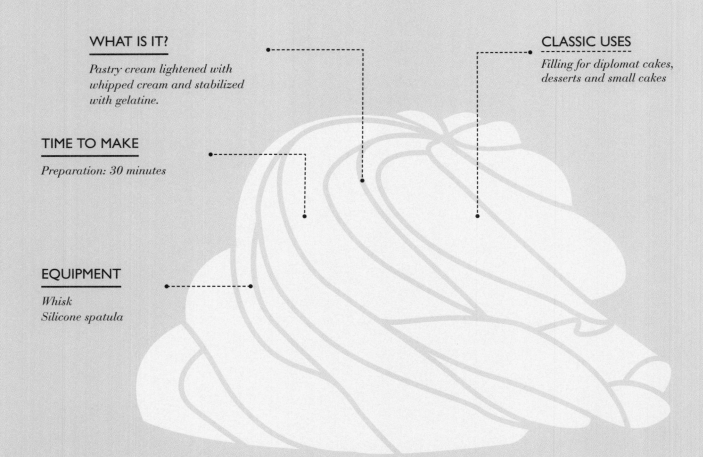

WHAT IS IT?

Pastry cream lightened with whipped cream and stabilized with gelatine.

TIME TO MAKE

Preparation: 30 minutes

EQUIPMENT

Whisk
Silicone spatula

CLASSIC USES

Filling for diplomat cakes, desserts and small cakes

WHY IS IT BETTER TO USE THE CREAM IMMEDIATELY?

In diplomat cream, the pastry cream is "glued" together by the gelatine to obtain a cream that will set well, before adding the whipped cream. The diplomat cream is therefore easiest to work with before it is chilled and the gelatine network has developed. It will take on its definitive texture in the assembled dessert.

TRICKY ASPECT
Cooking the pastry cream

TECHNIQUES TO MASTER
Hydrating gelatine (page 270)
Incorporating with a whisk then a silicone spatula (page 270)

ORGANIZATION & STORAGE
Pastry cream – cooling – whipped cream – mixing the two creams
Keeps for 3 days in the refrigerator.

TO MAKE 2 LB 3 OZ CREAM

1 PASTRY CREAM

¼ oz leaf gelatine
3½ oz egg yolk (about 6 yolks)
4¼ oz (.6 cup) superfine sugar
1¾ oz (about .4 cup) cornstarch
1 lb 2 oz (2¼ cups) milk
1 vanilla bean
1¾ oz (3½ tbsp) butter

2 WHIPPED CREAM

7 oz (about .9 cup) whipping cream (30% fat)

1 Hydrate the gelatine (page 270).

2 Make a vanilla pastry cream (page 52). At the end of cooking, whisk in the drained gelatine at the same time as the butter. Set aside to cool.

3 Whip the cream as for chantilly cream (page 62). Whisk the cooled pastry cream, then whisk in one-third of the whipped cream. Once the mixture is smooth, fold in the remaining whipped cream using a silicone spatula. Use immediately.

BAVAROIS

WHAT IS IT?

Delicate cream, composed of a base of crème anglaise to which whipped cream has been added.

TIME TO MAKE

Preparation: 15 minutes
Resting: about 30 minutes

EQUIPMENT

Candy thermometer

WHAT DOES THE GELATINE DO?

The gelatine is added to the warm custard so that it dissolves in it. After the addition of the whipped cream and cooling, the gelatine will set and stabilize the airy texture of this bavarois.

TRICKY ASPECTS
Cooking the custard
Incorporating the cream

TECHNIQUES TO MASTER
Hydrating gelatine (page 270)
Incorporating with a whisk then a silicone spatula (page 270)

TO MAKE 2 LB 3 OZ CREAM

1 CRÈME ANGLAISE

3½ oz egg yolk (about 6 yolks)
2¾ oz (about .4 cup) superfine sugar
1 vanilla bean, scraped
9 oz (1 cup 2 tbsp) milk
9 oz (1 cup 2 tbsp) whipping cream (30% fat)

2 WHIPPED CREAM

¼ oz leaf gelatine
14 oz (1¾ cups) whipping cream (30% fat)

1 Hydrate the gelatine (page 270). Make the crème anglaise (page 60). Drain the gelatine and whisk into the crème anglaise. Cool to room temperature.

2 Whip the cream as for chantilly cream (page 63). Whisk one-third of the cream into the crème anglaise and gelatine mixture.

3 Once the mixture is smooth, gently fold in the remaining whipped cream using a silicone spatula. Use immediately, as the mousse will set.

CREAMY
GANACHE

Understand

WHAT IS IT?
Thick and gooey chocolate mixture, made using a base of crème anglaise.

TIME TO MAKE
Preparation: 30 minutes

CLASSIC USES
Filling for desserts and macarons

OTHER USES
Filling for chocolate bonbons

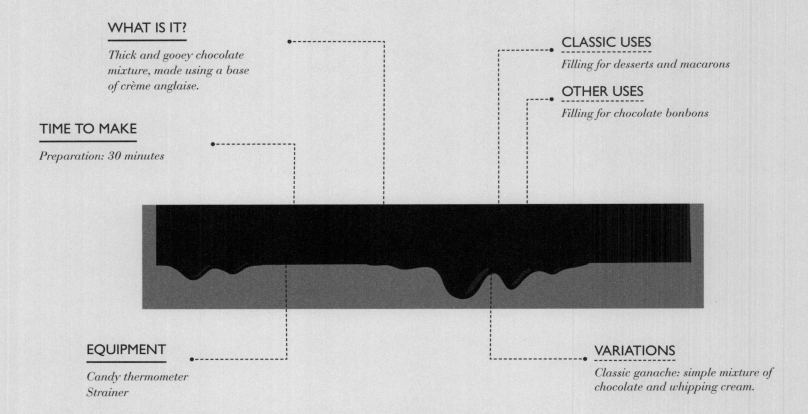

EQUIPMENT
*Candy thermometer
Strainer*

VARIATIONS
Classic ganache: simple mixture of chocolate and whipping cream.

WHAT GIVES THE GANACHE ITS TEXTURE?
When the chocolate and custard mixture cools, the cocoa butter crystallizes, which hardens the mixture to the desired texture. This texture depends on the proportion of chocolate: if too much is incorporated, the ganache will be difficult to cut.

WHAT MAKES THIS GANACHE CREAMY?
This ganache is particularly creamy thanks to the addition of crème anglaise, which gives great fluidity to the final texture.

TRICKY ASPECT
Cooking the crème anglaise

TECHNIQUES TO MASTER
Straining (page 270)
Blanching egg yolks (page 279)

TIP
For some uses, slightly increase the quantity of chocolate in order to obtain a stiffer mixture.

TO MAKE 2 LB GANACHE

3½ oz (about 6 yolks) egg yolk
3½ oz (½ cup) superfine sugar
1 lb 2 oz (2¼ cups) milk
9 oz dark chocolate

1   Blanch the egg yolk and sugar (page 279) using a whisk.

2   Bring the milk to the boil. When it rises to the top of the pan, pour half of it into the egg yolk and sugar mixture. Stir, then pour back into the saucepan.

3   Return to the cooktop over medium heat, stirring constantly with a spatula, until the crème anglaise coats the back of the spatula (181–185°F).

4   Strain (page 270) the crème anglaise into the chocolate. Mix. Refrigerate until ready to use.

LEMON CURD

Understand

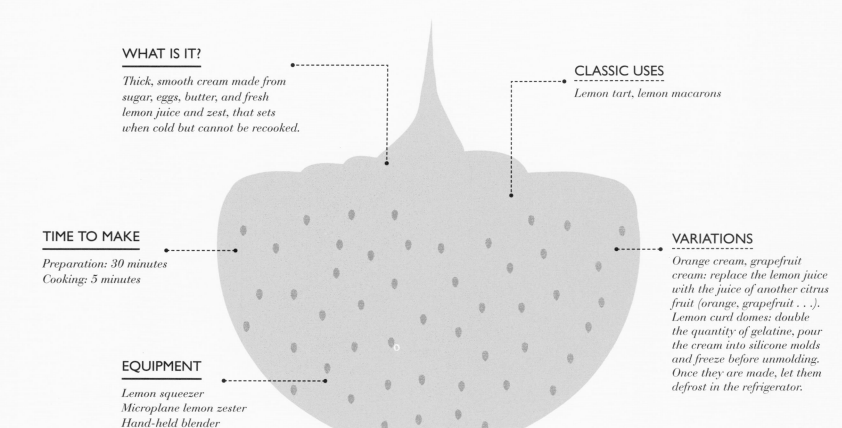

WHAT IS IT?

Thick, smooth cream made from sugar, eggs, butter, and fresh lemon juice and zest, that sets when cold but cannot be recooked.

CLASSIC USES

Lemon tart, lemon macarons

TIME TO MAKE

Preparation: 30 minutes
Cooking: 5 minutes

VARIATIONS

Orange cream, grapefruit cream: replace the lemon juice with the juice of another citrus fruit (orange, grapefruit . . .). Lemon curd domes: double the quantity of gelatine, pour the cream into silicone molds and freeze before unmolding. Once they are made, let them defrost in the refrigerator.

EQUIPMENT

Lemon squeezer
Microplane lemon zester
Hand-held blender

WHY ROLL THE LEMONS BEFORE SQUEEZING THEM?

This breaks the juice sacs in the lemon, which makes it easier to extract the juice.

WHAT MAKES THE MIXTURE SO THICK AND CREAMY?

The addition of the eggs provides creaminess because the eggs encourage the formation of an emulsion. They stabilize the fat in the lemon base provided by the butter. Cooking will then coagulate the egg proteins, making the curd more viscous.

TRICKY ASPECTS
Cooking
Incorporating the butter

TECHNIQUES TO MASTER
Zesting (page 281)
Hydrating gelatine (page 270)

TO MAKE 1 LB 3 OZ CURD

¹⁄₁₆ oz leaf gelatine
5 oz (about ⅔ cup) lemon juice (about 7 lemons)
7 oz egg (4 eggs)
5⅝ oz (.8 cup) superfine sugar
2¾ oz (5½ tbsp) butter

1 Soak the gelatine in cold water (page 270). Zest the lemons using a grater.

2 Roll the lemons on the work surface while pressing on them, to make them easier to juice. Squeeze them until you obtain 5 oz (about ⅔ cup) juice.

3 Break the eggs into a stainless-steel bowl and whisk them lightly.

4 Put the lemon zest and juice and the sugar in a saucepan. Whisk a little to dissolve the sugar and place over heat.

5 When it boils, remove from the heat and pour over the egg while whisking energetically so the egg doesn't cook.

6 Pour back into the saucepan, return to the heat and continue to whisk. As soon as it starts to boil, remove from the heat. Whisk in the butter and the drained gelatine, then blend for 2–3 minutes using a hand-held blender.

SHINY DARK CHOCOLATE
FROSTING

Understand

WHAT IS IT?

Very shiny frosting made from cocoa, used to cover desserts and cakes.

TIME TO MAKE

Preparation: 15 minutes

EQUIPMENT

Strainer
Hand-held blender

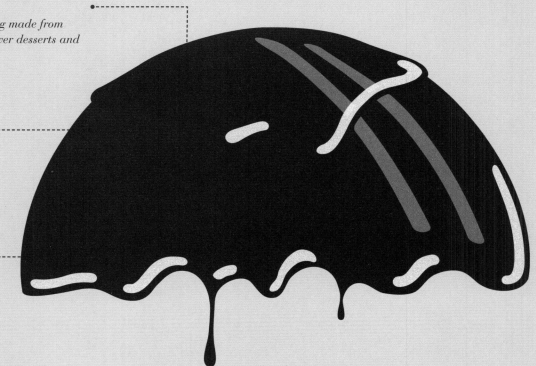

HOW DOES THE FROSTING SET UPON CONTACT WITH THE CAKE?

When the frosting is cooled, the gelatine it contains sets. It must reach 50°F to set completely.

WHY STRAIN THE FROSTING?

Straining creates a very smooth, even shinier frosting.

CLASSIC USE

Topping on a dessert

TRICKY ASPECT
Blending sufficiently

TECHNIQUE TO MASTER
Straining (page 270)

ORGANIZATION & STORAGE
The frosting can be reheated in a water bath if necessary.
Keeps for 1 week in the refrigerator and for 3 months in the freezer.

TO MAKE 1 LB 2 OZ FROSTING

¼ oz leaf gelatine

4¼ oz (½ cup ½ tbsp) water

3½ oz (7 tbsp) whipping cream (30% fat)

7¾ oz (1.1 cups) superfine sugar

2¾ oz (about .9 cups) bitter Dutch
   (unsweetened) cocoa powder

1   Hydrate the gelatine (page 270). Put the water,
cream and sugar on to boil. Stir.

2   Remove from the cooktop and add the drained
gelatine and the cocoa. Whisk to combine.

3   Blend with a hand-held blender to avoid lumps
and bubbles of cocoa. Strain (page 270). Use warm.

WHITE CHOCOLATE
FROSTING

Understand

WHAT IS IT?

Very white frosting with a white chocolate base.

TIME TO MAKE

Preparation: 15 minutes

EQUIPMENT

Whisk
Stainless-steel bowl

CLASSIC USE

Frosting on desserts or cakes

HOW CAN SOMETHING BE COLORED WHITE?

Thanks to titanium dioxide.

VARIATIONS

Colored frosting: add a touch of food coloring; mix it in well to obtain a homogeneous result.

TECHNIQUES TO MASTER
Hydrating gelatine (page 270)
Straining (page 270)
Preparing a water bath (page 270)

TO MAKE 9 OZ FROSTING

⅛ oz leaf gelatine
9 oz white chocolate
2 oz (¼ cup) milk
½ oz (1 tbsp) water
⅞ oz (1¼ tbsp) glucose syrup
⅛ oz food-grade titanium dioxide
   powder (white coloring)

1 Hydrate the gelatine (page 270). Melt the white chocolate in a water bath.

2 Put the milk, water and glucose on to boil. Once it boils, remove from the heat. Drain the gelatine and whisk into the milk mixture.

3 Whisk this mixture into the white chocolate. Add the titanium dioxide, remove the bowl from the water bath, then whisk for several minutes. Strain (page 270). Set aside in the refrigerator or use immediately.

MILK CHOCOLATE
FROSTING

Understand

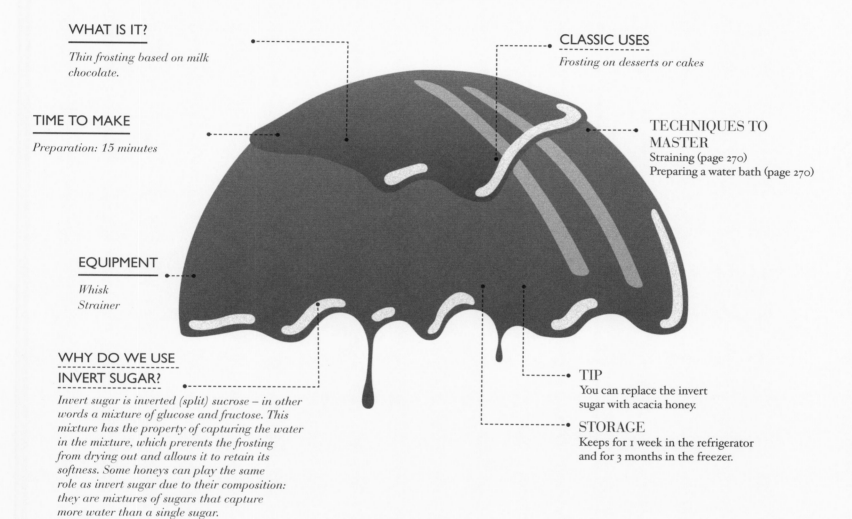

WHAT IS IT?

Thin frosting based on milk chocolate.

TIME TO MAKE

Preparation: 15 minutes

EQUIPMENT

*Whisk
Strainer*

**WHY DO WE USE
INVERT SUGAR?**

Invert sugar is inverted (split) sucrose – in other words a mixture of glucose and fructose. This mixture has the property of capturing the water in the mixture, which prevents the frosting from drying out and allows it to retain its softness. Some honeys can play the same role as invert sugar due to their composition: they are mixtures of sugars that capture more water than a single sugar.

CLASSIC USES

Frosting on desserts or cakes

**TECHNIQUES TO
MASTER**
Straining (page 270)
Preparing a water bath (page 270)

TIP
You can replace the invert
sugar with acacia honey.

STORAGE
Keeps for 1 week in the refrigerator
and for 3 months in the freezer.

TO MAKE 1 LB 3 OZ FROSTING

9 oz milk chocolate
3 oz dark chocolate
8 oz (1 cup) whipping cream (30% fat)
1⅜ oz (2 tbsp) invert sugar

1 Melt the milk chocolate and the dark chocolate together in a water bath (page 270).

2 In a saucepan, heat the cream with the invert sugar, mixing with a whisk.

3 When the cream mixture boils, whisk it into the chocolate mixture. Strain.

FONDANT
FROSTING

Understand

WHAT IS IT?

Frosting mixture, based on sugar, glucose syrup and water, that is available from specialist pastry suppliers in the form of a white paste to be reheated.

CLASSIC USES

Frosting on choux puffs and mille-feuilles.

EQUIPMENT

Candy thermometer

VARIATIONS

Colored frosting

TRICKY ASPECT

Getting the temperature right. If the fondant is overheated, the frosting won't be shiny.

TIP

Adding 1 oz (1½ tbsp) glucose syrup per 1 lb 2 oz fondant makes the frosting easier to use: with glucose the frosting will be shiny even if you overcook it a little.

PREPARATION

Put the fondant in a saucepan (add the glucose if using), then heat gently while stirring until it reaches 90–93°F at the most. If coloring is necessary, add it at the beginning.

FROSTING A CHOUX PUFF

Dipping: plunge the choux puff into the fondant, drain, then distribute it evenly with a finger.

As a shell: pour the fondant into half-sphere silicone molds, place the choux puffs on top of the fondant and push them in lightly. Put the whole thing in the freezer for 30 minutes, then unmold.

FROSTING AN ÉCLAIR

With spatula: let a ribbon of fondant fall from the spatula. When it runs evenly, pass the éclair under it.

With a basket-weave decorating tip: pipe the fondant using the smooth or fluted side of the tip.

FROSTING A MILLE-FEUILLE

If the pastry is not caramelized (page 208), brush a thin layer of glaze (page 275) over it. Melt 1⅜ oz dark chocolate in a water bath, then put in a pastry bag and make a small hole. Spread the fondant over the pastry using a frosting spatula. Pipe parallel chocolate lines, then score with a knife, perpendicular to the chocolate, first in one direction, then the other.

ROYAL
ICING

WHAT IS IT?

*Smooth and shiny white
frosting made using egg white,
confectioners' sugar and
lemon juice.*

TIME TO MAKE

Preparation: 15 minutes

EQUIPMENT

*Sieve
Whisk*

CLASSIC USES

*Decorating cakes or desserts,
decorating with a cone (page 273)*

VARIATIONS

*Colored royal icing: gradually
incorporate powdered
coloring (page 281)*

TRICKY ASPECTS

Sifting the sugar well to avoid it becoming grainy.
Not leaving the icing exposed to the air (it is at
risk of forming a crust).

HOW DOES THE ICING HARDEN?

*The confectioners' sugar is a mixture of sugar
and starch. When the ingredients are mixed,
the starch absorbs water, leaving less water
available to the sugar. The sugar then crystallizes,
triggering the hardening of the icing.*

TO MAKE 12 OZ ICING

10½ oz (2½ cups) confectioners' sugar
1 oz egg white (1 white)
⅜ oz (¾ tbsp) lemon juice

1   Sift the confectioners' sugar.

2   Whisk the egg white with an electric beater
at half-speed, adding the confectioners' sugar
little by little, until the mixture is smooth.

3   Incorporate the lemon juice. Cover
with plastic wrap, with the plastic
touching the surface of the icing.

TIPS

Depending on the intended use, you can vary
the consistency of the icing. By increasing
the quantity of confectioners' sugar, you
will move from a more supple consistency
(piping with a cone, covering an entire cake)
to a firm one (piping with a pastry bag).

STORAGE

Keeps for 1 week in the refrigerator with
plastic wrap touching the surface of the
icing. Keeps for 3 months in the freezer.

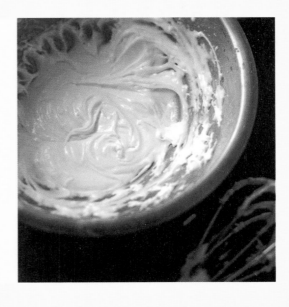

MARZIPAN

Understand

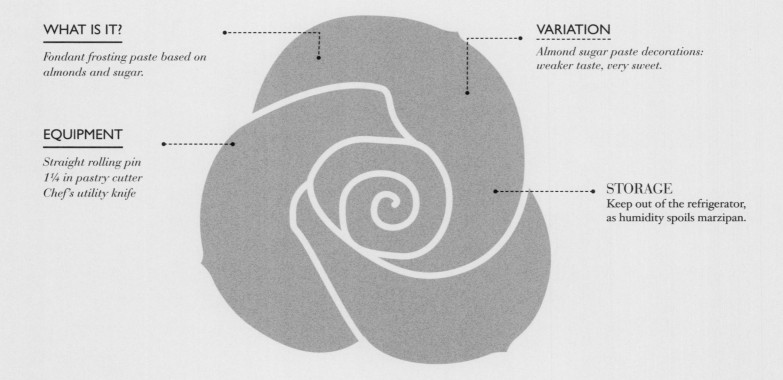

WHAT IS IT?

Fondant frosting paste based on almonds and sugar.

EQUIPMENT

*Straight rolling pin
1¼ in pastry cutter
Chef's utility knife*

VARIATION

Almond sugar paste decorations: weaker taste, very sweet.

STORAGE

Keep out of the refrigerator, as humidity spoils marzipan.

COLORING MARZIPAN

Sprinkle powdered coloring on the marzipan and knead until the color is even. Add gradually.

SPREADING MARZIPAN

Use potato starch rather than confectioners' sugar, to ensure the marzipan doesn't stick to the work surface. Dust (page 284) the work surface with the potato starch, then roll out the marzipan with a rolling pin.

COVERING A CAKE

Roll the marzipan to ½ in thickness. Curl the marzipan onto the rolling pin then unroll delicately over the cake. Press down on top with one hand, then smooth out the sides little by little, from top to bottom. With your other hand, lift the edge of the marzipan lightly to avoid pleats. Using a moist pastry brush, remove any visible potato starch. Trim off any excess marzipan using a utility knife.

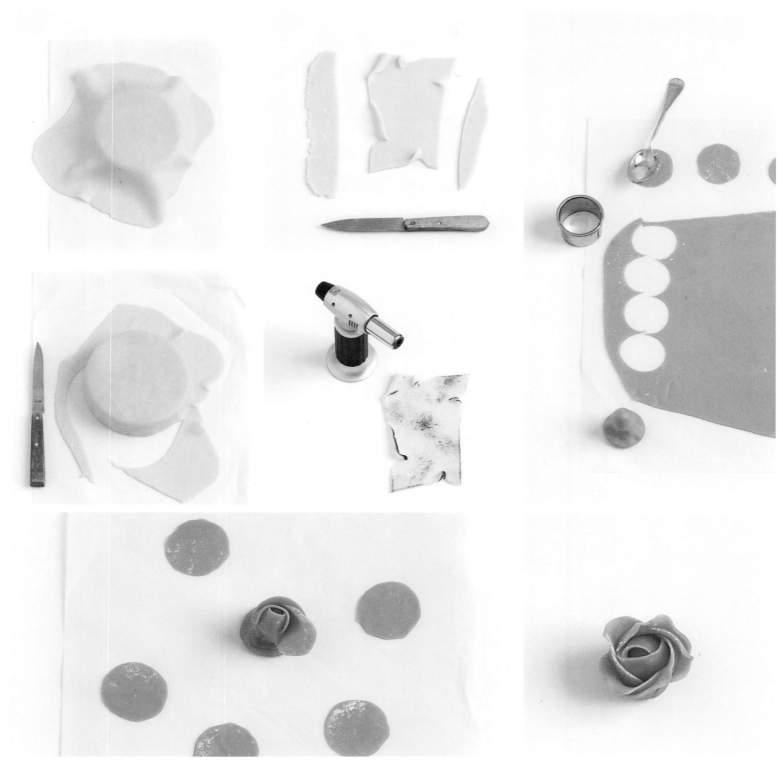

MAKING A SHEET

Roll the marzipan to ¹⁄₁₂ in thickness. Cut out a rectangle about 4¾ in × 3¼ in. Nick the edges three or four times to a depth of ⅜ in. Roll the corners and the edges of the nicks on themselves. Color using a kitchen blowtorch.

MAKING A ROSE

Roll the marzipan to ¹⁄₁₂ in thickness. Using a pastry cutter, cut out seven 1¼ in circles. With the aid of a spoon, thin out the circles. Make the rosebud with offcuts of the marzipan. Make a ball, then form a point. At the opposite end of the point, separate the ball into two with your fingers, without cutting, to make a base to put on the work surface, which will make it easier to arrange the petals. Put two petals on the bud, almost completely covering it. Press them down on the base to make them stick. Put the other petals over these, overlapping them. Press down to make them stick. Cut off the base with a utility knife.

SUGAR
DECORATIONS

Understand

WHAT ARE THEY?

Hard decorations made using classic caramel (with water).

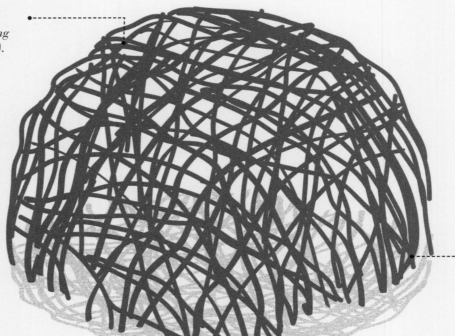

STORAGE
Use rapidly, as caramel is quickly affected by moisture in the air.

CARAMEL CAGE

1 Very lightly oil the back of a ladle by rubbing it with paper towel moistened with oil.

2 Make a classic caramel (page 48). When it is slightly thick, let it trickle from a tablespoon in a fine thread, then shake rapidly over the ladle. Repeat until you achieve the desired result.

3 Wait a few minutes, then lightly turn the caramel on the ladle to dislodge it.

TUILES

1 Make a classic caramel (page 48).

2 Using a spoon, make the caramel trickle in a fine thread over a sheet of baking paper, passing back and forth several times over the same spot to form a tuile. Let it harden completely.

SPUN-SUGAR HAZELNUTS

1 Make a classic caramel (page 48). Stick the hazelnuts on the ends of toothpicks.

2 When the caramel is slightly thick, dip the nuts in it.

3 Stick them in a block of polystyrene foam until the caramel hardens. Remove the toothpicks.

CHOCOLATE
DECORATIONS

Understand

WHAT ARE THEY?

Pieces made from couverture chocolate, which must be tempered for ease of manipulation and to obtain smooth and shiny decorations.

EQUIPMENT

Candy thermometer
Traditional work surface: marble
Alternative work surface: underside of a cookie sheet, silicone mat, guitar sheets or acetate sheets (baking paper gives a less shiny result)
Frosting spatula
Knife
Ruler

STORAGE

Chocolate decorations must be used quickly or kept in a box protected from moisture and heat. Don't put them in the refrigerator, which is too humid.

IS CHALKY CHOCOLATE BAD CHOCOLATE ?

No, it's chocolate that has not been subjected to a good tempering regime. It won't necessarily be bad, but it will melt more easily in the hand and will tend to turn white during storage.

DOES USING A MICROWAVE ALTER THE QUALITY OF THE CHOCOLATE?

Microwaves don't alter the quality of the chocolate if it isn't overheated during melting.

TEMPERING CHOCOLATE

Tempering the chocolate makes it melt-in-the-mouth and shiny, breaking with a crisp snap, and allows it to be handled without melting immediately. If it isn't tempered, when it cools it will take on a slightly grainy appearance and will turn white; poured into a mold, it won't unmold.

Tempering is carried out by following a precise tempering regime (heating, cooling, heating), which stabilizes the chocolate.

Cover the work surface, which will be slightly humid, with plastic wrap. Put the chocolate in a stainless-steel bowl.

DARK CHOCOLATE

Melt the chocolate in a warm water bath (page 270) until it reaches 122–131°F. Pour cold water into a stainless-steel bowl larger than the one holding the chocolate, and place a tart ring in the bottom for stability. Place the bowl containing the chocolate in the cold water bath: the water should reach the level of the chocolate. Let the temperature fall to 81–82°F, stirring regularly with a silicone spatula. Return to the warm water bath for 10 seconds at a time, stirring constantly, until the temperature rises to 88°F. It must not exceed 90°F. Use as quickly as possible. To maintain the temperature, regularly return the chocolate to the warm water bath, checking the temperature frequently to ensure a good tempering regime.

MILK CHOCOLATE

Melt to 113–122°F, cool to 79–81°F, reheat to 84–86°F.

WHITE CHOCOLATE

Melt to 104–113°F, cool to 77–79°F, reheat to 82–84°F.

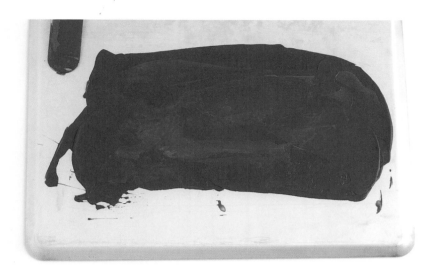

SHAVINGS

Temper the chocolate. Using a frosting spatula, spread it out in a thin layer on an overturned cookie sheet. When it has crystallized (wait about 30 minutes), scrape the surface, ideally with a fillet knife or a small pointed knife, and form shavings. To make curls, use a triangular frosting spatula.

DROPS

Temper the chocolate. Using a tablespoon, drop the equivalent of half a spoonful on an acetate sheet or guitar sheet or a cookie sheet, then, with the back of the spoon, press on the spoonful while pulling it along to form a drop.

SHEETS

Temper the chocolate. Pour it over an acetate sheet or guitar sheet and spread it out to 1/12 in thickness using a frosting spatula. When the chocolate is thick but not hard to the touch, it is ready to shape. Cut to the desired size and shape using a utility knife. Place a sheet of baking paper and a cookie sheet over the top and allow to crystallize. Detach the slabs from the backing sheet and manipulate them quickly (they melt fast).

RIBBONS FOR EDGING

Put a cookie sheet in the freezer for 30 minutes. Melt the chocolate in a water bath to about 104°F. Remove the sheet from the oven and very quickly spread a fine layer of chocolate over it using a frosting spatula. Using a utility knife and a ruler, cut a strip of the desired dimensions. Delicately detach the strip with the knife and apply to the dessert immediately.

PROFITEROLE
SAUCE

Understand

WHAT IS IT?

Dark chocolate and cocoa sauce, served warm as an accompaniment.

CLASSIC USES

Accompaniment to profiteroles, sauce for desserts

TECHNIQUES TO MASTER
Straining (page 270)

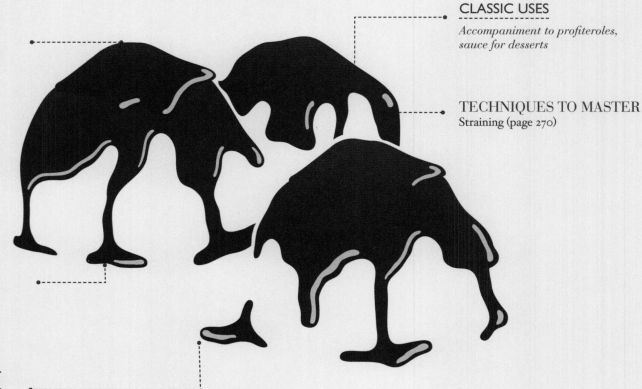

TIME TO MAKE

Preparation: 20 minutes
Cooking: 5 minutes

EQUIPMENT

Strainer
Whisk

TO MAKE 12½ OZ SAUCE

5¼ oz (⅔ cup) water
1¾ oz (¼ cup) superfine sugar
½ oz (2⅔ tbsp) Dutch (unsweetened)
    cocoa powder
4½ oz dark chocolate
Put the water and sugar in a saucepan, bring to the boil, add the cocoa powder and whisk. Add the chocolate and cook for 2 minutes, stirring with a spatula. Pass through a strainer. Serve warm.

MILK CHOCOLATE
SAUCE

Understand

WHAT IS IT?

Milk chocolate sauce, served as
an accompaniment.

CLASSIC USE

Sauce for cakes

TECHNIQUE TO MASTER
Straining (page 270)

TIME TO MAKE

Preparation: 20 minutes
Cooking: 5 minutes

STORAGE
Cover with plastic wrap with the plastic
touching the surface of the sauce.
Keeps for 1 week in the refrigerator
and for 3 months in the freezer.

EQUIPMENT

Strainer
Whisk

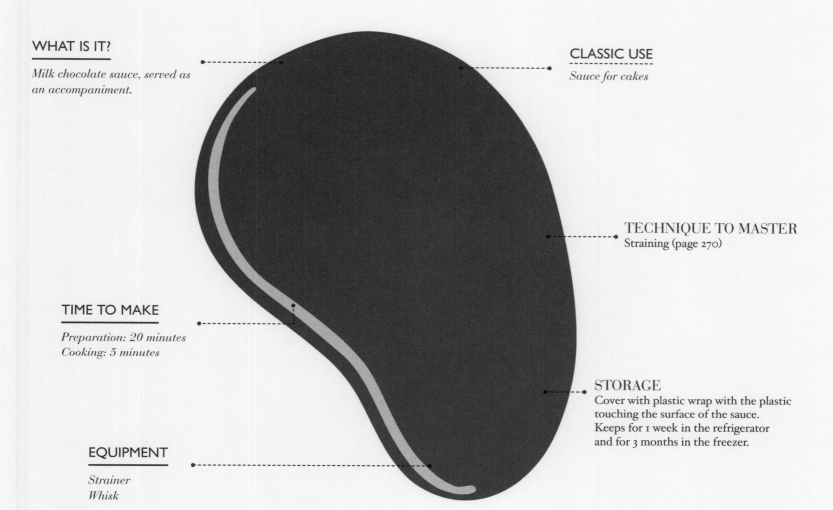

TO MAKE 11½ OZ SAUCE

5¼ oz (⅔ cup) milk
1 oz (1½ tbsp) glucose syrup
5¼ oz milk chocolate
Put the milk and glucose in a saucepan and
bring to the boil. Add the chocolate and cook
for 2 minutes while whisking. Whisk until
the chocolate is completely melted. Strain.
Serve warm.

RASPBERRY COULIS

Understand

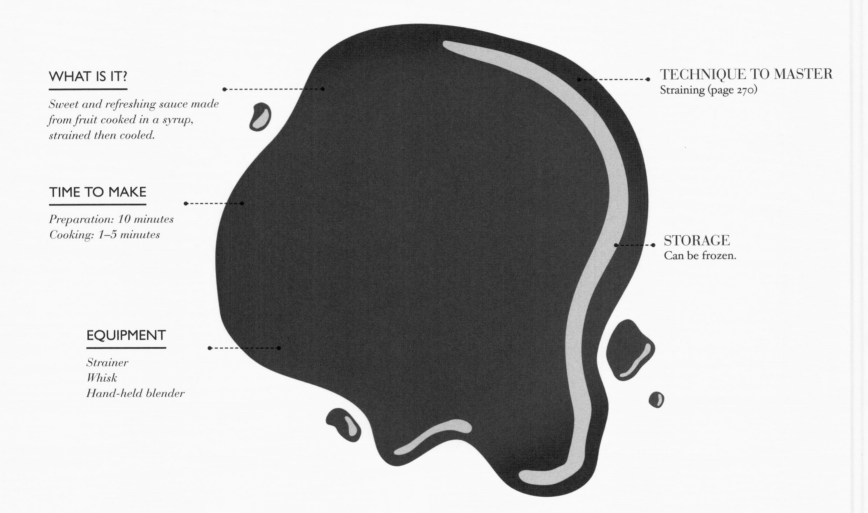

WHAT IS IT?

Sweet and refreshing sauce made from fruit cooked in a syrup, strained then cooled.

TIME TO MAKE

Preparation: 10 minutes
Cooking: 1–5 minutes

EQUIPMENT

Strainer
Whisk
Hand-held blender

TECHNIQUE TO MASTER
Straining (page 270)

STORAGE
Can be frozen.

TO MAKE 1 LB 9 OZ COULIS

3½ oz (7 tbsp) water
4¼ oz (.6 cup) superfine sugar
1 lb 11 oz raspberries

1 Put the water and sugar on to boil in a saucepan, add the raspberries and let them cook for 1 minute while mixing with a whisk.

2 Blend using a hand-held blender, then strain.

CARAMEL
SAUCE

Understand

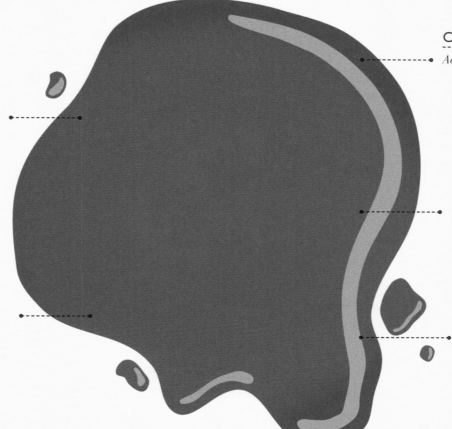

WHAT IS IT?

Caramel sauce containing cream, great as a topping.

TIME TO MAKE

Preparation: 20 minutes
Cooking: 5 minutes

CLASSIC USE

Accompaniment for cakes

TRICKY ASPECT

Incorporating the cream in the caramel

TECHNIQUES TO MASTER

Making dry caramel (page 49)
Straining (page 270)

WHY MAKE A DRY CARAMEL?

The flavoring capability of a dry caramel is much more powerful than that of a caramel made with water, and so is more useful for a sauce.

TO MAKE 6 OZ SAUCE

3½ oz (½ cup) superfine sugar
3½ oz (7 tbsp) whipping cream (30% fat)
1⁄16 oz (⅔ tsp) sea salt

1 Make a dry caramel (page 49). When the caramel develops a dark color, remove the saucepan from the heat and add the cream little by little, mixing well after each addition. Watch out for splashes.

2 Add the salt, then bring to the boil and cook for about 30 seconds. Strain (page 270).

CHAPTER 2
PASTRIES

BLACK FOREST
CAKE

CHOCOLATE
GENOESE
SPONGE

CHANTILLY
CREAM

CREAMY
CHOCOLATE
GANACHE

CHABLON

CHERRIES

SHINY DARK
CHOCOLATE
FROSTING

CHOCOLATE
SHAVINGS

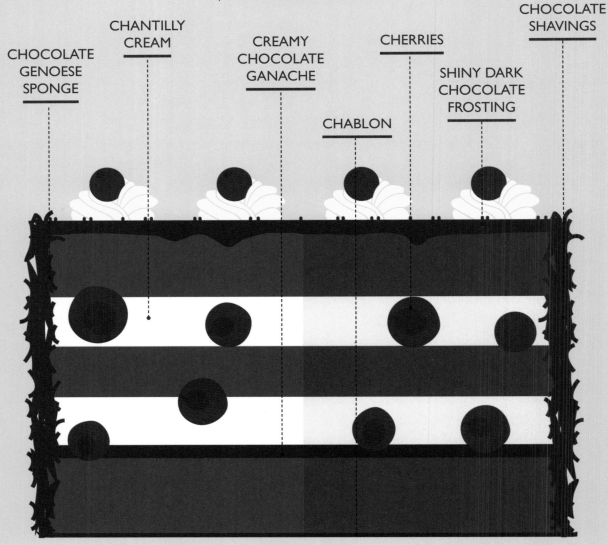

WHAT IS IT?

Dessert composed of a base of chocolate Genoese sponge with ganache, Chantilly cream and Morello and/or Amarena cherries.

TIME TO MAKE

*Preparation: 2 hours
Cooking: 15–25 minutes
Refrigeration: 30 minutes
Freezing: 40 minutes*

EQUIPMENT

*Large serrated knife
9½ in dessert ring 2 in high
Acetate cake band (used to prevent desserts from sticking to the cake tin when unmolding)*

VARIATION

For a traditional finish, simply cover the dessert in chantilly cream and add chocolate shavings (page 274).

TRICKY ASPECTS
Cooking the Genoese sponge perfectly
Frosting

TECHNIQUES TO MASTER
Creating a chablon layer (page 280)
Dousing desserts in syrup (page 278)
Piping (page 273)
Covering a cake with chocolate shavings (page 274)

ORGANIZATION
Sugar syrup – Genoese sponge – ganache – chantilly cream – assembly – frosting – chocolate shavings

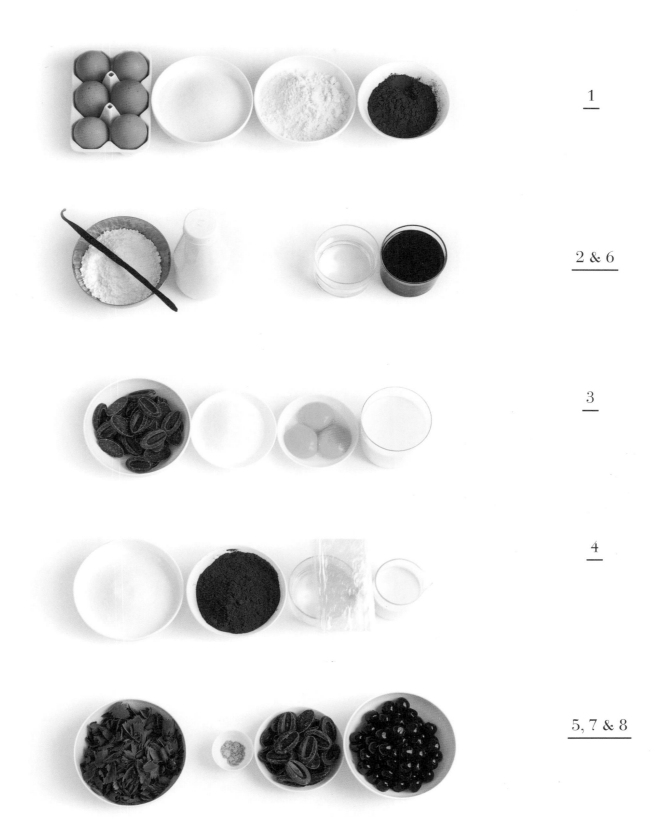

1

2 & 6

3

4

5, 7 & 8

TO SERVE 10

1 CHOCOLATE GENOESE SPONGE

10½ oz egg (6 eggs)
6¾ oz (about 1 cup) superfine sugar
5 oz (1 cup 2 tbsp) all-purpose flour
1½ oz (½ cup) Dutch
   (unsweetened) cocoa powder

2 CHANTILLY CREAM

14 oz (1¾ cups) whipping
   cream (30% fat)
2 oz (about ½ cup)
   confectioners' sugar
1 vanilla bean

3 CREAMY GANACHE

9 oz (1 cup 2 tbsp) milk
1¾ oz egg yolk (3 yolks)
1¾ oz (¼ cup) superfine sugar
4⅜ oz dark chocolate

4 SHINY DARK CHOCOLATE FROSTING

3½ oz (7 tbsp) whipping
   cream (30% fat)
7¾ oz (1.1 cups) superfine sugar
2¾ oz (about .9 cup) Dutch
   (unsweetened) cocoa powder
¼ oz leaf gelatine

5 FILLING

9 oz Morello cherries in syrup
   or Amarena cherries

6 CHERRY SOAKING SYRUP

7 oz syrup from the cherry tin or jar
2¾ oz (about .4 cup) superfine sugar
2¾ oz (⅓ cup) water

7 CHABLON

1 oz cooking chocolate

8 DECORATION

Chocolate shavings (page 274)
Gold powder

1 To make the cherry soaking syrup, bring the cherry syrup and the sugar to the boil. Remove from the heat and set aside. Reserve ten cherries as decoration. Make the Genoese sponge (page 33) and let it cool. Sit the dessert ring on a cookie sheet lined with baking paper. Line the insides of the ring with a strip of acetate cake band.

2 Using a large serrated knife, cut the cake in three horizontally. Add a chablon to the base of the bottom layer (page 280), then place in the prepared tin with the chablon side sitting on the baking paper.

3 Douse this layer in the soaking syrup (page 278).

4 Make the creamy ganache (page 72). Using a dough scraper or a silicone spatula, cover the bottom layer with 9 oz ganache and half the cherries, pushing them in gently. Refrigerate for 30 minutes.

5 Fill a pastry bag (page 272) with 7 oz chantilly cream (page 63), and distribute the cream over the ganache layer. Lay the second cake layer on top and douse it in the soaking syrup. Pipe the remaining chantilly cream over this layer and add the rest of the cherries.

6 Cover with the last cake layer, douse it in the remaining soaking syrup, and cover with the remaining ganache, setting aside 3½ oz for the end, and smooth out with a frosting spatula (page 274). Freeze for 30 minutes.

7 Make the shiny dark chocolate frosting (page 76) and let it cool. Take the cake out, remove from the tin and take off the acetate band. Using a frosting spatula, spread the reserved 3½ oz ganache around the sides and return to the freezer for 30 minutes. Place the cake on a wire rack over a cookie sheet,

then pour over the dark chocolate frosting and smooth it out with a frosting spatula to make a thin layer all over. Return to the freezer for 10 minutes.

8 Collect the surplus frosting and remelt it in a water bath or in the microwave. Fill a pastry bag. Take out the cake, make a small hole in the bag and pipe lines of frosting over the top of the cake. Garnish the sides with chocolate shavings (page 274), pipe ten little rosettes of chantilly cream on top, with a cherry in the middle of each, and dust the cake with the gold powder.

FRAISIER CAKE

Understand

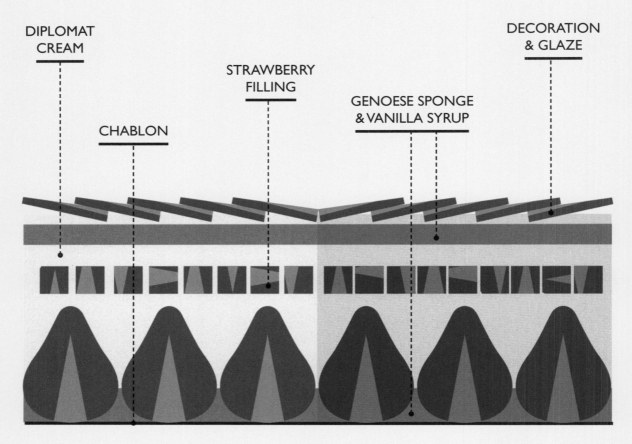

DIPLOMAT
CREAM

CHABLON

STRAWBERRY
FILLING

GENOESE SPONGE
& VANILLA SYRUP

DECORATION
& GLAZE

WHAT IS IT?

Dessert composed of a Genoese sponge base, with diplomat cream and fresh strawberries.

TIME TO MAKE

Preparation: 1 hour 30 minutes
Cooking: 20–30 minutes
Refrigeration: 5 hours

EQUIPMENT

9½ in dessert ring
Acetate cake band
Pastry bag
No. 12 plain decorating tip
Frosting spatula

VARIATION

Classic fraisier cake: made with German butter cream, decorated with marzipan

TRICKY ASPECT
Assembly

TECHNIQUES TO MASTER
Creating a chablon layer (page 280)
Dousing desserts in syrup (page 278)
Using a pastry bag (page 272)

ORGANIZATION
Pastry cream – Genoese sponge – syrup – diplomat cream – assembly – decoration

2

1

3

4, 5 & 6

TO SERVE 10

1 GENOESE SPONGE

7 oz egg (4 eggs)
4⅜ oz (about .6 cup)
    superfine sugar
4⅜ oz (1 cup) all-purpose flour

2 DIPLOMAT CREAM

pastry cream
3½ oz egg yolk (6 yolks)
4¼ oz (.6 cups) superfine sugar
1¾ oz (about .4 cup) cornstarch
1 lb 2 oz (2¼ cups) milk
1¾ oz (3½ tbsp) butter
1 vanilla bean

whipped cream
7 oz (about .9 cup)
    whipping cream (30% fat)
¼ oz leaf gelatine

3 VANILLA SYRUP

2 vanilla beans
11½ oz (about 1.4 cups) water
5¼ oz (¾ cup) superfine sugar

4 CHABLON

1 oz chocolate

5 FILLING

2 lb 3 oz gariguette strawberries
    or another conical variety

6 GLAZE

about 3½ oz apricot jelly or
    apricot glaze
½ oz (1 tbsp) water

1   To make the vanilla syrup, split the vanilla beans lengthways, scrape out the seeds and put both seeds and beans in a saucepan with the water and sugar. Bring to the boil. Remove from the heat.

2   Make the vanilla pastry cream (page 52) for the diplomat cream and set aside to cool. Make the Genoese sponge (page 32) in a 9½ in dessert frame over a lined cookie sheet, then set aside to cool. Make the diplomat cream (page 68). Hull the strawberries and cut about fifteen of them lengthways for the outside of the fraisier cake.

3   Cut the cooled Genoese sponge in two horizontally. Melt the chocolate for the chablon layer. Add a chablon to the base of the bottom layer (page 280).

4   Sit the dessert ring on a cookie sheet lined with baking paper. Line the insides of the ring with a band of acetate cake wrap. Place the chocolate-coated sponge layer in the ring, chablon side down. Fill a pastry bag fitted with a no. 12 decorating tip with diplomat cream. Pipe a ring of cream between the sponge and the dessert ring. Slide half-strawberries all around the ring, with the cut side against the ring.

5   Douse this layer in the vanilla syrup (page 278).

6   Cover the ring of strawberries with piped diplomat cream. Using a frosting spatula, smooth the cream over the strawberries all around the ring.

7   Dice the strawberries for the filling. Cover the bottom cake layer with piped diplomat cream, then distribute half of the strawberries over it, pushing them down lightly. Cover with the rest of the diplomat cream, taking care to reserve 3 tablespoons for the last layer.

8   Douse the second sponge layer in the vanilla syrup, then place the doused side on the cream. Douse the other side. Spread the rest of the cream over the top using a frosting spatula. Refrigerate for 2 hours.

DECORATION

Warm the apricot glaze or jelly in a saucepan with the water. Spread a fine layer over the top of the fraisier cake, smoothing it with a spatula. Leave the acetate band until ready to serve, to protect the strawberries from oxidation. Cut the remaining strawberries in thin slices and arrange them in a rosette on top of the cake. Using a pastry brush, cover with a thin layer of apricot glaze, to protect the fruit.

OPERA CAKES

Understand

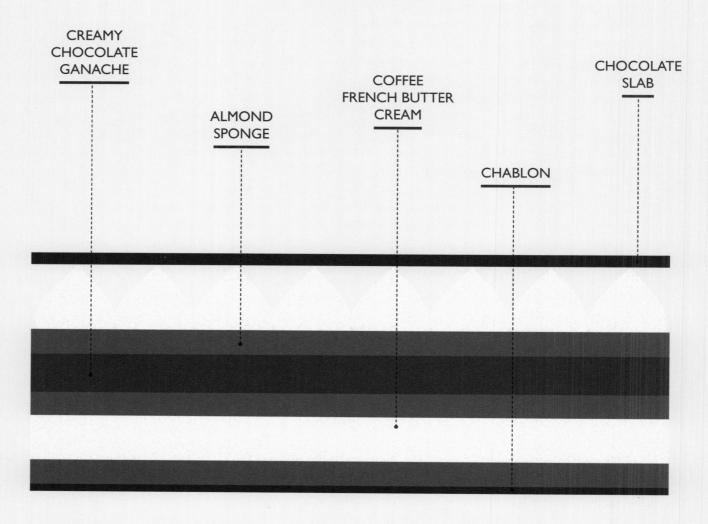

CREAMY
CHOCOLATE
GANACHE

ALMOND
SPONGE

COFFEE
FRENCH BUTTER
CREAM

CHOCOLATE
SLAB

CHABLON

WHAT ARE THEY?

Desserts composed of almond sponge, creamy ganache and a coffee-flavored French butter cream, topped with a slab of snappy chocolate.

TIME TO MAKE

Preparation: 2 hours
Cooking: 8–15 minutes
Refrigeration: 4 hours

EQUIPMENT

9½ in square dessert frame
Chef's knife
Pastry bag fitted with a no. 8 plain decorating tip

TRICKY ASPECTS
Assembly
Piping

TECHNIQUES TO MASTER
Creating a chablon layer (page 280)
Preparing a water bath (page 270)
Using a pastry bag (page 272)

ORGANIZATION
Syrup – almond sponge – ganache – French butter cream – chocolate slab

VARIATION

To make a vanilla opera cake: place 1 scraped vanilla bean in the syrup and add ¾ oz (1⅓ tbsp) vanilla extract + 1 scraped bean to the butter cream.

TO MAKE 16

1 ALMOND SPONGE

base
7 oz (1⅔ cups) confectioners' sugar
7 oz (about 2.1 cups) almond meal
10½ oz egg (6 eggs)
1 oz (¼ cup) all-purpose flour

meringue
7 oz egg white (about 7 whites)
1 oz (2¼ tbsp) superfine sugar

2 CREAMY CHOCOLATE GANACHE

1⅜ oz egg yolk (2 yolks)
1⅜ oz (.2 cup) superfine sugar
7 oz (about .9 cup) milk
3½ oz dark chocolate

3 COFFEE FRENCH BUTTER CREAM

7 oz egg (4 eggs)
2¾ oz (⅓ cup) water
9¼ oz (1⅓ cup) superfine sugar
14 oz (1¾ cups) butter, softened
2 oz (¼ cup) coffee extract

4 COFFEE SYRUP

11½ oz (about 1.4 cups) water
5¼ oz (¾ cup) superfine sugar
1 oz (2 tbsp) coffee extract

5 CHOCOLATE SLAB

7 oz dark chocolate

6 CHABLON

1 oz dark cooking chocolate

1   Make the coffee syrup. Bring the sugar and water to the boil. Remove from the heat and add the coffee extract. Set aside. Make three almond sponge slabs (page 35). Make the coffee French butter cream (page 54). Make the ganache (page 72). Line a cookie sheet with baking paper and place the dessert frame on top. Melt the chocolate for the chablon.

2   Cut one piece of sponge to the size of the frame. Add a chablon to the base (page 280) and place it in the frame, chocolate side down.

3   Douse the sponge (page 278) in the warm coffee syrup; when you touch the cake, syrup should appear.

4   Spread 1 lb of the butter cream over the first sponge layer using a frosting spatula.

5   Cut a second piece of sponge. Place it on top of the cream layer and douse in the coffee syrup. Spread the creamy ganache on top using a frosting spatula.

6   Place the third piece of trimmed sponge on top and douse in the syrup (page 278). Refrigerate for 2 hours. Remove from the frame and neatly trim the edges. Put the remaining butter cream in a pastry bag fitted with a no. 8 plain decorating tip and pipe domes of cream all over the top of the dessert.

7   Prepare a water bath (page 270). Melt the chocolate for the slab, then spread it over a marble block (page 87).

8   Cut sixteen small slabs of chocolate 4¼ in × 1 in (page 87).

FINAL PRESENTATION

Cut the opera cake into sixteen 4¼ in × 1 in pieces using a chef's knife dipped in hot water. Place a chocolate slab on top of each piece.

MOCHA CAKE

CARAMELIZED
ALMONDS

COFFEE
FRENCH BUTTER
CREAM

GENOESE
SPONGE

CRUNCHY BASE

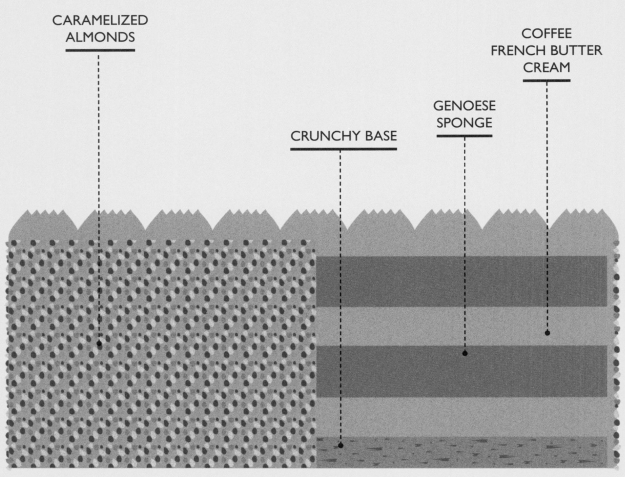

WHAT IS IT?

Coffee-flavored dessert composed of Genoese sponge and French butter cream, assembled on a crunchy base and covered in caramelized almonds.

TIME TO MAKE

Preparation: 1 hour 30 minutes
Cooking: 35 minutes to 1 hour
Resting: 4 hours

EQUIPMENT

2 × 9½ in dessert rings
Pastry bag
Basket-weave decorating tip
Acetate cake band
Large serrated knife

VARIATIONS

Classic mocha cake: replace the crumble base with a first layer of Genoese sponge. Chocolate mocha cake: omit the coffee extract and add 1 oz (⅓ cup) Dutch (unsweetened) cocoa powder to the Genoese sponge and 5¼ oz melted chocolate to the butter cream.

TRICKY ASPECTS

Getting the temperature of the French butter cream right
Dousing the Genoese sponge in syrup

TECHNIQUES TO MASTER

Making a sugar syrup (page 278)
Roasting nuts (page 281)
Preparing a water bath (page 270)
Dousing desserts in syrup (page 278)

ORGANIZATION

Crumble – crunchy base – Genoese sponge – coffee French butter cream – assembly

<u>1</u>

<u>2</u>

<u>3</u>

<u>4 & 5</u>

TO SERVE 10

1 GENOESE SPONGE

7 oz egg (4 eggs)
4⅜ oz (about ⅔ cup)
   superfine sugar
4⅜ oz (1 cup) all-purpose flour

2 COFFEE BUTTER CREAM

10½ oz egg (6 eggs)
4¼ oz (about ½ cup) water
14¾ oz (about 2.1 cups) superfine sugar
1 lb 5 oz (about 2⅔ cups) butter, softened
1 oz (2 tbsp) coffee extract

3 COFFEE SYRUP

11½ oz (about 1.4 cups) water

5¼ oz (¾ cup) superfine sugar
1 oz (2 tbsp) coffee extract

4 CRUNCHY BASE

1¾ oz (½ cup) almond meal
1¾ oz (¼ cup) superfine sugar
1¾ oz (.4 cup) all-purpose flour
1¾ oz (3½ tbsp) butter
¾ oz (about ¼ cup) hazelnut meal
2 oz white chocolate

1 oz praline (ground caramelized
   almonds)
1 oz pailleté feuilletine (crumbled
   crêpes dentelles – lacy crepes)

5 CARAMELIZED ALMONDS

¾ oz (1½ tbsp) water
¾ oz (1⅔ tbsp) superfine sugar
7 oz (about 1.8 cups) chopped
   almonds

1 To make the coffee syrup, bring the water and sugar to the boil. Remove from the heat and add the coffee extract. Set aside. To make the caramelized almonds, preheat the oven to 320°F, bring the water and sugar to the boil in a saucepan. Remove from the heat. Let it cool to lukewarm, then add the almonds. Spread over a cookie sheet lined with baking paper and bake for 15–25 minutes, stirring regularly. Remove from the oven when golden and set aside to cool. Leave the oven at 320°F. To make the crumble for the crunchy base, mix the almond meal, sugar and flour, then rub in the butter with your hands. Spread in a thin layer over a cookie sheet lined with baking paper. Bake for 15–20 minutes, stirring from time to time with a spatula. Remove from the oven when the crumble is golden, then set aside to cool. Leave the oven at 320°F.

2 Toast the hazelnut meal in the oven for 15 minutes (page 281). Melt the white chocolate in a water bath. Add the praline, toasted hazelnut meal, pailleté feuilletine and the crumble. Mix using a spatula.

3 Line a cookie sheet with baking paper. Line a 9½ in dessert ring with acetate cake band. Turn the crunchy base mixture into the ring and smooth the top with a frosting spatula. Refrigerate.

4 Make the Genoese sponge (page 32) in 9½ in dessert ring on a lined cookie sheet. Allow to cool. Make the butter cream, adding the coffee extract at the end (page 54). With a large serrated knife, cut a thin layer off the bottom of the Genoese sponge, to allow the syrup to penetrate better. Cut in two horizontally.

5 Put 14 oz of the coffee butter cream on top of the crunchy base and smooth the top with a frosting spatula. Place the first layer of sponge on top and douse in coffee syrup using a pastry brush (page 278). Repeat these steps: put 14 oz butter cream on top, then the second layer of sponge and douse it with the syrup.

6 Put half the remaining butter cream in a pastry bag fitted with a basket-weave decorating tip and use the rest to cover the dessert: smooth over the top, remove the cake band and cover the sides (page 274). Decorate the top by piping on waves (page 273).

7 Cover the sides with the caramelized almonds, using the same method as for chocolate shavings (page 274).

TRIPLE-CHOCOLATE
MOUSSE CAKE

Understand

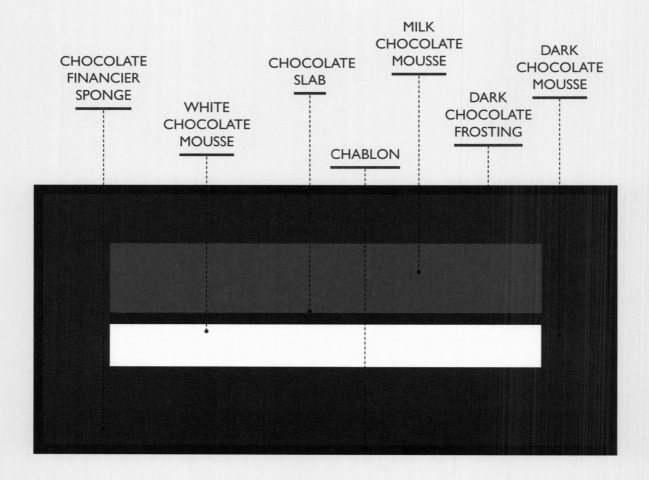

CHOCOLATE
FINANCIER
SPONGE

WHITE
CHOCOLATE
MOUSSE

CHOCOLATE
SLAB

CHABLON

MILK
CHOCOLATE
MOUSSE

DARK
CHOCOLATE
FROSTING

DARK
CHOCOLATE
MOUSSE

WHAT IS IT?

Dessert composed of a chocolate financier sponge base and three chocolate mousses (dark, milk, white) between which is interposed a snappy chocolate layer.

TIME TO MAKE

Preparation: 2 hours
Cooking: 15 minutes
Freezing: at least 6 hours

EQUIPMENT

4¾ in × 9½ in rectangular dessert frame
3¼ in × 8¾ in rectangular cake tin
Wire rack
Frosting spatula

TRICKY ASPECTS

Making the crème anglaise
Freezing the insert well enough
to manipulate it
Manipulating the chocolate slab

TECHNIQUES TO MASTER

Preparing a water bath (page 270)
Hydrating gelatine (page 270)
Making a chocolate slab (page 87)

ORGANIZATION

Insert (milk chocolate mousse, white chocolate mousse and slab of chocolate) – sponge – dark chocolate mousse – frosting

TO SERVE 8–10

1 CHOCOLATE FINANCIER SPONGE

1 oz dark chocolate

2⅝ oz (¾ cup) almond meal

2 oz (about ½ cup) confectioners' sugar

³⁄₁₆ oz (2 tbsp) cornstarch

4 oz egg white (4 whites)

1 oz (2 tbsp) whipping cream (30% fat)

2 CHABLON

1 oz dark chocolate

3 CRÈME ANGLAISE

3⅝ oz (.45 cup) whipping cream (30% fat)

3⅝ oz (.45 cup) milk

1⅜ oz egg yolk (2 yolks)

⅞ oz (2 tbsp) superfine sugar

4 CHOCOLATE MOUSSES

base

3 oz milk chocolate

¹⁄₃₂ oz leaf gelatine

2¾ oz white chocolate

6⅛ oz dark chocolate

whipped cream

13¼ oz (1⅔ cup) whipping cream (30% fat)

5 SHINY DARK CHOCOLATE FROSTING

8½ oz (1 cup 1 tbsp) water

7 oz (about .9 cup) whipping cream (30% fat)

15½ oz (2.2 cups) superfine sugar

5⅝ oz (about 1.9 cups) bitter Dutch (unsweetened) cocoa powder

³⁄₁₆ oz leaf gelatine

6 CHOCOLATE SLAB

5¼ oz dark chocolate

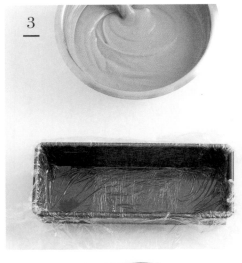

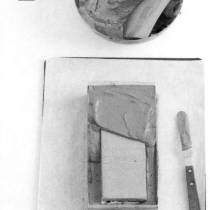

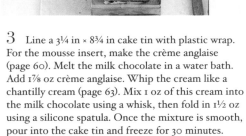

1   Preheat the oven to 360°F. To make the sponge, melt the chocolate in a water bath. In another bowl, mix the almond meal, confectioners' sugar and cornstarch. Add the egg white and the cream, and mix with a spatula until smooth. Add the melted chocolate and mix it in. Line a cookie sheet with baking paper and place a 4¾ in × 9½ in frame on top. Pour the mixture into the frame and bake for 14 minutes. Remove from the oven, allow to cool and remove the frame.

2   Melt the chocolate for the chablon in a water bath. Turn the sponge upside down on a sheet of baking paper. Remove the baking paper from the base and add a layer of chocolate to the bottom of the cake. Line a cookie sheet with baking paper and place the frame on top. Once the chablon has hardened, place the sponge in the frame, chocolate side down.

3   Line a 3¼ in × 8¾ in cake tin with plastic wrap. For the mousse insert, make the crème anglaise (page 60). Melt the milk chocolate in a water bath. Add 1⅞ oz crème anglaise. Whip the cream like a chantilly cream (page 63). Mix 1 oz of this cream into the milk chocolate using a whisk, then fold in 1½ oz using a silicone spatula. Once the mixture is smooth, pour into the cake tin and freeze for 30 minutes.

4   Make a chocolate slab (page 87) 8 in long, 2¾ in wide and ⅜ in thick. Freeze for 30 minutes.

5   Hydrate the gelatine (page 270). Melt the white chocolate in a water bath. Drain the gelatine and whisk into the white chocolate. Make the white chocolate mousse the same way as the milk chocolate mousse. Take the cake tin out of the freezer, put the chocolate slab on top of the milk chocolate mousse and pour the white chocolate mousse on top. Return to the freezer for 2 hours, or ideally overnight.

6   Make the dark chocolate mousse the same way as the milk chocolate mousse, whisking in half the remaining cream, then folding in the rest with a silicone spatula. Pour one-third of the dark chocolate mousse over the sponge and freeze for 30 minutes.

7   Remove the sponge/dark chocolate mousse and the insert from the freezer. If necessary, cut down the insert so that it is 3¼ in × 8¾ in. Place on top of the dark chocolate mousse base.

8   Pour over the remaining dark chocolate mousse. Freeze for 2 hours.

9   Make the shiny dark chocolate frosting (page 76) and let it cool. Remove the dessert from the freezer and unmold. Place on a wire rack over a cookie sheet with sides. Pour over the frosting. Smooth using a frosting spatula to obtain a thin layer (page 280).

Triple-chocolate mousse cake

CARAMEL
DESSERT

Understand

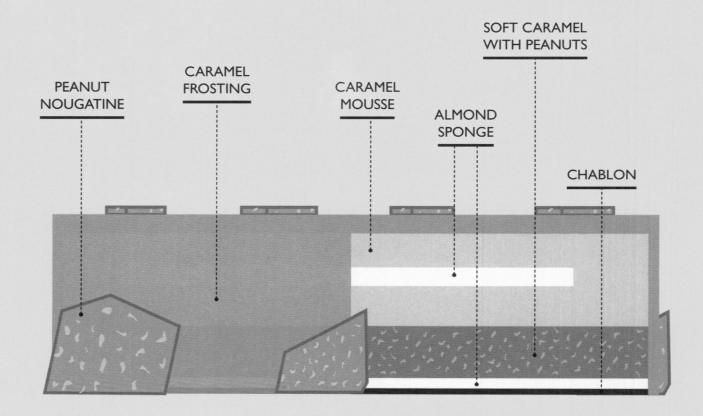

PEANUT
NOUGATINE

CARAMEL
FROSTING

CARAMEL
MOUSSE

ALMOND
SPONGE

SOFT CARAMEL
WITH PEANUTS

CHABLON

WHAT IS IT?

Dessert composed of an almond sponge base, soft caramel with peanuts and caramel mousse, covered with caramel frosting and peanut nougatine.

TIME TO MAKE

Preparation: 2 hours
Cooking: 15 minutes
Freezing: at least 6 hours

EQUIPMENT

7 in dessert ring
9½ in dessert ring
Acetate cake band
Candy thermometer
Wire rack
Frosting spatula

TRICKY ASPECTS
Making the caramels

TECHNIQUES TO MASTER
Making dry caramel (page 49)
Using a pastry bag (page 272)

ORGANIZATION
Soft caramel – almond sponge – mousse – frosting – nougatine

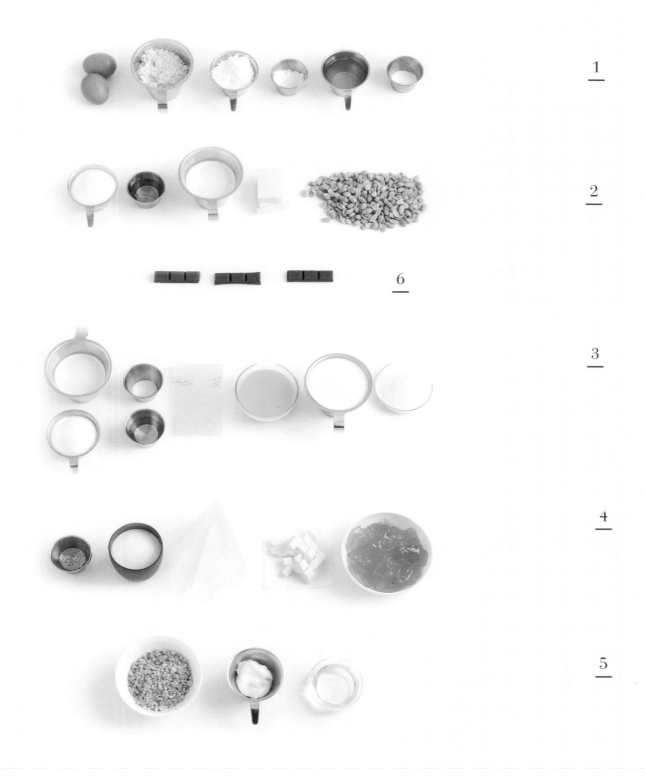

1

2

6

3

4

5

TO SERVE 8

1 ALMOND SPONGE

sponge base

2½ oz (about .6 cup)
  confectioners' sugar
2½ oz (¾ cup) almond meal
3½ oz egg (2 eggs)
⅜ oz (1⅓ tbsp) all-purpose flour

meringue

2½ oz egg white (2 whites)
⅜ oz (2½ tbsp) superfine sugar

2 SOFT CARAMEL WITH PEANUTS

4½ oz (.9 cup) salted roasted peanuts
3½ oz (½ cup) superfine sugar
4½ oz (9 tbsp) whipping
  cream (30% fat)
2½ oz (5 tbsp) butter
1¾ oz (2½ tbsp) glucose syrup

3 CARAMEL MOUSSE

bombe mixture

3½ oz egg yolk (6 yolks)
1¼ oz (2½ tbsp) water
4½ oz (⅔ cup) superfine sugar

caramel

⅜ oz leaf gelatine
3½ oz (½ cup) superfine sugar
4½ oz (9 tbsp) whipping cream (30% fat)
³⁄₁₆ oz (2 tbsp) sea salt

whipped cream

9 oz (1 cup 2 tbsp) whipping cream
  (30% fat)

4 CARAMEL FROSTING

⅜ oz leaf gelatine
6⅛ oz (about .9 cup) superfine sugar
3 oz (about ¼ cup) glucose syrup
9 oz apricot glaze
1⅜ oz (2¾ tbsp) butter

5 NOUGATINE

2¼ oz (about ½ cup) salted
  roasted peanuts, chopped
2⅝ oz white fondant
2¼ oz (3⅓ tbsp) glucose syrup

6 CHABLON

1 oz dark chocolate

1 To make the soft caramel with peanuts, roughly chop the peanuts in a food processor. Make a dry caramel (page 49). As soon as the caramel turns dark, remove from the heat and pour in a little of the cream. When it is incorporated, add a little bit more cream and mix. Repeat until all the cream has been incorporated. Add the butter, then the chopped peanuts. Line a cookie sheet with baking paper and sit a 9½ in dessert ring on top. Pour the caramel mixture into the ring and freeze for at least 2 hours.

2 Make the almond sponge (page 34). Unmold the soft caramel, return it to the freezer and clean the dessert ring. Once the sponge has cooled, cut out one 7 in disc and one 9½ in disc. Melt the chablon chocolate and add a layer to the larger disc.

3 Line the 9½ in dessert ring with acetate cake band and place it on a cookie sheet lined with baking paper. Place the larger sponge piece in the ring, chocolate side down. Put the soft caramel on the almond sponge. Set sponge and caramel aside in the refrigerator.

4 To make the caramel mousse, hydrate the gelatine (page 270). Make a dry caramel (page 49). As soon as the caramel turns dark, remove from the heat, deglaze with the cream, then whisk. Drain the gelatine, incorporate it into the caramel, sift then add the salt, then set aside to cool to room temperature.

5 Whip the cream for the mousse like a chantilly cream (page 63). Make the bombe mixture (page 58). Whisk one-third of the cream into the caramel. Add the bombe mixture and fold in gently using a silicone spatula. Add the remaining whipped cream and fold in gently with the silicone spatula until the mixture is smooth.

6 Spread a layer of mousse over the soft caramel. Place the small piece of sponge in the middle, then cover with the remaining mousse and freeze for at least 2 hours, ideally overnight

7 To make the caramel frosting, hydrate the gelatine (page 270). Make a dry caramel with the sugar and glucose (page 49). As soon as the caramel turns dark, remove from the heat, deglaze with the glaze, mix using a whisk, then add the butter. Drain the gelatine, then incorporate it. Blend, strain and cool to 104°F. Take out the dessert, then remove the ring and the cake band. Place on a wire rack, pour over the frosting and smooth it out (page 274).

8 Make the nougatine (page 50), smash it into pieces with a rolling pin and use it to decorate the dessert.

TIRAMISU

Understand

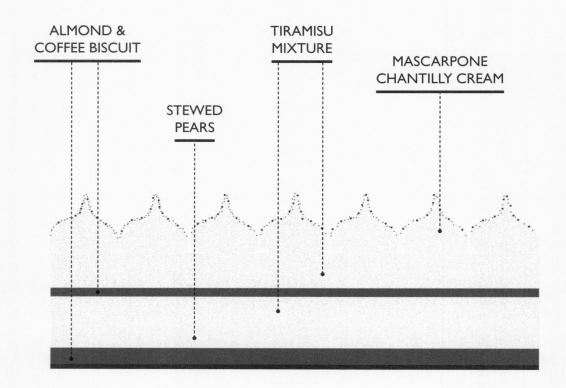

ALMOND &
COFFEE BISCUIT

STEWED
PEARS

TIRAMISU
MIXTURE

MASCARPONE
CHANTILLY CREAM

WHAT IS IT?

Dessert composed of an almond and coffee biscuit, tiramisu mousse and stewed pears.

TIME TO MAKE

Preparation: 2 hours
Cooking: 15–25 minutes
Freezing: 4 hours 30 minutes

EQUIPMENT

4¾ in × 9½ in rectangular dessert frame
Food processor
Electric mixer with whisk or beater attachment
Pastry bag
St Honoré decorating tip

TRICKY ASPECT
Assembly

TECHNIQUES TO MASTER
Piping with a St Honoré decorating tip (page 273)

TIP
For a quicker version, omit the stewed pear layer.

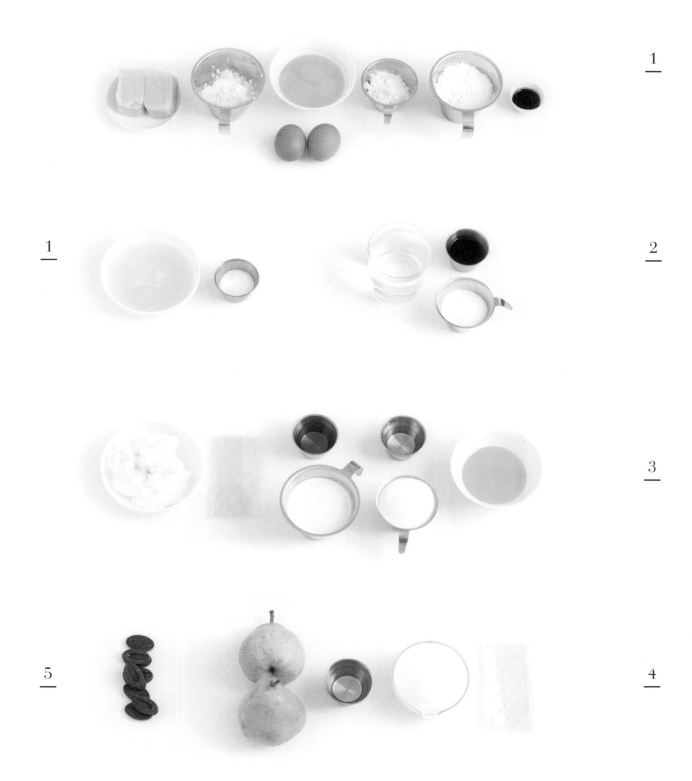

TO SERVE 6–8

1 ALMOND AND COFFEE BISCUIT

2⅝ oz (⅓ cup) almond paste
   (made using raw almonds at 50%)
1⅜ oz egg yolk (2 yolks)
1¾ oz egg (1 egg)
1½ oz (⅓ cup) confectioners' sugar
⅜ oz (2¼ tsp) coffee extract
½ oz (1¾ tbsp) all-purpose flour
1 oz (3½ tbsp) cornstarch

French meringue
4⅜ oz egg white (4 whites)
1 oz (2¼ tbsp) superfine sugar

2 COFFEE SYRUP

11½ oz (about 1½ cups) water
5¼ oz (¾ cup) superfine sugar
1 oz (2 tbsp) coffee extract

3 TIRAMISU MIXTURE

³⁄₁₆ oz leaf gelatine
13¼ oz mascarpone
9 oz (1 cup 2 tbsp) whipping
   cream (30% fat)
1 oz (2 tbsp) Marsala

bombe mixture
2½ oz egg yolk (4 yolks)
1 oz (2 tbsp) water
4 oz (about .6 cup) superfine sugar

4 STEWED PEARS

14 oz pears
1 oz (2 tbsp) water
2 oz (4½ tbsp) superfine sugar
³⁄₁₆ oz leaf gelatine

5 CHABLON

1 oz dark chocolate

6 DECORATION

1 oz (⅓ cup) Dutch (unsweetened)
   cocoa powder

1   To make the almond and coffee biscuit, preheat the oven to 360°F. Using a food processor, mix the almond paste with the egg yolk and the whole egg. Transfer to an electric mixer fitted with the whisk attachment. Add the confectioners' sugar and beat for several minutes to obtain a very airy mixture. Add the coffee extract. Whisk gently until the mixture is uniform. Transfer to a large stainless-steel bowl.

2   Make the French meringue (page 42). Gently fold one-third into the almond mixture using a silicone spatula. Fold in the sifted flour and cornstarch using a silicone spatula. Fold in the remaining meringue using a silicone spatula.

3   Pour the mixture into a cookie sheet lined with baking paper and spread out using a frosting spatula. Bake for 15–25 minutes. Allow to cool.

4   Core the pears, cut them into ¾ in cubes, and put them in a saucepan with the water and sugar. Hydrate the gelatine (page 270). Cook the pears over high heat until the mixture is very dry, almost candied, stirring frequently with a spatula. Drain the gelatine and add.

5   Cut two pieces of almond and coffee biscuit. Melt the chocolate for the chablon in a water bath. To make the coffee syrup, bring the water and sugar to the boil. Remove from the heat and add the coffee extract. Place a 4¾ in × 9½ in dessert frame on a cookie sheet lined with baking paper. Add a chablon layer to one of the biscuit pieces.

6   Place the coated biscuit in the frame, chablon side down. Douse the biscuit with the coffee syrup (page 278). Spread all the stewed pear over the biscuit using a silicone spatula. Freeze for 3 hours.

7   To make the tiramisu mixture, soak the gelatine in cold water. Whip the mascarpone with the cream using an electric mixer. Set aside 7½ oz for the decoration and add the confectioners' sugar. Refrigerate. Make the bombe mixture (page 58). Warm the Marsala and melt the drained gelatine in it. Gently whisk the Marsala into the whipped mascarpone and cream, then whisk in one-third of the bombe mixture. Gently fold in the rest of the bombe mixture using a silicone spatula.

8   Using a silicone spatula, spread 9 oz of the tiramisu mixture over the stewed fruit layer. Freeze for 30 minutes. Add the second piece of biscuit on top and douse it with the coffee syrup (page 278). Fill the frame with the rest of the tiramisu mix and freeze for 1 hour.

9   Remove the frame. Pipe on the reserved cream using a St Honoré tip (page 273) and dust with cocoa powder.

GIANDUJA
BARS

Understand

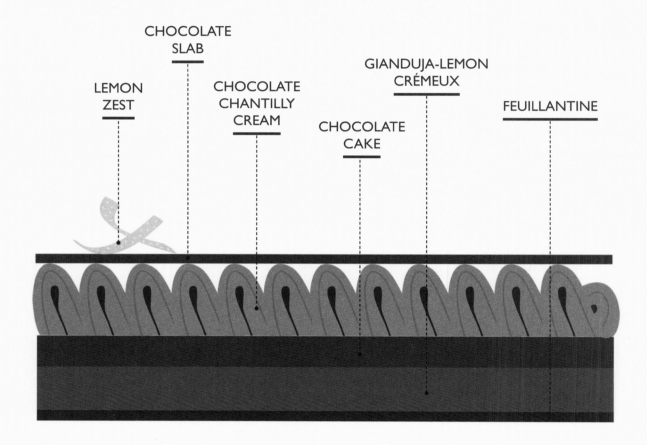

LEMON ZEST

CHOCOLATE SLAB

CHOCOLATE CHANTILLY CREAM

CHOCOLATE CAKE

GIANDUJA-LEMON CRÉMEUX

FEUILLANTINE

WHAT ARE THEY?

Praline and lemon desserts on a crispy feuillantine base, garnished with chantilly cream and milk chocolate.

TIME TO MAKE

Preparation: 2 hours
Cooking: 15 minutes
Resting: 4 hours

EQUIPMENT

9½ in square dessert frame
Pastry bag

Basket-weave decorating tip with eight teeth
Toothpicks
Piece of polystyrene foam
Bent frosting spatula
Chef's knife

WHY IS CHOCOLATE CHANTILLY CREAM GRAINIER THAN CLASSIC CHANTILLY CREAM?

The graininess that is sometimes visible is linked to the crystallization of the chocolate during cooling. To avoid this, mix the chocolate cream well to form a stable emulsion.

TRICKY ASPECT
Making the chocolate chantilly cream

TECHNIQUES TO MASTER
Using a pastry bag (page 272)
Preparing a water bath (page 270)
Making caramel (pages 48 and 278)

ORGANIZATION
Lemon zest – chantilly cream base –
flourless chocolate cake – feuillantine –
gianduja-citron cream – assembly –
chocolate slab – caramelized hazelnuts

TO MAKE 12 INDIVIDUAL BARS (4¾ IN × 4¾ IN)

1 FLOURLESS CHOCOLATE CAKE

cake base
5 oz chocolate (66% cacao)
2½ oz (⅓ cup) Provence almond paste (50% almonds)
1 oz egg yolk (2 yolks)
1⅜ oz (2¾ tbsp) butter

French meringue
5⅝ oz egg white (5 whites)
2 oz (4½ tbsp) superfine sugar

2 FEUILLANTINE

5¼ oz dark chocolate
7½ oz pailleté feuilletine (crumbled crêpes dentelles – lacy crepes)
13 oz praline (ground caramelized almonds)

3 GIANDUJA-LEMON CRÉMEUX

4¼ oz dark chocolate
3½ oz (7 tbsp) lemon juice (from about 6 lemons)

4¼ oz (about ½ cup) hazelnut paste
1¾ oz (3½ tbsp) whipping cream (30% fat)

4 CHOCOLATE CHANTILLY CREAM

1 lb 2 oz (2¼ cups) whipping cream (30% fat)
7 oz milk chocolate

5 SPUN-SUGAR HAZELNUTS

1¾ oz (3½ tbsp) water
7 oz (1 cup) superfine sugar

1⅜ oz (2 tbsp) glucose syrup
5¼ oz (about 1.1 cups) hazelnuts, skins removed

6 CHOCOLATE SLABS

7 oz dark chocolate

7 CANDIED LEMON ZEST

3½ oz (7 tbsp) water
4½ oz (⅔ cup) superfine sugar
2 lemons

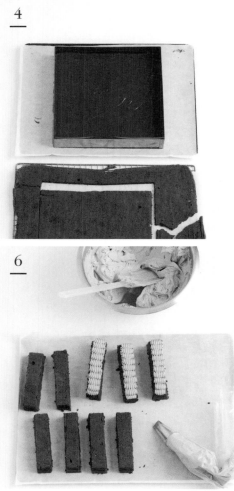

1   Make the flourless chocolate cake (page 40). Make the feuillantine: melt the chocolate in a water bath (page 270). Put the pailleté feuilletine and the praline in the bowl of an electric mixer and mix at low speed with the paddle. Once the mixture is smooth, pour in the melted chocolate and mix it in, still using the paddle. Line a baking sheet with baking paper and place a 9½ in dessert frame on top. Put the feuillantine in the frame and smooth the top using a palette knife. Refrigerate for 30 minutes.

2   To make the gianduja-lemon crémeux, melt the dark chocolate in a water bath. Put the hazelnut paste in a stainless-steel bowl and mix in the melted chocolate using a spatula. Heat the cream and pour over the hazelnut and chocolate mixture. Add the lemon juice and combine.

3   Pour the crémeux over the feuillantine. Refrigerate for 30 minutes.

4   Remove from the frame. Cut the chocolate cake to size using the frame.

5   Put the flourless chocolate cake on the crémeux. Set aside in the refrigerator.

6   To make the chocolate chantilly cream, boil the cream. Put the chocolate in a stainless-steel bowl and pour over the cream. Mix using a whisk. Pour into a container, cover with plastic wrap with the plastic touching the surface and refrigerate overnight so the mixture is very cold. Using a chef's knife, cut the assembled cake into twelve 4¾ in × ¾ in bars. Separate the pieces slightly. Take out the chocolate cream and

whip it like a classic chantilly cream (page 63). Use it to fill a pastry bag fitted with a basket-weave decorating tip with eight teeth and decorate each piece (page 273).

7   Make twelve chocolate slabs of 4¾ in × ¾ in (page 87). Make the candied lemon zest (page 281). Drain the strips of zest and tie in knots. Distribute the chocolate slabs and zest knots over the desserts.

8   To make the spun-sugar hazelnuts, make a caramel (page 49). Put the nuts on toothpicks. When the caramel is slightly thick, dip the nuts in it and stick the toothpicks in a piece of polystyrene foam until the caramel hardens. Remove the toothpicks and distribute the nuts among the bars.

Giandvja bars

MORELLO CHERRY
DOMES

Understand

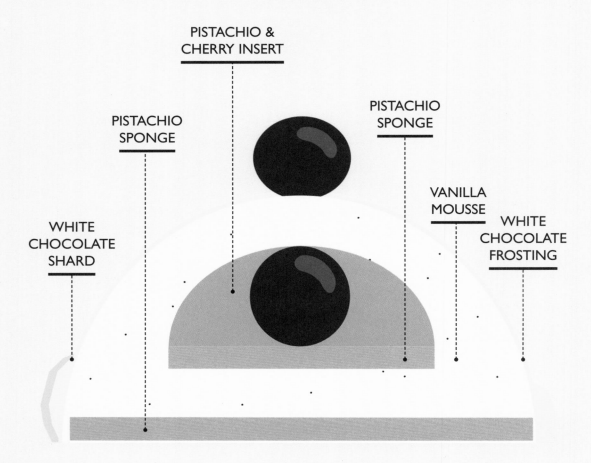

PISTACHIO &
CHERRY INSERT

PISTACHIO
SPONGE

PISTACHIO
SPONGE

WHITE
CHOCOLATE
SHARD

VANILLA
MOUSSE

WHITE
CHOCOLATE
FROSTING

WHAT ARE THEY?

Desserts made in a dome mold with a moist pistachio sponge base, vanilla mousse and a creamy Morello cherry and pistachio insert.

TIME TO MAKE

Preparation: 2 hours
Cooking: 1 hour
Freezing: at least 6 hours

EQUIPMENT

2 half-sphere silicone molds (one with 3¼ in diameter holes and one with 1¼ in diameter holes)
2¾ in round cookie cutter
1¼ in round cookie cutter
Pastry bag
Wire rack

VARIATIONS

Classic dome: chocolate mousse, vanilla insert (replace the pistachio paste with the seeds of 1 vanilla bean)

TRICKY ASPECT
Assembly

TECHNIQUES TO MASTER
Blanching egg yolks (page 279)
Hydrating gelatine (page 270)
Creating a chablon layer (page 280)
Using a pastry bag (page 272)

ORGANIZATION
Insert – sponge – mousse – assembly – frosting – chocolate decorations

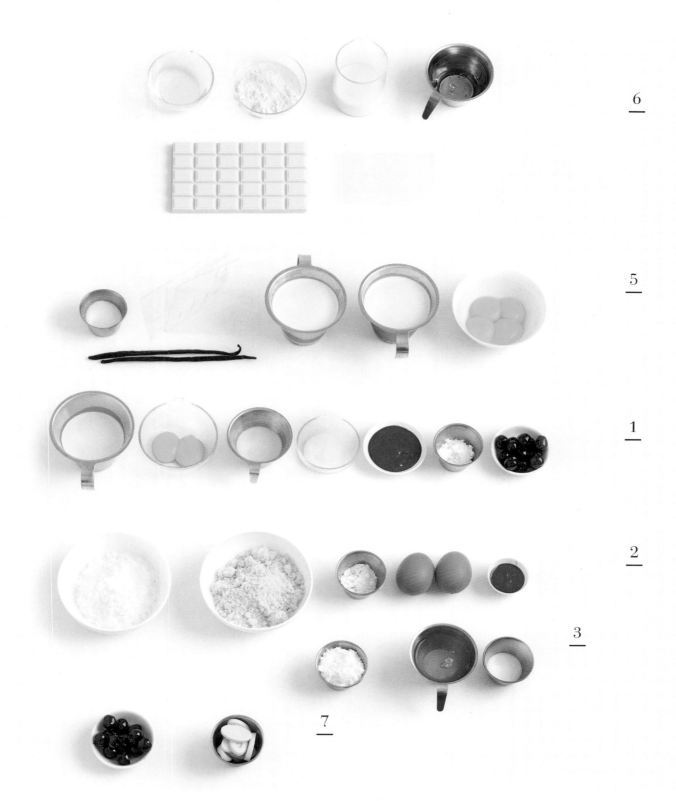

TO MAKE 6 DOMES

1 PISTACHIO AND CHERRY INSERT

¾ oz egg yolk (1 yolk)
¼ oz (½ tbsp) superfine sugar
⅛ oz (1⅓ tbsp) cornstarch
¾ oz (1½ tbsp) milk
2 oz (¼ cup) whipping cream (30% fat)
⅜ oz (2½ tbsp) pistachio paste
6 Morello or Amarena cherries in syrup

2 PISTACHIO SPONGE

2½ oz (about .6 cup) confectioners' sugar
2½ oz (¾ cup) almond meal
3½ oz egg (2 eggs)
⅜ oz (1⅓ tbsp) all-purpose flour
⅜ oz (2½ tbsp) pistachio paste
1 oz (¼ cup) confectioners' sugar, for dusting

3 MERINGUE

2½ oz egg white (about 2 whites)
⅜ oz (2½ tbsp) superfine sugar

4 CHABLON

1 oz white chocolate

5 VANILLA MOUSSE

crème anglaise

³⁄₁₆ oz leaf gelatine
2 oz egg yolk (3 yolks)
1 oz (2¼ tbsp) superfine sugar
6½ oz (about .8 cup) whipping cream (30% fat)
2 vanilla beans

whipped cream

6½ oz (about .8 cup) whipping cream (30% fat)

6 WHITE CHOCOLATE FROSTING

⅛ oz leaf gelatine
5¼ oz white chocolate
2 oz (¼ cup) milk
½ oz (1 tbsp) water
⅞ oz (1¼ tbsp) glucose syrup
⅛ oz titanium dioxide

7 DECORATION

1¾ oz white chocolate
6 Amarena cherries in syrup

1   To make the pistachio and cherry insert, preheat the oven to 195°F. In a stainless-steel bowl, blanch (page 279) the egg yolk with the sugar and cornstarch. Put the milk, cream and pistachio paste in a saucepan and heat while whisking. As soon as it boils, pour it over the egg yolk mixture and whisk.

2   Put one cherry in each of six holes of the small half-sphere mold. Pour over the pistachio mixture. Bake for 20–30 minutes. When you shake the mold gently, the mixture should not move. Cool to room temperature, then freeze (for at least 3 hours) to be able to unmold them.

3   Preheat the oven to 375°F. Make the dough for the pistachio sponge as for an almond sponge (page 35). Take out 1 oz of the dough, add the pistachio paste, then return to the rest of the dough and fold in using a silicone spatula. Line a baking sheet with

baking paper. Spread out the dough uniformly using frosting spatula, then bake for 10 minutes. Let the sponge cool on a wire rack. Dust a sheet of baking paper with confectioners' sugar and turn out the sponge onto it. Detach the bottom sheet of baking paper. Using two cookie cutters, cut out six 2¾ in discs and six 1¼ in discs. Melt the white chocolate for the chablon in a water bath. Using a pastry brush, coat the larger pieces of sponge (page 280).

4   To make the vanilla mousse, hydrate the gelatine (page 270). Make the crème anglaise (page 60) using cream instead of milk. Drain the gelatine and whisk into the crème anglaise. Strain, cover with plastic wrap with the plastic touching the surface, then set aside to cool to room temperature. Whip the cream as for a chantilly cream (page 63). Mix one-third into the crème anglaise with a whisk. Fold in the remaining cream using a silicone spatula.

5   Use the vanilla mousse to fill pastry bag without a decorating tip. Cut the end off the bag with scissors. This will allow you to pinch the end of the bag and move cleanly between domes. Take the large half-sphere mold. Half-fill each hole with the mousse.

6   Place a pistachio-cherry insert in the middle of the mousse in each hole, then a 1¼ in piece of sponge. Fill each hole with the mousse, stopping ¹⁄₁₂ in from the top. Cover with the 2¾ in disc, chablon side up. Freeze for at least 3 hours, ideally overnight.

7   Make the white chocolate frosting (page 78). Put a wire rack over a baking sheet. Unmold the domes on the rack and pour over the white chocolate frosting using ladle. Arrange the white chocolate shards (page 274) around the sides and a cherry on top.

TROPICAL FRUIT
TART

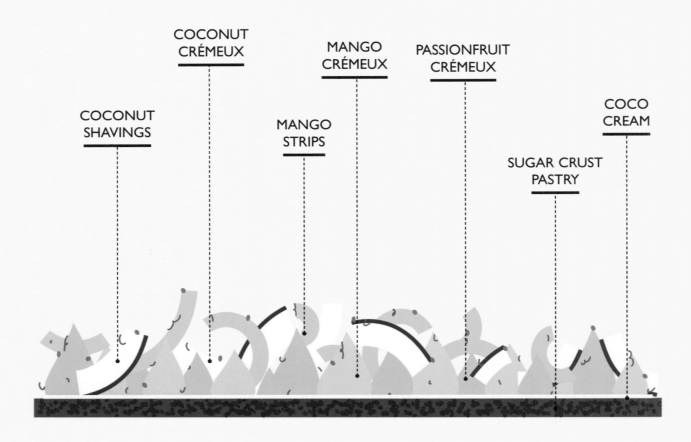

COCONUT
CRÉMEUX

MANGO
CRÉMEUX

PASSIONFRUIT
CRÉMEUX

COCONUT
SHAVINGS

COCO
CREAM

MANGO
STRIPS

SUGAR CRUST
PASTRY

WHAT IS IT?

Sugar crust pastry base covered with coco cream, domes of three tropical fruit crémeux and fresh fruit.

TIME TO MAKE

Preparation: 2 hours
Cooking: 30 minutes
Refrigeration: 4 hours

EQUIPMENT

3 pastry bags
3 no. 8 plain decorating tips
8¾ in dessert ring
Microplane grater
Hand-held blender

TRICKY ASPECTS

Cooking the pastry
Piping the domes

TECHNIQUES TO MASTER

Blanching egg yolks (page 279)
Using a pastry bag (page 272)
Zesting (page 281)

ORGANIZATION

Sugar crust pastry – coco cream –
coconut crémeux – passionfruit crémeux –
mango crémeux – filling

TO SERVE 8

1 SUGAR CRUST PASTRY

7 oz (1.6 cups) all-purpose flour
1/32 oz (1/3 tsp) salt
2½ oz (5 tbsp) butter
2½ oz (.6 cup) confectioners' sugar
1¾ oz egg (1 egg)

2 COCO CREAM

2 oz (4 tbsp) butter
1⅜ oz (.2 cup) superfine sugar

2 oz desiccated coconut
1¾ oz egg (1 egg)
⅜ oz (1⅓ tbsp) all-purpose flour

3 COCONUT CRÉMEUX

1/32 oz leaf gelatine
⅞ oz egg yolk (about 1½ yolks)
¾ oz (1⅔ tbsp) superfine sugar
1 oz egg (about ½ egg)
3½ oz coconut purée
1 oz (2 tbsp) butter
1 oz desiccated coconut

4 PASSIONFRUIT CRÉMEUX

1/32 oz leaf gelatine
1¼ oz egg yolk (2 yolks)
1¼ oz (3 tbsp) superfine sugar
1¾ oz egg (1 egg)
4⅜ oz passionfruit purée
1¾ oz (3½ tbsp) butter

5 MANGO CRÉMEUX

1/32 oz leaf gelatine
1¼ oz egg yolk (2 yolks)
1¼ oz (3 tbsp) superfine sugar
1¾ oz egg (1 egg)

4⅜ oz mango purée
1¾ oz (3½ tbsp) butter

6 FILLING

1 mango
1 coconut
2 passionfruit
1 lime

1 Make the sugar crust pastry (page 12). After resting, roll it out to ¹⁄₁₂ in thickness. Butter the dessert ring then cut out a 8¾ in disc, leaving the ring in place on a cookie sheet lined with baking paper.

2 Preheat the oven to 320°F. Make the coco cream in the same way as an almond cream (page 64), replacing the almond meal with the desiccated coconut.

3 Pour over the pastry disc and bake for 20–30 minutes. Lift the disc using a frosting spatula: the pastry should be uniformly golden. Remove the ring and let the pastry cool on a wire rack.

4 To make the passionfruit crémeux, hydrate the gelatine (page 270). Blanch the egg yolk with the sugar and egg (page 279). At the same time, heat the passionfruit purée. When it boils, pour half over the egg yolk mixture, mixing with a whisk.

5 Pour this mixture back into the saucepan and return to the heat, whisking constantly. As soon as it boils, remove from the heat, add the butter and drained gelatine, mix with a whisk, then blend using a hand-held blender for 2–3 minutes. Transfer to a container and refrigerate for at least 2 hours.

6 Whisk the set cream to make it smooth. Fill a pastry bag fitted with a no. 8 plain decorating tip and pipe little domes over the pastry base in a random manner. Cover about one-third of the surface.

7 Make the mango crémeux in the same way, using the mango purée. Pipe little domes on the pastry base.

8 Make the coconut crémeux the same way, using the coconut purée. When adding the butter and gelatine, add the desiccated coconut. Pipe little domes on the pastry base. Stone the mango. Cut into strips. Crack the coconut and take off long shavings using a utility knife. Remove the pulp from the passionfruit. Arrange all the elements on the tart.

DECORATION

Zest the lime over the tart using a microplane grater.

PISTACHIO & RED FRUIT
CHARLOTTE

Understand

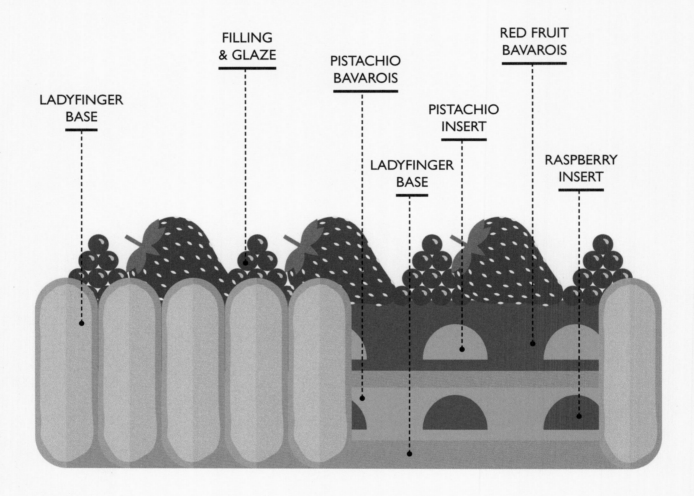

LADYFINGER
BASE

FILLING
& GLAZE

PISTACHIO
BAVAROIS

LADYFINGER
BASE

PISTACHIO
INSERT

RED FRUIT
BAVAROIS

RASPBERRY
INSERT

WHAT IS IT?

Dessert structured with a "cartridge belt" of ladyfingers containing two layers of bavarois: raspberry with pistachio insert, and pistachio with raspberry insert. The whole is garnished with fruit and glazed.

TIME TO MAKE

Preparation: 2 hours
Cooking: 30 minutes
Freezing: 4 hours
Refrigeration: 4 hours

EQUIPMENT

Pastry bag
No. 10 plain decorating tip
8¾ in dessert ring
Acetate cake band
Half-sphere silicone mold with 24 holes of 1¼ in diameter

TECHNIQUE TO MASTER
Using a pastry bag (page 272)

ORGANIZATION
Inserts – ladyfinger – bavarois – assembly – resting – decoration

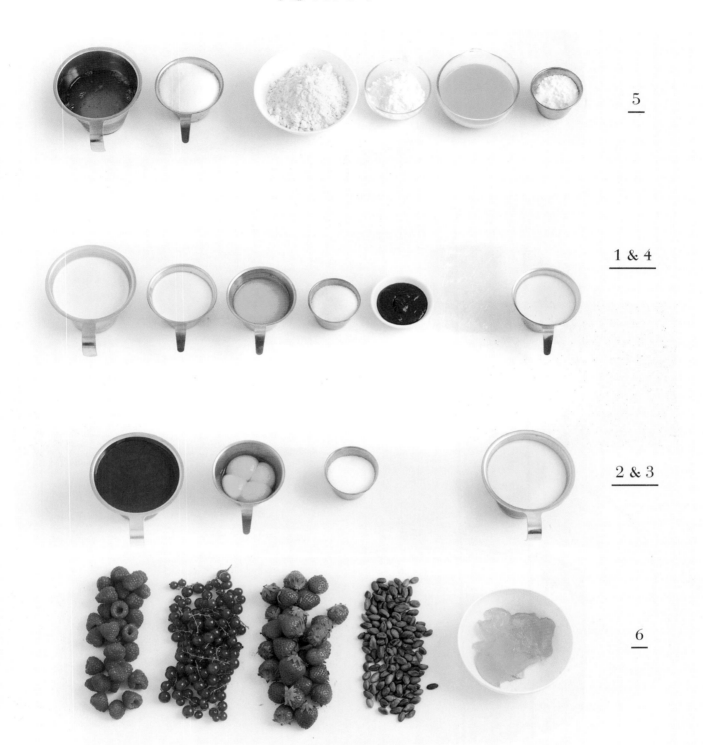

TO SERVE 8

1 PISTACHIO BAVAROIS

crème anglaise
1¾ oz egg yolk (about 3 yolks)
1⅜ oz (.2 cup) superfine sugar
4⅜ oz (.55 cup) milk
4⅜ oz (.55 cup) whipping cream
   (30% fat)
1 oz (about 2 tbsp) pistachio paste

whipped cream
⅛ oz leaf gelatine
7 oz (about .9 cup) whipping cream
   (30% fat)

2 RED FRUIT BAVAROIS

crème anglaise
9 oz purée of red fruit
1¾ oz egg yolk (about 3 yolks)
1⅜ oz (.2 cup) superfine sugar

whipped cream
⅛ oz leaf gelatine
7 oz (.9 cup) whipping cream
   (30% fat)

3 RASPBERRY INSERT

1⁄16 oz leaf gelatine
7 oz raspberry purée
¾ oz (1⅔ tbsp) superfine sugar

4 PISTACHIO INSERT

crème anglaise
2 oz (¼ cup) milk
2 oz (¼ cup) whipping cream
   (30% fat)
⅞ oz egg yolk (about 1½ yolks)
½ oz (3½ tsp) superfine sugar

flavoring
⅜ oz (1½ tbsp) pistachio paste
1⁄16 oz leaf gelatine

5 LADYFINGER COOKIE

French meringue
5¼ oz egg white (5 whites)
4⅜ oz (about ⅔ cup) superfine
   sugar

cookie base
3½ oz (about .8 cup) all-purpose
   flour
⅞ oz (3 tbsp) potato starch
2¾ oz egg yolk (about 4½ yolks)

dusting
1 oz (¼ cup) confectioners' sugar

6 GARNISH

1¾ oz glaze
3½ oz (.8 cup) raspberries
3½ oz (.7 cup) strawberries
3½ oz (.7 cup) blueberries
1¾ oz (.4 cup) unsalted
   shelled pistachios
1¾ oz (.4 cup) red currants

1 Make the ladyfinger mixture (page 37). Pipe two "cartridge belts" 16 in long and 2 in wide, and two discs of 8¾ in diameter (page 37). Bake (page 37). Cool on a wire rack.

2 To make the pistachio inserts, soak the gelatine in cold water. Make the crème anglaise (page 60) using both milk and cream. At the end of cooking, add the pistachio paste and the drained gelatine. Whisk, pour into twelve of the half-sphere molds and set aside in the freezer for 2 hours. To make the raspberry inserts, soak the gelatine in cold water. Heat the purée with the sugar. As soon as it boils, remove from the heat and whisk in the drained gelatine. Pour the mixture into the other twelve half-spheres. Set aside in the freezer for 2 hours.

3 To make the two bavarois, whip the 14 oz (1¾ cups) cream needed for both as for chantilly cream (page 62) and set aside in the refrigerator before adding half to each bavarois. Make the pistachio bavarois (page 70), adding the pistachio paste at the end of cooking the crème anglaise.

4 Make the red fruit bavarois (page 70), replacing the milk and cream with the red fruit purée.

5 Put a 8¾ in dessert ring lined with acetate cake band on a cookie sheet lined with baking paper. Put a "cartridge belt" around the sides and slide a ladyfinger disc into the bottom.

6 Pour in the pistachio bavarois and level with a silicone spatula. Unmold the raspberry inserts and distribute them in the bavarois.

7 Put the second ladyfinger disc on the pistachio bavarois. Pour the red fruit bavarois over the disc. Unmold the pistachio inserts and distribute them in the bavarois. Refrigerate for at least 3 hours.

8 Warm the glaze in a large saucepan. Remove from the heat, add the raspberries, strawberries cut in quarters, blueberries and pistachios, then mix gently using a spoon.

9 Distribute the glazed fruit over the charlotte and top with the currants.

MILK CHOCOLATE
LOG

Understand

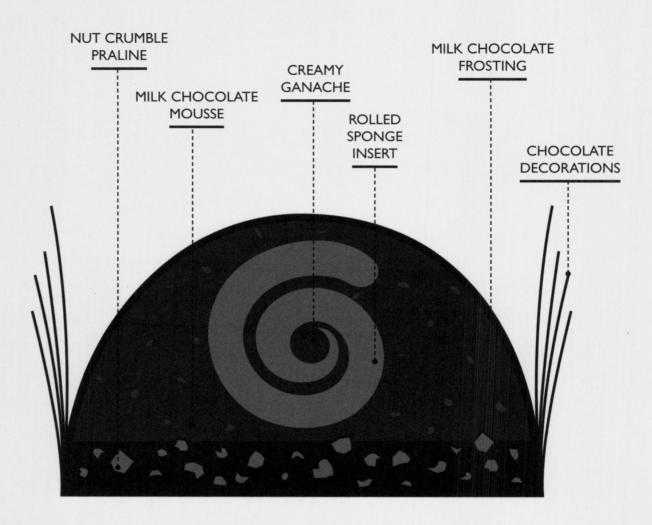

NUT CRUMBLE
PRALINE

MILK CHOCOLATE
MOUSSE

CREAMY
GANACHE

ROLLED
SPONGE
INSERT

MILK CHOCOLATE
FROSTING

CHOCOLATE
DECORATIONS

WHAT IS IT?

Log composed of a crunchy base of nuts in praline, a milk chocolate and cinnamon mousse and a rolled insert filled with ganache, the whole covered with milk chocolate frosting and decorated with stripes of white chocolate frosting.

TIME TO MAKE

Preparation: 2 hours
Cooking: 10–20 minutes
Freezing: at least 7 hours

EQUIPMENT

Yule log tin/guttered cake tin (4 in × 12 in)
Dessert frame (4 in × 12 in) or cake tin (4 in × 12 in) or cookie sheet and chopping board
Pastry bag

VARIATION

Replace the milk chocolate and cinnamon mousse with a white chocolate mousse (page 112).

TRICKY ASPECT
Frosting

TECHNIQUES TO MASTER
Roasting nuts (page 281)
Whipping cream (page 277)
Making a chocolate slab (page 87)

TIP
For easier unmolding, dip the mold in hot water for a few seconds.

ORGANIZATION
Ganache – Genoese sponge – crumble – mousse – assembly – frosting – decoration

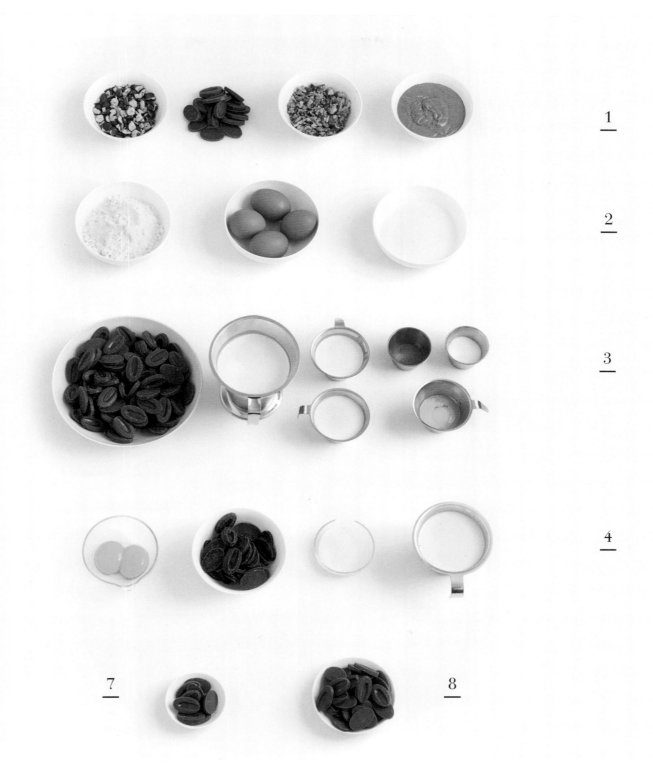

TO SERVE 10

1 NUT CRUMBLE PRALINE

2¾ oz milk chocolate
5¼ oz praline (ground caramelized almonds)
2 oz (½ cup) chopped hazelnuts
2 oz (½ cup) chopped walnuts

2 GENOESE SPONGE

2 eggs
2¼ oz (⅓ cup) superfine sugar
2¼ oz (½ cup) all-purpose flour

3 CHOCOLATE & CINNAMON MOUSSE

crème anglaise
14½ oz milk chocolate
1⅜ oz egg yolk (2 yolks)
¾ oz (1⅔ tbsp) superfine sugar
3 oz (6 tbsp) milk
3 oz (6 tbsp) whipping cream (30% fat)
⅜ oz (⅓ tbsp) ground cinnamon

whipped cream
12 oz (1½ cups) whipping cream (30% fat)

4 CREAMY GANACHE

¾ oz egg yolk (about 1 yolk)
¾ oz (1⅔ tbsp) superfine sugar
3½ oz (7 tbsp) milk
1¾ oz dark chocolate

5 MILK CHOCOLATE FROSTING

1½ oz dark chocolate
4⅜ oz milk chocolate
4 oz (½ cup) whipping cream (30% fat)
¾ oz (3⅓ tsp) invert sugar

6 WHITE CHOCOLATE FROSTING

1⁄16 oz leaf gelatine
2⅝ oz white chocolate
1 oz (2 tbsp) milk
¼ oz (½ tbsp) water
⅜ oz (1⅔ tsp) glucose syrup
1⁄16 oz titanium dioxide

7 CHABLONS

1 oz white chocolate

8 DECORATION

3½ oz dark chocolate

1 Preheat the oven to 340°F, spread the nuts over a cookie sheet lined with baking paper and roast them (page 281) for 15–20 minutes.

2 To make the nut crumble praline, melt the milk chocolate in a water bath. In a stainless-steel bowl, mix the praline and the nuts using a spatula. Incorporate the melted chocolate. Pour into a 4 in × 12 in frame and refrigerate until set.

3 Make the creamy ganache (page 72), then set aside in the refrigerator. Make the Genoese sponge (page 32). Cut out a 4 in × 12 in strip. Spread with the creamy ganache, roll into a cylinder, wrap in plastic wrap and freeze for 1 hour.

4 To make the chocolate and cinnamon mousse, melt the milk chocolate in a water bath. Make the crème anglaise with the milk, cream, egg, and sugar (page 279), adding the cinnamon to the milk at the beginning. Remove the milk chocolate from the water bath and incorporate the crème anglaise. Whip the whipping cream as for chantilly cream (page 62).

5 Whisk 3½ oz of the whipped cream into the chocolate crème anglaise. Fold in the remaining whipped cream using a silicone spatula (page 270). Once the mixture is smooth, pour half the mousse into the yule log tin.

6 Take out the roll, place it on the mousse and pour over the rest of the mousse.

7 Add the nut crumble praline, and add a white chocolate chablon on top (page 280). Freeze for at least 6 hours.

8 Make the milk chocolate frosting and the white chocolate frosting (pages 78–79), and keep them at about 115°F. Unmold the log and place it on a wire rack, then frost with the milk chocolate frosting by pouring it over (page 280). Put the white chocolate frosting in a pastry bag, cut a small hole in the end, then pipe fine stripes over the milk chocolate frosting.

CHOCOLATE DROP DECORATIONS

Make chocolate drops (page 87) and stick them along the sides of the log.

Milk chocolate log

LEMON
MERINGUE PIE

Understand

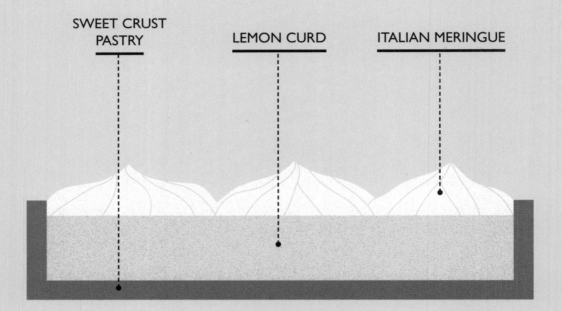

SWEET CRUST PASTRY

LEMON CURD

ITALIAN MERINGUE

WHAT IS IT?

Sweet crust pastry filled with lemon curd set cold and Italian meringue colored using a kitchen blowtorch.

TIME TO MAKE

Preparation: 1 hour
Cooking: 30 minutes
Resting: 1 hour
Refrigeration: 30 minutes

EQUIPMENT

9½ in dessert ring

Pastry bag
St Honoré decorating tip
Kitchen blowtorch

VARIATIONS

Traditional meringue topping: pipe using a fluted decorating tip.
Simple meringue topping: spread using a spatula.
Lime meringue pie: replace the lemons with limes (same weight of juice).
Yuzu meringue pie: replace the lemons with yuzus (same weight of juice).

TRICKY ASPECTS

Cooking the pastry
Adding and coloring the meringue

TECHNIQUES TO MASTER

Dusting with flour (page 284)
Aerating dough (page 284)
Lining a mold with pastry (page 284)
Coloring with a kitchen blowtorch (page 275)
Using a pastry bag (page 272)

ORGANIZATION

Sweet crust pastry – curd – meringue – assembly – cooking

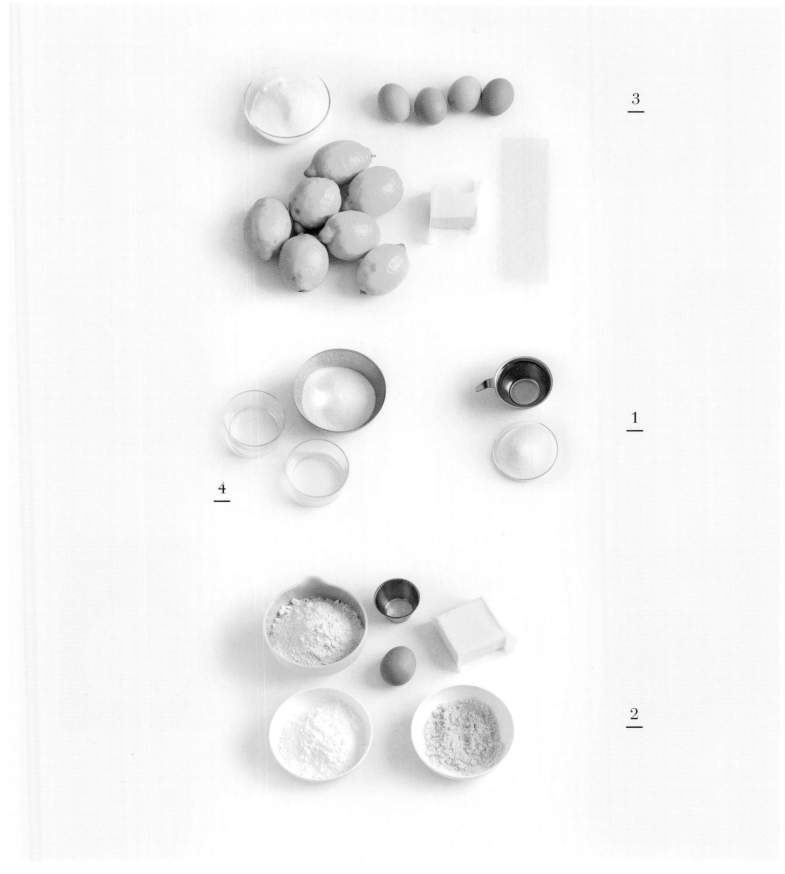

TO SERVE 8

1 SYRUP

3½ oz (7 tbsp) water
1¾ oz (¼ cup) superfine sugar

2 SWEET CRUST PASTRY

4 oz (½ cup) butter
2¾ oz (⅔ cup) confectioners' sugar
1¾ oz egg (1 egg)
1/32 oz (⅛ tsp) fine salt
7 oz (1.6 cups) all-purpose flour
¾ oz (about ¼ cup) almond meal

3 LEMON CURD

⅛ oz leaf gelatine
5 oz (about .6 cup) lemon
   juice (from 7 lemons)
zest from 7 lemons
7 oz egg (4 eggs)
5⅝ oz (.8 cup) superfine sugar
2¾ oz (5½ tbsp) butter

4 ITALIAN MERINGUE

1⅜ oz (2¾ tbsp) water
4⅜ oz (about .6 cup)
   superfine sugar
1¾ oz egg white (about 1½ whites)

1   Make the sweet crust pastry (page 15). Take the pastry out of the refrigerator 30 minutes in advance. Dust the work surface with flour (page 284), roll out the dough to 1/12 in thickness and aerate it (page 284). Grease a 9½ in tart ring with butter and place on a cookie sheet lined with baking paper. Line the ring with the pastry (page 284).

2   Trim off the surplus pastry with a knife or by rolling the rolling pin over the top (page 285). Prick the bottom of the tart and/or prepare to bake it blind, as a precaution (page 285).

3   Bake for 30 minutes at 340°F. Carefully lift the bottom of the tart shell to check if it is cooked: it should be uniformly colored.

4   Bring a small saucepan of water to the boil. Zest the lemons using a potato peeler, removing any white pith if necessary (page 281) then cut these pieces into thin strips 1/12 in wide (or remove the zest with a zester). Put the zest in the boiling water for 30 seconds. Drain.

5   Make a sugar syrup by putting the water and sugar in a saucepan, stirring and bringing to the boil, then removing from the heat. Put the zest in the syrup, leave it to marinate for at least 1 hour, then drain.

6   Make the lemon curd (page 74). Pour it into the tart shell while still hot, filling it to the brim, then refrigerate for 30 minutes.

7   Scatter the zest over the lemon curd.

8   Make the Italian meringue (page 44). Using a St Honoré decorating tip, pipe little lines of meringue on the tart, drawing circles, from the outside in (or use a spoon).

9   Color the meringue using a kitchen blowtorch (page 275) or leave the tart under the broiler for 30 seconds, watching carefully.

LIME
TARTLETS

Understand

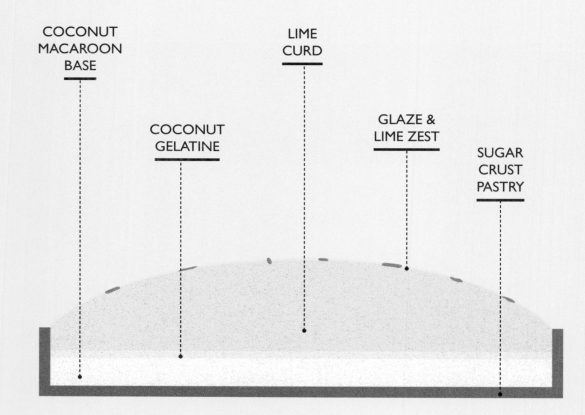

COCONUT
MACAROON
BASE

COCONUT
GELATINE

LIME
CURD

GLAZE &
LIME ZEST

SUGAR
CRUST
PASTRY

WHAT ARE THEY?

Sugar crust pastry filled with a base of coconut macaroon, topped with melt-in-the-mouth coconut gelatine and lime curd.

TIME TO MAKE

Preparation: 1 hour 30 minutes
Cooking: 30 minutes
Resting: 4 hours

EQUIPMENT

6 × 4 in tart rings
4¾ in cookie cutter
Pastry bag fitted with a no. 10 plain decorating tip
Frosting spatula
Microplane grater

VARIATION

Lemon tartlets (same weight of lemon juice)

TRICKY ASPECTS

Cooking the pastry
Shaping with a frosting spatula

TECHNIQUES TO MASTER

Dusting with flour (page 284)
Aerating dough (page 284)
Lining a mold with pastry (page 284)
Zesting (page 281)
Making a dome with a frosting
spatula (page 275)

TIPS

To check the pastry is cooked, lift the tart base: it should be uniformly colored. The coconut macaroon base layer acts to balance the textures in the tart between crumbly and creamy.

ORGANIZATION

Sugar crust pastry – lime curd – macaroon base – coconut gelatine – decoration

TO MAKE 6 TARTLETS

1 MACAROON BASE

2⅝ oz desiccated coconut
2⅝ oz (6 tbsp) superfine sugar
1¾ oz coconut purée
1 oz egg white (1 white)

2 SUGAR CRUST PASTRY

7 oz (1.6 cups) all-purpose flour
1/32 oz (⅓ tsp) salt
2½ oz (5 tbsp) butter
2½ oz (.6 cup) confectioners' sugar
1¾ oz egg (1 egg)

3 COCONUT GELATINE

1/16 oz leaf gelatine
3½ oz coconut purée
¾ oz (1⅔ tbsp) superfine sugar

4 LIME CURD

⅛ oz leaf gelatine

4¼ oz (about .6 cup)
   lime juice (from 8 limes)
5¼ oz egg yolk (about 8 yolks)
5¼ oz (¾ cup) superfine sugar
7 oz (14 tbsp) butter

5 DECORATION

1 lime
9 oz glaze

1   Make the sugar crust pastry (page 12). Take the pastry out of the refrigerator 30 minutes in advance. Preheat the oven to 340°F, dust the work surface (page 270), roll out the pastry using a rolling pin to ⁵⁄₆₄ in thickness, then aerate the pastry (page 284). Cut out six discs using a 4¾ in cookie cutter.

2   Line a cookie sheet with baking paper. Grease six 4 in tart rings with butter and place them on the prepared sheet. Line the rings with the pastry, being careful to make a right angle between the sides and the bottom (page 284). Cut off any excess level with the top of the ring. Precook at 340°F. Allow to cool, then remove from rings.

3   Make the coconut macaroon base by mixing all the ingredients in a stainless-steel bowl.

4   Spread ¼ oz of the macaroon mix in each tart shell, using a tablespoon. Bake for about 15 minutes to finish the cooking. Remove from the oven and cool on a wire rack.

5   To make the coconut gelatine, hydrate the gelatine (page 270). Heat 1¾ oz coconut purée in a saucepan with the sugar. Once it boils, remove from the heat. Add the drained gelatine, then the remaining coconut purée. Pour 1 oz of the coconut gelatine into each tart shell. Set aside in the refrigerator.

6   Make the lime curd (page 74), pour into a container, cover with plastic wrap, with the plastic touching the surface, and refrigerate for at least 2 hours. Stir with a whisk to smooth out the curd. Use the curd to fill a pastry bag fitted with a no. 10 plain tip, then pipe the curd in a dome in each tartlet shell (page 275).

7   Smooth into a pyramid shape using a frosting spatula (page 275), then freeze for at least 2 hours.

8   Grate the lime zest using a microplane grater. Warm the glaze slightly and add to the zest. Remove the tartlets from the freezer and dip the curd domes into the glaze.

CHIBOUST & RASPBERRY
TARTLETS

Understand

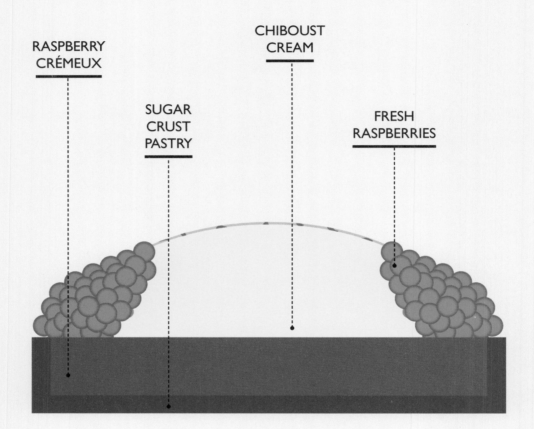

RASPBERRY
CRÉMEUX

SUGAR
CRUST
PASTRY

CHIBOUST
CREAM

FRESH
RASPBERRIES

WHAT ARE THEY?

Sugar crust pastry filled with a raspberry crémeux and caramelized chiboust cream, garnished with fresh raspberries.

TIME TO MAKE

Preparation: 1 hour 30 minutes
Cooking: 15–25 minutes
Refrigeration: 30 minutes
Freezing: 4 hours 30 minutes

EQUIPMENT

8 × 3¼ in tart rings
Half-sphere silicone mold (2½ in diameter holes)
Hand-held blender
Kitchen blowtorch, pastry brush

TRICKY ASPECT
Cooking the pastry

TECHNIQUES TO MASTER
Dusting with flour (page 284)
Aerating dough (page 284)
Lining a mold with pastry (page 284)
Hydrating gelatine (page 270)

TIP
If you don't have a silicone half-sphere mold, you can make domes by piping the chiboust cream (page 275). The result will be less neat.

ORGANIZATION
Sugar crust pastry – raspberry crémeux – chiboust cream – assembly

1

3

4

2

**TO MAKE 8 TARTLETS
(OR 1 × 9½ IN TART)**

1 SUGAR CRUST PASTRY

7 oz (1.6 cups) all-purpose flour
1/32 oz (⅓ tsp) salt
2½ oz (5 tbsp) butter
2½ oz (.6 cup) confectioners' sugar
1¾ oz egg (1 egg)

2 CHIBOUST CREAM

pastry cream
1¾ oz egg yolk (about 3 yolks)
2 oz (4½ tbsp) superfine sugar
⅞ oz (1¼ tbsp) cornstarch
9 oz (1 cup 2 tbsp) milk
⅞ oz (1¾ tbsp) butter
¼ oz leaf gelatine

Italian meringue
1⅜ oz (2¾ tbsp) water
4⅜ oz (about ⅔ cup)
   superfine sugar
1¾ oz egg white (about 2 whites)

3 RASPBERRY CRÉMEUX

2 oz egg yolk (3 yolks)
2¾ oz egg (about 1½ eggs)
2 oz (4½ tbsp) superfine sugar

1/16 oz leaf gelatine
7 oz raspberry purée
   (or 1⅜ oz raspberry coulis)
2¾ oz (5½ tbsp) butter,
   softened and cut into cubes

4 GARNISH

7 oz glaze
9 oz raspberries

1 Make the sweet crust pastry (page 15). Take the pastry out of the refrigerator 30 minutes in advance. Preheat the oven to 340°F, dust the work surface with flour (page 284), roll out the pastry using a rolling pin to 1⁄12 in thickness and aerate the pastry (page 284). Cut out six discs using a 4 in cookie cutter.

2 Grease six 3¼ in tart rings with butter and place them on a cookie sheet lined with baking paper. Line the rings with the pastry (page 284) and cut off any excess level with the top of the rings, using a utility knife or by pressing on the rings using a rolling pin (page 284). Prick the bottom with a fork and/or prepare to bake it blind (page 285), as a precaution.

3 Bake for 15 minutes at 340°F. Carefully lift the bottom of the tartlet shells to check if they are cooked: they should be evenly colored. Allow to cool, then remove the ring.

4 To make the raspberry crémeux, blanch the egg yolk with the sugar (page 279) in a stainless-steel bowl. Hydrate the gelatine (page 270).

5 Heat up the raspberry purée. When it boils, pour half into the egg yolk and sugar mixture and add whole eggs. Whisk, then pour back into the saucepan. Continue to cook, whisking constantly.

6 As soon as it boils, remove from the heat and add the butter and drained gelatine. Whisk, then blend using a hand-held blender for 2–3 minutes.

7 Pour directly into the tartlet shells, filling them to the brim, then refrigerate for 30 minutes.

8 Make the chiboust cream (page 66). Pour into the half-sphere mold and set in the freezer for at least 4 hours, ideally overnight.

9 Unmold the half-spheres of cream and place them on top of the tartlets. Color the tops with a kitchen blowtorch (page 275). Freeze for 20 minutes, glaze with a pastry brush, then add a row of raspberries around the edge of each dome.

STRAWBERRY
TART

Understand

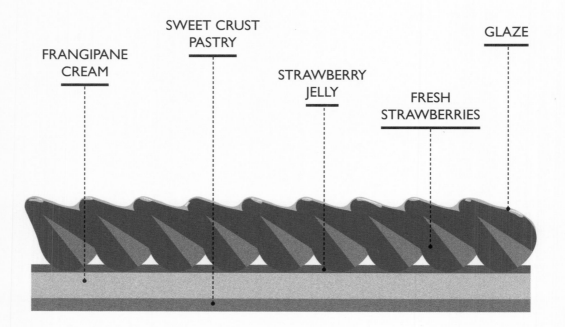

FRANGIPANE
CREAM

SWEET CRUST
PASTRY

STRAWBERRY
JELLY

GLAZE

FRESH
STRAWBERRIES

WHAT IS IT?

Sweet crust pastry filled with frangipane, jelly and fresh strawberries.

TIME TO MAKE

Preparation: 1 hour
Cooking: 25–35 minutes
Refrigeration: 1 hour

EQUIPMENT

9½ in tart ring
Pastry bag
No. 8 plain decorating tip

VARIATIONS

Pastry cream or chantilly cream filling.
Decoration with whole strawberries.

TRICKY ASPECT
Cooking the pastry

TECHNIQUES TO MASTER
Dusting with flour (page 284)
Aerating dough (page 284)
Lining a mold with pastry (page 284)
Using a pastry bag (page 272)

ORGANIZATION
Sweet crust pastry – pastry cream – assembly

TO SERVE 8

1 SWEET CRUST PASTRY

5 oz (10 tbsp) butter
3½ oz (about .8 cup) confectioners' sugar
1¾ oz egg (1 egg)
1⁄32 oz (⅛ tsp) fine salt
9 oz (2 cups) all-purpose flour
⅞ oz (¼ cup) almond meal

2 CRÈME FRANGIPANE

almond cream
1¾ oz (3½ tbsp) butter
1¾ oz (¼ cup) superfine sugar

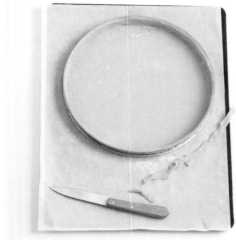

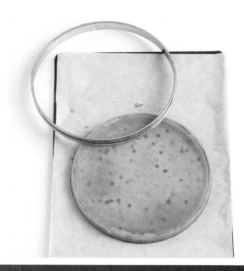

1¾ oz (½ cup) almond meal
1¾ oz egg (1 egg)
⅜ oz (1⅓ tbsp) all-purpose flour

pastry cream
¼ oz egg yolk (about ½ yolk)
¼ oz (½ tbsp) superfine sugar
⅛ oz (1⅓ tsp) cornstarch
1 oz (2 tbsp) milk
⅛ oz (¼ tbsp) butter

3 FILLING

3½ oz strawberry jelly
1 lb 11 oz strawberries
1¾ oz glaze
¾ oz (1½ tbsp) water

1 Make the sweet crust pastry (page 15). Take the pastry out of the refrigerator 30 minutes in advance. Dust the work surface with flour (page 284), roll out the pastry using a rolling pin to 1/12 in thickness and aerate it (page 284).

2 Grease a 9½ in tart ring with butter and sit it on a cookie sheet lined with baking paper. Line the ring with the pastry (page 284). Cut off any excess at the brim using a utility knife or by pressing the rolling pin on the ring. Refrigerate for 30 minutes. Preheat the oven to 320°F.

3 To make the frangipane, make the pastry cream (page 53) and let it cool in the refrigerator. Make the almond cream (page 64), then whisk the pastry cream into it. Fill a pastry bag fitted with a plain no. 10 tip, and fill the bottom of

the tart by piping in a snail shell (page 273).

4 Bake for 30 minutes at 320°F. Watch the cooking (page 285). Allow to cool, then remove the ring.

5 Spread the jelly over the frangipane.

6 Set aside a good whole strawberry. Halve all the others lengthways. Arrange them in a rosette, overlapping them and alternating one ring with the cut side down and one ring with the cut side up. Start from the outside and work inward. Place the whole strawberry in the middle.

7 Boil the glaze with ¾ oz water. Glaze the strawberries immediately, using a pastry brush (page 275).

PASSIONFRUIT
TART

Understand

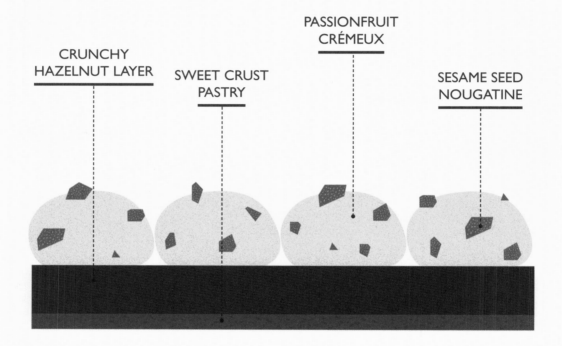

CRUNCHY
HAZELNUT LAYER

SWEET CRUST
PASTRY

PASSIONFRUIT
CRÉMEUX

SESAME SEED
NOUGATINE

WHAT IS IT?

Sweet crust pastry filled with a hazelnut crumble layer, passionfruit crémeux domes and shards of sesame seed nougatine.

TIME TO MAKE

Preparation: 1 hour 30 minutes
Cooking: 40–50 minutes
Refrigeration: 3 hours

EQUIPMENT

4¾ in × 9½ in rectangular dessert frame
Pastry bag
No. 12 plain decorating tip
Hand-held blender

TRICKY ASPECT
Cooking the pastry

TECHNIQUES TO MASTER
Dusting with flour (page 284)
Aerating dough (page 284)
Using a pastry bag (page 272)

ORGANIZATION
Sweet crust pastry – hazelnut crumble – passionfruit crémeux – sesame seed nougatine

TO SERVE 8

1 SWEET CRUST PASTRY

2½ oz (5 tbsp) butter
1¾ oz (.4 cup) confectioners' sugar
1 oz egg (about ½ egg)
1/32 oz (⅛ tsp) fine salt
4⅜ oz (1 cup) all-purpose flour
1¾ oz (⅔ cup) hazelnut meal

2 CRUNCHY HAZELNUT LAYER

3½ oz (7 tbsp) cold butter, cut into small cubes
3½ oz (.8 cup) all-purpose flour
3½ oz (1⅓ cups) hazelnut meal
1¾ oz (¼ cup) superfine sugar
3½ oz milk chocolate
1¾ oz praline (crushed caramelized almonds)
1¾ oz pailleté feuilletine (crumbled crêpes dentelles – lacy crepes)

3 PASSIONFRUIT CRÉMEUX

1/16 oz leaf gelatine
2⅝ oz egg yolk (about 4 yolks)
3½ oz egg (2 eggs)
2⅝ oz (6 tbsp) superfine sugar
9 oz passionfruit purée
3½ oz (7 tbsp) butter

4 SESAME SEED NOUGATINE

1¾ oz sesame seeds
2 oz fondant
1¾ oz (2½ tbsp) glucose syrup

1 Make the sweet crust pastry (page 15). Take it out of the refrigerator 30 minutes in advance. Preheat the oven to 340°F. Dust the work surface with flour. Roll the pastry into a rectangle ¹⁄₁₂ in thick and aerate it (page 284). Place it on a baking sheet lined with baking paper and cut out a 4¾ in × 9½ in piece using the dessert frame. Prick with a fork (as a precaution).

2 Bake for 20 minutes. The pastry should be uniformly golden. Cool on a wire rack.

3 To make the crunchy hazelnut layer, keep the oven at 340°F. Rub the butter into the flour, hazelnut meal and sugar, rubbing the mixture between your hands (page 284). Spread this crumble over a cookie sheet lined with baking paper and bake for 20–30 minutes, stirring regularly with a spatula. Allow to cool.

4 Melt the milk chocolate in a water bath (page 270), add the praline, pailleté feuilletine and the hazelnut crumble, and mix with a spatula. With the frame over the pastry, spread the mixture over the pastry using a silicone spatula. Leave in the refrigerator to harden.

5 To make the passionfruit crémeux, hydrate the gelatine (page 270). Blanch the egg yolk and whole eggs with the sugar (page 279). At the same time, heat the passionfruit purée. When it boils, pour half into the egg and sugar mixture. Whisk.

6 Return this mixture to the saucepan and cook while whisking. As soon as it boils, remove from the heat and add the butter and drained gelatine. Whisk, then blend for 2–3 minutes using a hand-held blender. Pour into a container and refrigerate for at least 2 hours.

7 To make the sesame seed nougatine, preheat the oven to 360°F. Lightly toast the sesame seeds in the oven for 10–15 minutes (page 281). They should be blond.

8 Make the nougatine (page 50), replacing the almonds with the toasted sesame seeds. Roll out thinly using a rolling pin and allow to cool. Break into little pieces.

9 Take the tart out of the refrigerator and remove the frame. As soon as the passionfruit cream is set, whisk it to smooth it out. Fill a pastry bag (with a no. 12 plain tip) and pipe domes (page 275) over the crunchy hazelnut layer (put four 4 domes across the tart). Cover the whole surface. To make individual portions, cut the tart into six pieces before piping on the cream. Decorate with nougatine pieces.

CHOCOLATE
TART

Understand

FLOURLESS
CHOCOLATE CAKE

SWEET CRUST
PASTRY

CREAMY
GANACHE

DARK
CHOCOLATE
FROSTING

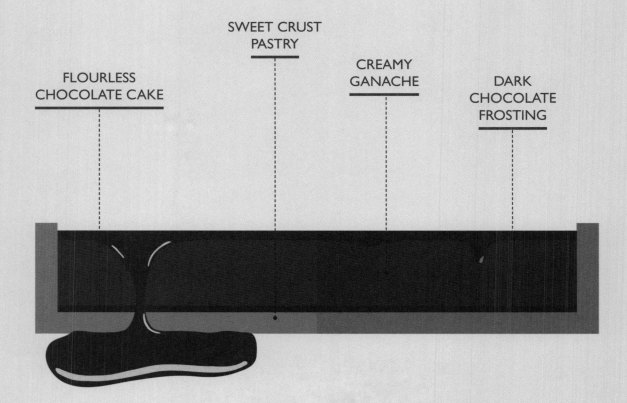

WHAT IS IT?

Base of sweet crust pastry filled with flourless chocolate cake, creamy ganache and chocolate frosting.

TIME TO MAKE

Preparation: 1 hour
Cooking: 40 minutes
Refrigeration: 3 hours

EQUIPMENT

9½ in tart ring (or 8 × 3¼ in tart rings)

VARIATIONS

Vanilla chocolate tart: replace the creamy ganache with vanilla mousse (see the recipe for Morello cherry domes, page 126). Chocolate tart shell: replace 1 oz (¼ cup) of the flour with 1 oz (⅓ cup) Dutch (unsweetened) cocoa powder.

TRICKY ASPECT
Frosting

TECHNIQUE TO MASTER
Lining a mold with pastry (page 284)

ORGANIZATION
Sugar crust pastry – chocolate cake – cooking the pastry – ganache – frosting

1

3

2

4

TO SERVE 8

1 SWEET CRUST PASTRY

5 oz (10 tbsp) butter
3½ oz (about .8 cup)
    confectioners' sugar
1¾ oz egg (1 egg)
1⁄32 oz (⅛ tsp) fine salt
6 oz (1⅓ cups) all-purpose flour
⅞ oz (¼ cup) almond meal

2 FLOURLESS
CHOCOLATE CAKE

2½ oz chocolate (66% cacao)
1¼ oz (2½ tbsp) Provence
    almond paste (50% almonds)
½ oz egg yolk (about 1 yolk)
¾ oz (1½ tbsp) butter
2¾ oz egg white (about 2½ whites)
1 oz (2¼ tbsp) superfine sugar

3 CREAMY GANACHE

1¾ oz egg yolk (about 3 yolks)
1¾ oz (¼ cup) superfine sugar
9 oz (1 cup 2 tbsp) milk
4⅜ oz dark chocolate

4 SHINY DARK
CHOCOLATE FROSTING

¼ oz leaf gelatine
4¼ oz (.56 cup) water
3½ oz (.44 cup) whipping cream
    (30% fat)
7¾ oz (1.1 cups) superfine sugar
2¾ oz (.9 cup) bitter Dutch
    (unsweetened) cocoa powder

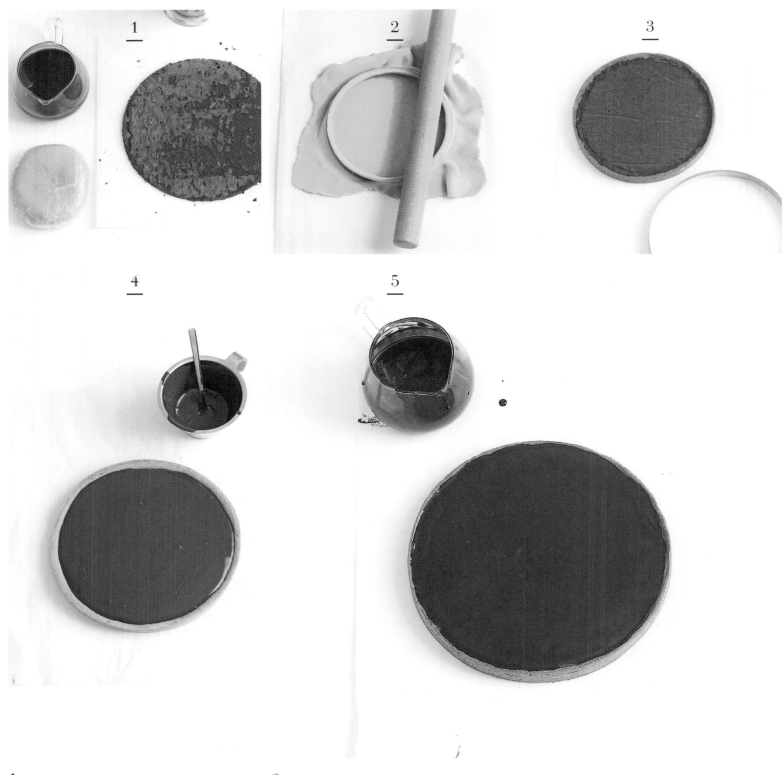

1 Make the sweet crust pastry (page 15). Make the shiny dark chocolate frosting (page 76) and allow to cool to lukewarm. Make the flourless chocolate cake; once it has cooled, cut to a diameter of 4¾ in.

2 Take out the pastry 30 minutes in advance. Grease a 9½ in tart ring with butter and place on a cookie sheet lined with baking paper. Preheat the oven to 300°F, dust the work surface with flour (page 284), roll the pastry using a rolling pin to 1/12 in thickness, aerate it (page 284) and use it to line the tart ring (page 284). Prick the bottom with a fork or prepare to bake it blind (page 285), as a precaution. Cut off any excess pastry at the brim. Bake for 25 minutes at 300°F.

3 Touch to the pastry with a finger to check if it is done: it should resist. Remove from the oven and allow to cool, then remove the tart ring. Place the disc of chocolate cake in the tart shell.

4 Make the creamy ganache (page 72), then pour it into the tart shell, leaving 1/12 in at the top. Refrigerate for 1 hour.

5 Using a ladle, pour frosting in the middle of the tart, then tilt the tart slightly to spread the frosting to the edges. Let it set in the refrigerator.

Chocolate tart

VANILLA
TART

Understand

SUGAR CRUST
PASTRY

VANILLA
MOUSSE

BISCUIT

CONFECTIONERS'
SUGAR

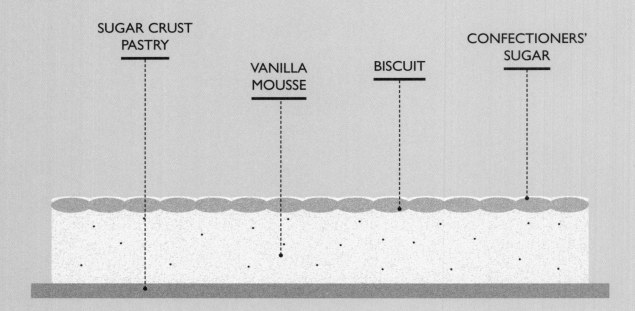

WHAT IS IT?

Tart composed of a sugar crust pastry base for crunch, vanilla mousse for creaminess and a biscuit layer for softness.

TIME TO MAKE

Preparation: 1 hour 30 minutes
Cooking: about 35 minutes
Freezing: 4 hours
Refrigeration: 30 minutes

EQUIPMENT

2 tart rings (1 × 8¾ in and 1 × 9½ in)
Pastry bag
No. 10 plain decorating tip
Acetate cake band

TRICKY ASPECTS
Cooking the pastry
Making the crème anglaise

TECHNIQUES TO MASTER
Dusting with flour (page 284)
Aerating dough (page 284)
Using a pastry bag (page 272)
Hydrating gelatine (page 270)

ORGANIZATION
Sugar crust pastry – vanilla
biscuit – vanilla mousse

1

2

3

4

TO SERVE 8

1 SUGAR CRUST PASTRY

7 oz (1.6 cups) all-purpose flour
1/32 oz (1/3 tsp) salt
2½ oz (5 tbsp) butter
2½ oz (.6 cup) confectioners' sugar
1¾ oz egg (1 egg)

2 VANILLA MOUSSE

crème anglaise
3/16 oz leaf gelatine
2 oz egg yolk (about 3 yolks)
1 oz (2¼ tbsp) superfine sugar
2 vanilla beans
6½ oz (.8 cup) whipping
   cream (30% fat)

whipped cream
6½ oz (.8 cup) whipping cream

3 BISCUIT

2 oz (.6 cup) almond meal
2 oz (about ½ cup)
   confectioners' sugar
½ oz (about 2 tbsp)
   all-purpose flour

1 vanilla bean
3½ oz egg white (about 3 whites)
2½ oz (1/3 cup) superfine sugar

4 DECORATION

1¾ oz (.4 cup) confectioners' sugar

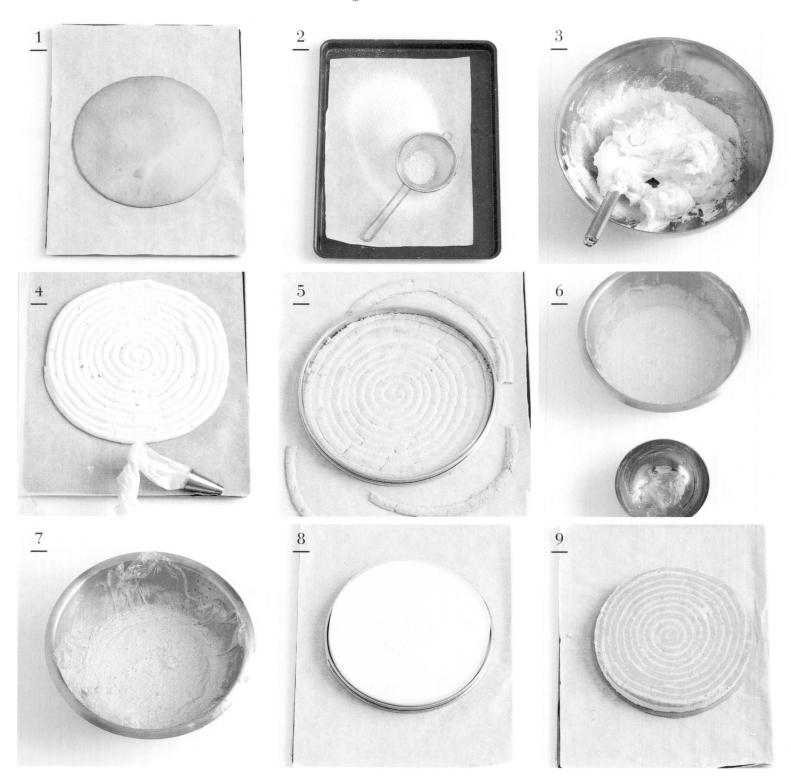

1 Make the sugar crust pastry (page 12). Take it out 30 minutes in advance. Dust the work surface with flour (page 284). Roll the pastry using a rolling pin to ⅛ in thickness, then aerate it (page 284). Using a 9½ in tart ring, cut out a disc of pastry and place it on a cookie sheet lined with baking paper. Refrigerate for 30 minutes. Preheat the oven to 340°F, then bake the pastry for 15–20 minutes. The pastry should be a uniform blond. Let it cool.

2 Change the oven temperature to 365°F. To make the biscuit, sift the almond meal with the confectioners' sugar, flour and the seeds from the vanilla bean. Make the French meringue (page 42) with the egg white and superfine sugar. Rain the dry ingredients into the meringue and fold them in using a silicone spatula until the mixture is smooth.

3 Draw a 9½ in circle on a sheet of baking paper. Put the biscuit mixture in a pastry bag with a plain no. 10 tip and pipe from the middle outward in a snail shell (page 273).

4 Bake for 15 minutes; the biscuit should be golden on top and detach from the paper easily. Allow to cool. If necessary, cut the biscuit to a diameter of 8¾ in. Place the cake band around the 8¾ in ring and put the biscuit in the bottom.

5 To make the vanilla mousse, hydrate the gelatine (page 270). Make the crème anglaise (page 60), using the cream in place of milk.

6 When the crème anglaise coats the spatula (a maximum of 185°F), drain the gelatine and whisk into the crème anglaise. Strain, cover with plastic wrap with the plastic touching the surface, then allow to cool to room temperature.

7 Whip the whipping cream like a chantilly cream (page 62). Add one-third to the crème anglaise and whisk vigorously. Delicately fold in the remaining cream using a silicone spatula. Pour the mousse over the biscuit. Freeze for several hours, ideally overnight.

8 Remove the ring and the cake band. Turn the biscuit and mousse combination upside down onto the pastry.

DECORATION

Dust liberally with confectioners' sugar.

PECAN TART

Understand

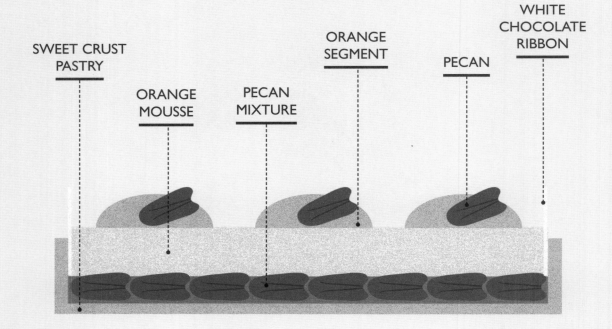

SWEET CRUST
PASTRY

ORANGE
MOUSSE

PECAN
MIXTURE

ORANGE
SEGMENT

PECAN

WHITE
CHOCOLATE
RIBBON

WHAT IS IT?

Sweet tart shell with a pecan filling topped with orange mousse encircled in white chocolate.

TIME TO MAKE

Preparation: 1 hour 30 minutes
Cooking: 45 minutes
Freezing: at least 3 hours

EQUIPMENT

9½ in tart ring
Acetate cake band, hand-held blender

TRICKY ASPECTS

Making the orange mousse
Putting up the chocolate ribbon

TECHNIQUES TO MASTER

Hydrating gelatine (page 270)
Zesting (page 281)
Lining a mold with pastry (page 284)
Making a chocolate ribbon (page 86)

ORGANIZATION

Sweet crust pastry – orange mousse –
pecan mixture – cooking – assembly –
caramelized pecans

TO SERVE 8

1 SWEET CRUST PASTRY

5 oz (10 tbsp) butter
3½ oz (about .8 cup) confectioners' sugar
1¾ oz egg (1 egg)
1/32 oz (⅛ tsp) fine salt
9 oz (2 cups) all-purpose flour
⅞ oz (¼ cup) almond meal

2 PECAN MIXTURE

1 vanilla bean
2¼ oz (4½ tbsp) butter
5¾ oz (¾ cup) soft brown sugar
7 oz (⅔ cup) glucose syrup
7 oz egg (4 eggs)
1/32 oz (⅓ tsp) salt

1/32 oz (⅓ tsp) ground cinnamon
5¼ oz (1½ cups) pecans

3 ORANGE MOUSSE

⅛ oz leaf gelatine
zest of 2 oranges
5 oz orange juice (from about 2 oranges)
7 oz egg (4 eggs)
2¾ oz (about .4 cup) superfine sugar
1⅜ oz (2¾ tbsp) butter

bombe mixture
2¾ oz egg yolk (about 4½ yolks)
¾ oz (1½ tbsp) water
2¾ oz (about .4 cup) superfine sugar

whipped cream
5¼ oz (⅔ cup) whipping cream (30% fat)

4 DECORATION

3½ oz white chocolate
¾ oz (1⅔ tbsp) superfine sugar
8 pecans
1 orange

1   Make the sweet crust pastry (page 14). Take it out 30 minutes in advance. Grease a 9½ in tart ring with butter and place on a cookie sheet lined with baking paper. Preheat the oven to 320°F, dust the work surface with flour (page 284), roll the pastry using a rolling pin to 1/12 in thickness, aerate it (page 284) then use it to line the ring (page 284). Prick the bottom with a fork and/or prepare it for blind baking (page 285), as a precaution. Precook for 15 minutes.

2   To make the pecan mixture, scrape the seeds from the vanilla bean into a saucepan, then add the butter, brown sugar and glucose. Bring to the boil, stirring with a spatula. Remove from the heat and whisk in the egg, salt and cinnamon. Pour into the precooked tart shell, arrange the pecans in it, then bake for 20–30 minutes. When you lift the tart with a frosting spatula; the coloration should be uniform. Remove the ring.

3   To make the orange mousse, hydrate the gelatine (page 270).

4   Break the eggs into a stainless-steel bowl and whisk them lightly. Put the orange zest and juice and the sugar in a saucepan. Bring to the boil. Pour directly over the egg while whisking vigorously so the egg doesn't cook.

5   Pour this orange cream back into the saucepan, and return to the heat, whisking. As soon as it boils, remove from the heat and whisk in the butter and drained gelatine. Blend for 2–3 minutes using a hand-held blender. Allow to cool to room temperature.

6   Whip the cream (page 277) and set aside in the refrigerator. Make the bombe mixture (page 58), whisking until cooled. Whisk the orange cream, then whisk in one-third of the whipped cream. Fold in the bombe mixture using a silicone spatula, then fold in the rest of the whipped cream. Line the tart ring with acetate cake band and sit it on a cookie sheet lined with baking paper. Pour the mousse into the ring and freeze for at least 3 hours, ideally overnight.

7   Remove the ring from the frozen mousse, Place it on the pecan pie and remove the cake band.

8   Make two white chocolate ribbons 12–16 in long (page 87), and apply them around the orange mousse while they are still supple. Make a caramel with sugar (page 49) and roll the pecans in it. Cut out eight orange segments. Decorate the tart.

CARAMEL & APPLE
SHORTBREADS

Understand

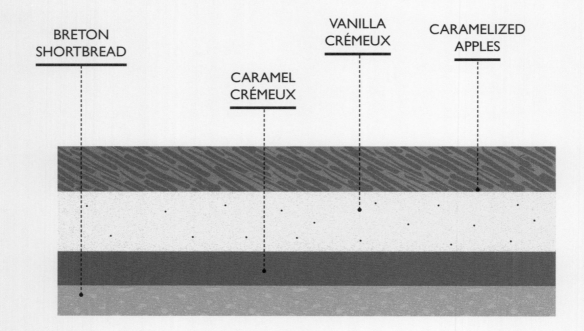

BRETON
SHORTBREAD

CARAMEL
CRÉMEUX

VANILLA
CRÉMEUX

CARAMELIZED
APPLES

WHAT ARE THEY?

*Breton shortbread topped with vanilla
crème brûlée, caramel crémeux and
caramelized stewed apples.*

TIME TO MAKE

*Preparation: 2 hours
Cooking: 2 hours 50 minutes to
3 hours 20 minutes
Freezing: 4 hours
Resting: 3 hours*

EQUIPMENT

*4¾ in × 9½ in dessert frame, 2 in high
Plastic wrap (oven safe)
Strainer*

VARIATION

*Tropical desserts: replace the
apples with mangoes. Reduce
cooking time to 30 minutes.*

TRICKY ASPECT
Cooking the caramelized apples

TECHNIQUES TO MASTER
Hydrating gelatine (page 270)
Making dry caramel (page 49)

ORGANIZATION
& STORAGE
Vanilla crémeux – caramel crémeux – stewed
apples – Breton shortbread – assembly

TO MAKE 6 BARS

1 BRETON SHORTBREAD

2⅝ oz (⅓ cup) butter
2½ oz (⅓ cup) superfine sugar
1 oz egg yolk (about 1½ yolks)
3½ oz (.8 cup) all-purpose flour

1⁄16 oz (.4 tsp) baking powder
1⁄16 oz (⅔ tsp) salt

2 VANILLA CRÉMEUX

2¾ oz egg yolk (about 4 yolks)
1 oz (2¼ tbsp) superfine sugar
⅜ oz (1⅓ tbsp) cornstarch
2¾ oz (⅓ cup) milk

8½ oz (1 cup 1 tbsp) whipping
 cream (30% fat)
1 vanilla bean

3 CARAMEL CRÉMEUX

3⁄16 oz leaf gelatine
5¼ oz (¾ cup) superfine sugar
9 oz (1 cup 2 tbsp) whipping
 cream (30% fat)

1¾ oz (3½ tbsp) butter

4 CARAMELIZED APPLES

6 royal gala apples
7 oz (1 cup) superfine sugar
1¾ oz (3½ tbsp) butter

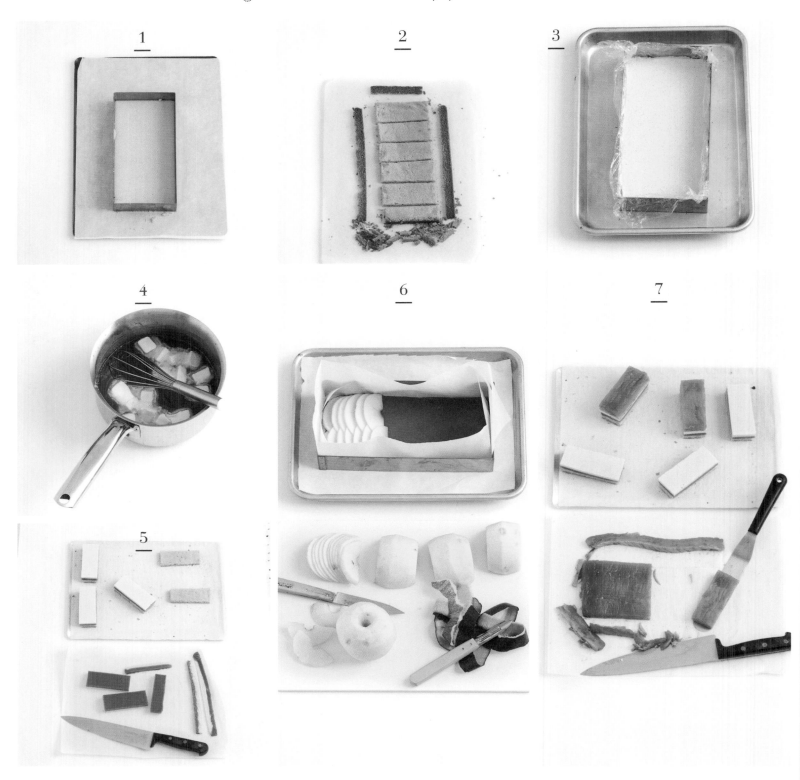

1   2   3

4   6   7

5

1   To make the Breton shortbread, preheat the oven to 340°F. Work the butter until it is smooth and soft (page 276), add the sugar and mix using a spatula (creaming, page 276). Add the egg yolk then the flour, baking powder and salt, and mix until smooth. Line a cookie sheet with baking paper. Put the shortbread mixture in a 4¾ × 9½ × 2 in dessert frame, smooth the top and bake for 20–30 minutes.

2   Remove from the oven, wait a few minutes, pass the blade of a knife around the sides, then lift off the frame. Cut into six bars 1½ in wide. Cutting while hot prevents the shortbread crumbling.

3   To make the vanilla crémeux, preheat the oven to 195°F. Blanch the egg yolk with the sugar and cornstarch by whisking in a stainless-steel bowl. In a saucepan, heat the milk, cream and split and scraped vanilla bean. Whisk frequently. As

soon as it boils, strain into the egg yolk mixture and whisk. Line the dessert frame with oven-safe plastic wrap, pour in the vanilla crémeux and bake for 30–50 minutes. When you shake the mold gently, the crémeux should not move. Let it cool to room temperature, then freeze for 1 hour.

4   Once the vanilla crémeux is chilled, make the caramel crémeux. Hydrate the gelatine (page 270). Make a caramel sauce (page 91), then add the butter and the drained gelatine. Blend, then allow to cool to lukewarm (the crémeux should not go below 85°F). Pour the caramel crémeux over the vanilla crémeux, then freeze for about 3 hours.

5   Once the caramel crémeux is set, remove the frame and the plastic wrap, then cut into rectangles the same size as the shortbread pieces. Place on top of the Breton shortbread.

6   To make the caramelized apples, preheat the oven to 320°F. Core and peel the apples, then cut into very thin and even slices. Make the caramel as for the caramel sauce (page 91), adding the butter at the end of cooking, then blending. Pour half into the frame, arrange the apple slices on top, then cover with the rest of the caramel. Bake for 1 hour, then reduce the oven temperature to 250°F and bake for another 1 hour. Put a sheet of baking paper then a weight (such as a carton of milk) on top of the apples and leave them to rest for at least 3 hours.

7   Remove the frame, cut to the size of the desserts using a serrated knife and place on top of the vanilla crémeux.

CHOCOLATE
ÉCLAIRS

Understand

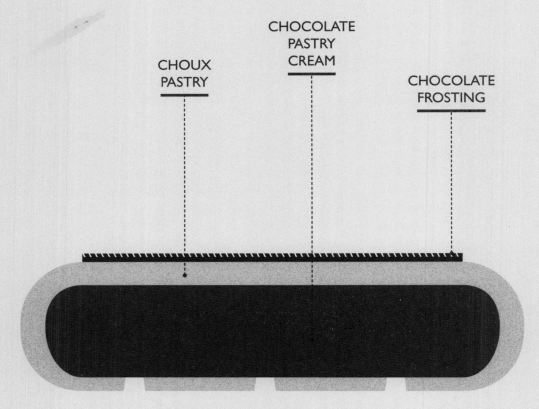

CHOCOLATE
PASTRY
CREAM

CHOUX
PASTRY

CHOCOLATE
FROSTING

WHAT ARE THEY?

Sticks of choux pastry filled with chocolate pastry cream and frosted with chocolate.

TIME TO MAKE

Preparation: 45 minutes
Cooking: 30–45 minutes
Resting: 2 hours

EQUIPMENT

3 pastry bags
No. 12 plain decorating tip
No. 6 plain decorating tip

VARIATION

Fondant frosting (shinier but less tasty):
2¾ oz white fondant frosting (page 80)
+ ⅜ oz melted dark chocolate

TRICKY ASPECTS

Cooking the éclairs (watch
them after 20 minutes)
Frosting

TECHNIQUES TO MASTER

Using a pastry bag (page 272)
Preparing a water bath (page 270)
Frosting (page 80) and filling an éclair
(page 282)

ORGANIZATION

Choux pastry – cooking – pastry
cream – filling – frosting

TO MAKE 15 ÉCLAIRS

1 CHOUX PASTRY

3½ oz (7 tbsp) milk
3½ oz (7 tbsp) water
1/16 oz (2/3 tsp) salt
1/16 oz (½ tsp) superfine sugar
3 oz (6 tbsp) butter
4 oz (.9 cup) all-purpose flour
7 oz egg (4 eggs)
1 egg, beaten

2 PASTRY CREAM

3½ oz egg yolk (about 5½ yolks)
4¼ oz (.6 cup) superfine sugar
1¾ oz (.4 cup) cornstarch
1 lb 2 oz (2¼ cups) milk
4¼ oz dark chocolate

3 CHOCOLATE FROSTING

7 oz dark chocolate
1¾ oz white chocolate

1 Preheat the oven to 450°F. Line a cookie sheet with baking paper. Make the choux pastry (page 30) and pipe éclairs (using a plain no. 12 tip) 6 in long. Glaze with the beaten egg. Reduce the oven to 340°F and put in the éclairs. At the end of 20 minutes, briefly open the oven door to let the steam out. Close immediately. Let them cook until light golden, about 25 minutes, then let them cool on a wire rack.

2 Melt the chocolate for the pastry cream in a water bath (page 270). Make the pastry cream (page 53), adding the melted chocolate at the end of cooking, then leave to cool. Whisk the cream to smooth it out. Fill a pastry bag (no. 6 plain tip). Using the point of a knife, make three holes in the underside of each éclair. Fill the éclairs via these holes, then feel their weight: they should be quite heavy.

3 Melt the dark chocolate for the frosting in a water bath (page 270). Frost the éclairs by dipping them in the chocolate. Drain off the surplus, then smooth out the chocolate using a finger. Melt the white chocolate in a water bath, put it in a pastry bag and cut off the end to make a very tiny hole. Pipe white lines on the éclairs. Refrigerate for 2 hours.

COFFEE
RELIGIEUSES

Understand

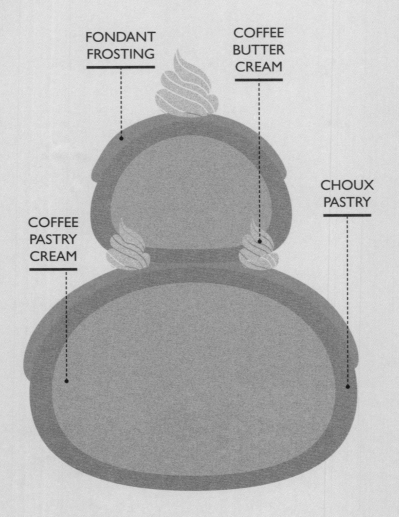

FONDANT
FROSTING

COFFEE
BUTTER
CREAM

COFFEE
PASTRY
CREAM

CHOUX
PASTRY

WHAT ARE THEY?

Large choux puffs topped with a small choux puff, both filled with coffee pastry cream, and decorated with coffee butter cream and fondant frosting.

TIME TO MAKE

Preparation: 45 minutes
Cooking: 20–40 minutes
Refrigeration: 4 hours

EQUIPMENT

Pastry bag

No. 12 plain decorating tip
No. 6 plain decorating tip
No.6 fluted decorating tip
2 silicone half-sphere molds (one with 1¼ in holes and one with 3¼ in holes)
Candy thermometer

VARIATIONS

Classic frosting: dip the choux puffs in hot fondant and remove the overflows with a finger.
Chocolate religieuses: chocolate pastry cream made with 7 oz chocolate, and 1 oz (⅓ cup) Dutch (unsweetened) cocoa powder in the fondant frosting.

TECHNIQUES TO MASTER
Using a pastry bag (page 272)
Toasting in the oven (281)
Making choux puffs (page 282)

TIP
The glucose syrup allows the fondant to be heated more.

ORGANIZATION
Pastry cream – choux pastry – frosting – French butter cream

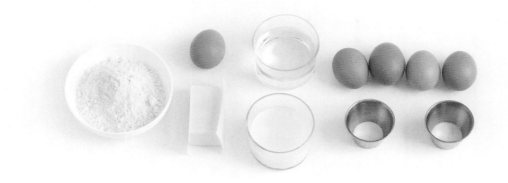

TO MAKE 12 RELIGIEUSES

1 CHOUX PASTRY

3½ oz (7 tbsp) milk
3½ oz (7 tbsp) water
1⁄16 oz (⅔ tsp) salt
1⁄16 oz (½ tsp) superfine sugar
3 oz (6 tbsp) butter
4 oz (.9 cup) all-purpose flour

7 oz egg (4 eggs)
1 egg, beaten

2 COFFEE PASTRY CREAM

3½ oz ground coffee
1 lb 2 oz (2¼ cups) milk
3½ oz egg yolk (about 5½ yolks)
4¼ oz (.6 cup) superfine sugar
1¾ oz (about .4 cup) cornstarch
4⅜ oz butter

3 COFFEE BUTTER CREAM

3½ oz egg (2 eggs)
1⅜ oz (2¾ tbsp) water
4½ oz (about ⅔ cup) superfine
   sugar
7 oz (14 tbsp) butter
½ oz (1 tbsp) coffee extract

4 FONDANT FROSTING

14 oz fondant
⅜ oz (¾ tbsp) coffee extract
1 oz (1½ tbsp) glucose syrup

1

2

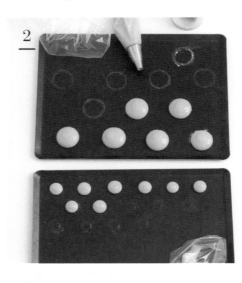

3

4

7

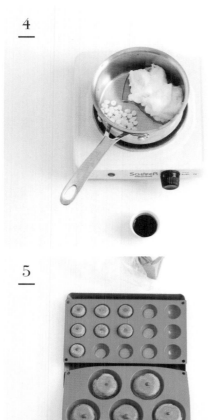

5

1   To make the coffee pastry cream, toast (page 281) the coffee on a cookie sheet lined with baking paper for 15 minutes in a 320°F oven. Put the milk in a saucepan with the coffee, cover and infuse for 30 minutes, then strain. Adjust the quantity of milk if necessary, to come to 1 lb 2 oz. Follow the recipe as indicated (page 53).

2   Preheat the oven to 450°F. Make the choux pastry (page 30). On a nonstick cookie sheet or a cookie sheet lined with baking paper, pipe twelve large choux puffs (using a no. 12 plain tip) of 1½ in diameter and ¾ in height. On another cookie sheet, pipe twelve "heads" of ⅝ in diameter and ⅜ in height. Glaze with the beaten egg. Lower the oven temperature to 340°F and bake. At the end of 20

minutes, briefly open the oven door to let the steam out. Close it again straightaway. Take out the small puffs as soon as they color up, before the large ones.

3   Using the point of a knife, make little holes in the bottom of the choux puffs. Fill a pastry bag (no. 6 plain tip) with coffee pastry cream and fill the choux puffs (page 282).

4   Put the fondant in a saucepan with the coffee extract and glucose syrup. Warm it up, stirring constantly with a spatula to 95°F.

5   Use it to fill a pastry bag and cut off the end (page 272). Pipe into ¾ in half-sphere molds for the large choux puffs and into ⅜ in half-sphere molds for the small choux puffs. Put all the choux puffs

upside down into the molds and press lightly. Freeze for about 1 hour so that you can unmold them.

6   Make the coffee French butter cream (page 54). Fill a pastry bag (no. 6 fluted tip) with the cream.

7   Put the small choux puffs on top of the large ones. Pipe "flames" between the bodies and heads of the religieuses and a little rose on top. Refrigerate for 2 hours before eating.

CRISPY PISTACHIO
CHOUX PUFFS

Understand

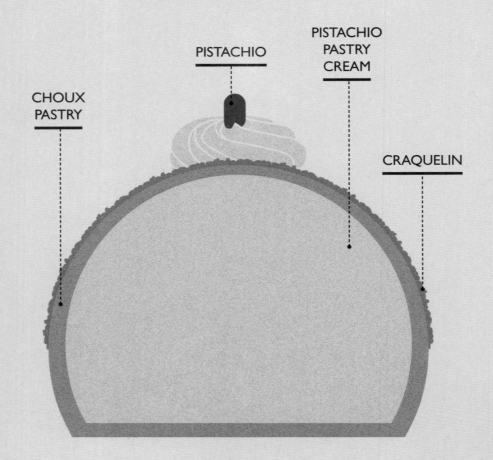

CHOUX
PASTRY

PISTACHIO

PISTACHIO
PASTRY
CREAM

CRAQUELIN

WHAT ARE THEY?

Pistachio cream puffs topped with a crispy, crackly craquelin layer and decorated with pistachio cream.

TIME TO MAKE

Preparation: 45 minutes
Cooking: 20–45 minutes
Refrigeration: 3 hours

EQUIPMENT

1¼ in round cookie cutter
Pastry bag
No. 10 and no. 6 plain decorating tips
No. 8 fluted decorating tip

TRICKY ASPECTS
Making choux pastry
Cooking the choux puffs (page 282)

TECHNIQUES TO MASTER
Using a pastry bag (page 272)
Glazing (page 270)

ORGANIZATION
Craquelin dough – pastry cream –
choux pastry – assembly

TIP
Craquelin adds crunchiness and allows the creation of very uniform choux puffs.

TO MAKE 20–25 CHOUX PUFFS

1 CHOUX PASTRY

3½ oz (7 tbsp) milk
3½ oz (7 tbsp) water
1⁄16 oz (⅔ tsp) salt
1⁄16 oz (½ tsp) superfine sugar
3 oz (6 tbsp) butter
4 oz (about .9 cup) all-purpose flour
7 oz egg (4 eggs)

2 GLAZE

1 egg, beaten

3 CRAQUELIN

1½ oz (3 tbsp) soft brown sugar
1½ oz (⅓ cup) all-purpose flour
1¼ oz (2½ tbsp) butter, softened

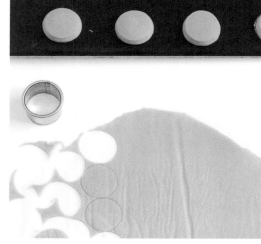

4 PASTRY CREAM

7 oz egg yolk (11 yolks)
8½ oz (about 1.2 cups) superfine sugar
3½ oz (about .8 cup) cornstarch
34 oz (4¼ cups) milk
4⅜ oz (8¾ tbsp) butter
1⅜ oz (about 3 tbsp) pistachio paste

5 DECORATION

¾ oz (about 3 tbsp) unsalted pistachios

1 Mix all the craquelin ingredients in a stainless-steel bowl using a spatula. Once the mixture is smooth, roll the pastry between two sheets of baking paper, using a rolling pin, to 1/12 in thickness. Set aside in the refrigerator.

2 Make the pastry cream (page 53). At the end of cooking, whisk in the pistachio jackke. Transfer to a container, cover with plastic wrap with the plastic touching the surface, and refrigerate.

3 Line a cookie sheet with baking paper. Make the choux pastry (page 30), use it to fill pastry bag (no. 10 plain tip) and pipe 20–25 choux dollops of 1½ in diameter, spacing them well (page 282). Glaze with the beaten egg.

4 Take the craquelin dough out of the refrigerator and peel off the top sheet of baking paper. Turn the dough upside down onto this sheet, then peel off the second sheet. Using a cookie cutter of 1¼ in diameter, cut out discs of dough and pop them on top of the choux.

5 Preheat the oven to 450°F. Reduce the temperature to 340°F and bake. Open the oven door briefly after 20 minutes, to let the steam escape. Cook until they are evenly colored, about 20 minutes more. Let them cool on a wire rack.

6 Smooth out the pastry cream by whisking for a few minutes. Using a fluted decorating tip, make a hole in the bottom of the choux puffs. Fill a pastry bag with the pastry cream (no. 6 plain tip) and fill the choux puffs with two-thirds of the cream (page 282). The puffs are well filled when they swell in your hand. Pipe the remaining cream in little roses on top of the choux, using a pastry bag fitted with a no. 6 fluted tip. Decorate each with a pistachio.

PARIS-BREST

Understand

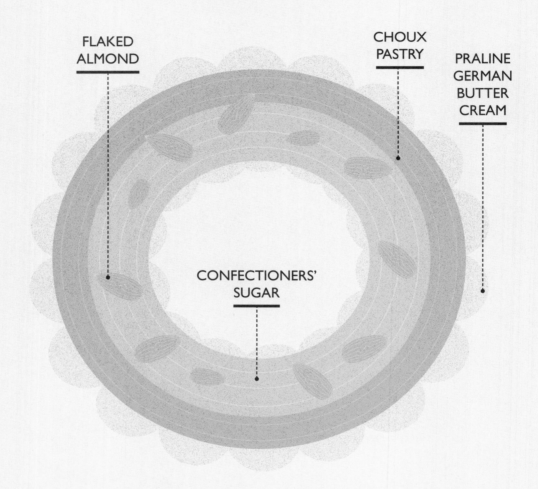

FLAKED
ALMOND

CHOUX
PASTRY

PRALINE
GERMAN
BUTTER
CREAM

CONFECTIONERS'
SUGAR

WHAT IS IT?

Grand dessert of choux pastry sprinkled with flaked almonds and filled with praline German butter cream.

TIME TO MAKE

*Preparation: 45 minutes
Cooking: 40 minutes
Refrigeration: 3 hours*

EQUIPMENT

*Pastry bag
No. 10 plain decorating tip
Serrated knife*

VARIATION

Classic version: choux piped in a ring to make a wreath (historically, the shape represents a bicycle wheel, in reference to the cycling race between Paris and Brest).

TRICKY ASPECTS

Making choux pastry
Cooking the choux pastry (page 282)

TECHNIQUES TO MASTER

Using a pastry bag (page 272)
Piping choux pastry (page 282)
Glazing (page 270)

ORGANIZATION

Pastry cream – choux pastry – German butter cream – assembly

TO MAKE 12

1 CHOUX PASTRY

3½ oz (7 tbsp) milk
3½ oz (7 tbsp) water
1/16 oz (⅔ tsp) salt
1/16 oz (½ tsp) superfine sugar
3 oz (6 tbsp) butter
4 oz (about .9 cup) all-purpose flour
7 oz egg (4 eggs)

2 GLAZE

1 egg, beaten

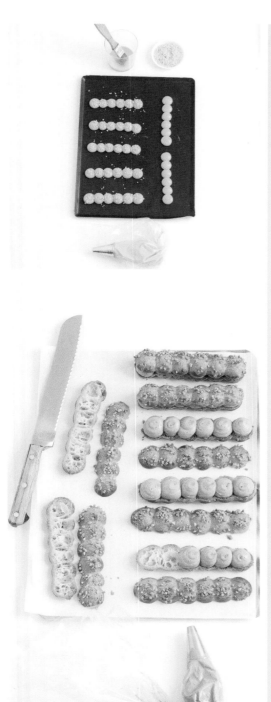

3 GERMAN BUTTER CREAM

4¼ oz (.6 cup) superfine sugar
1¾ oz (about .4 cup) cornstarch
3½ oz egg yolks (about 6 yolks)
1 lb 2 oz (2¼ cups) milk
4¼ oz (8½ tbsp) butter
4¼ oz (8½ tbsp) butter, softened
5⅝ oz praline (ground caramelized almonds)

4 DECORATION

flaked almonds
confectioners' sugar

1   Preheat the oven to 450°F. Make the choux pastry (page 30). Using a pastry bag (no. 10 plain tip), pipe twelve rows of six small choux balls stuck to each other on a cookie sheet lined with baking paper or a nonstick cookie sheet. Glaze with the beaten egg, then sprinkle with flaked almonds.

2   When you are ready to bake, reduce the oven temperature to 340°F. Briefly open the oven door at the end of 20 minutes, to let the steam out. Bake until uniformly colored, at least 20 minutes extra. Let them cool on a wire rack.

3   Make the German butter cream (page 57). At the end of cooking, add the praline. Allow to cool.

4   Once the Paris-Brests are cool, cut them in half horizontally using a serrated knife. Fill a pastry bag fitted with a no. 10 plain decorating tip with butter cream and pipe domes on the lower halves of the Paris-Brests. Put the tops on. Dust with confectioners' sugar just before serving.

ST HONORÉ
CAKE

Understand

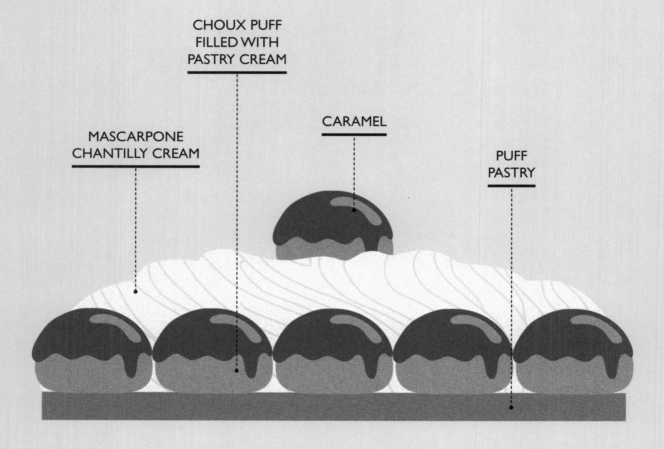

CHOUX PUFF
FILLED WITH
PASTRY CREAM

MASCARPONE
CHANTILLY CREAM

CARAMEL

PUFF
PASTRY

WHAT IS IT?

Choux gâteau on a puff pastry base, filled with chantilly cream.

TIME TO MAKE

Preparation: 1 hour
Cooking: 20–30 minutes
Refrigeration: 3 hours

EQUIPMENT

4 pastry bags
No. 6 plain decorating tip
No. 8 plain decorating tip
No. 10 plain decorating tip
St Honoré decorating tip
9½ in dessert ring
Electric mixer with whisk attachment

VARIATIONS

Classic decoration: pipe the cream in a continuous wave (page 273).
Square format: Cut a rectangle of puff pastry and arrange the choux puffs along the long sides. Pipe the cream in the middle, in a wave.
Classic version: replace the mascarpone chantilly cream with chiboust cream (page 66).

TRICKY ASPECTS

Piping the cream
Cooking the choux puffs (page 282)

TECHNIQUES TO MASTER

Using a pastry bag (page 272)
Decorating with a St Honoré
decorating tip (page 273)
Making caramel (pages 48 and 278)
Frosting (page 80) and filling
choux puffs (page 282)
Glazing (page 270)

ORGANIZATION

Puff pastry – choux pastry – piping –
baking – caramel pastry cream – assembly –
mascarpone chantilly cream – decoration

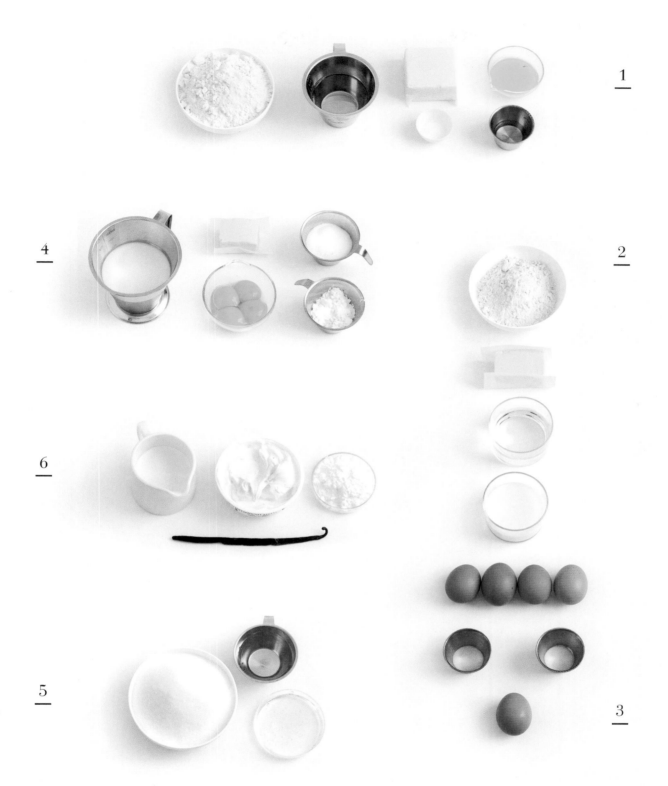

TO MAKE 8

1 PUFF PASTRY

9 oz (2 cups) all-purpose flour
3½ oz (7 tbsp) water
⅜ oz (2 tsp) white vinegar
³⁄₁₆ oz (2 tsp) salt
1 oz (2 tbsp) butter, melted
5¼ oz (⅔ cup) butter

2 CHOUX PASTRY

3½ oz (7 tbsp) milk
3½ oz (7 tbsp) water
⅟₁₆ oz (⅔ tsp) salt
⅟₁₆ oz (½ tsp) superfine sugar
3 oz (6 tbsp) butter
3½ oz (about .8 cup) all-purpose
    flour
7 oz egg (4 eggs)

3 GLAZE

1 egg, beaten

4 PASTRY CREAM

1¾ oz egg yolk (about 3 yolks)
2 oz (4½ tbsp) superfine sugar
⅞ oz (about 3 tbsp) cornstarch
9 oz (1 cup 2 tbsp) milk
2 oz (¼ cup) butter

5 CARAMEL

3½ oz (7 tbsp) water
12½ oz (about 1.8 cups) superfine
    sugar
2½ oz glucose syrup

**6 MASCARPONE
CHANTILLY CREAM**

5¼ oz mascarpone
1⅜ oz (⅓ cup) confectioners' sugar
1 vanilla bean
5¼ oz (⅔ cup) whipping cream

1   Make the puff pastry (page 18). Roll using a rolling pin to ¹⁄₁₂ in thickness. Place on a cookie sheet lined with baking paper and refrigerate for 30 minutes. Prick the pastry with a fork and, using a 9½ in dessert ring, cut out a disc.

2   Preheat the oven to 240°F. Make the choux pastry (page 30). Pipe 20 choux dollops of ½ in diameter (no. 8 plain tip) on a cookie sheet lined with baking paper or a nonstick cookie sheet. Glaze the choux with the beaten egg then bake. At the end of 20 minutes, briefly open the oven door to let the steam out. Cook until uniformly colored, about 20 minutes longer.

3   Put the remaining choux pastry in a pastry bag fitted with a no. 10 plain decorating tip. Take out the puff pastry. Pipe a band of pastry ⅜ in from

the edge, then pipe an open spiral in the middle and glaze it all with the beaten egg. Bake for 20–30 minutes at 340°F. Check whether it is cooked by lifting the pastry disc; it should be uniformly golden.

4   Make the pastry cream (page 53). Leave it to cool, then whisk to smooth it out. Fill the choux puffs using a pastry bag fitted with a no. 6 plain decorating tip (page 282).

5   Make the caramel (page 48), stopping the cooking when it is clear. Let it cool enough to thicken slightly, then caramelize the choux puffs by dipping the rounded side in the caramel. Let it harden. If the caramel cools too much and becomes too hard, reheat it gently.

6   Dip the bases of the choux puffs in the caramel, stick them on the pastry ring, then allow to harden.

7   To make the mascarpone chantilly cream, put the mascarpone, confectioners' sugar, scraped seeds from the vanilla bean and 1¾ oz of the cream in the bowl of an electric mixer. Beat gently. Add the rest of the cream in a thin thread. Once the mixture is smooth, increase the speed of the mixer and whip as for a chantilly cream. Spread a thin layer of cream in the middle of the cake, smoothing it with a frosting spatula. Put the rest of the cream in a pastry bag fitted with a St Honoré decorating tip and decorate the gâteau with a rosette (page 273).

CROQUEMBOUCHE

Understand

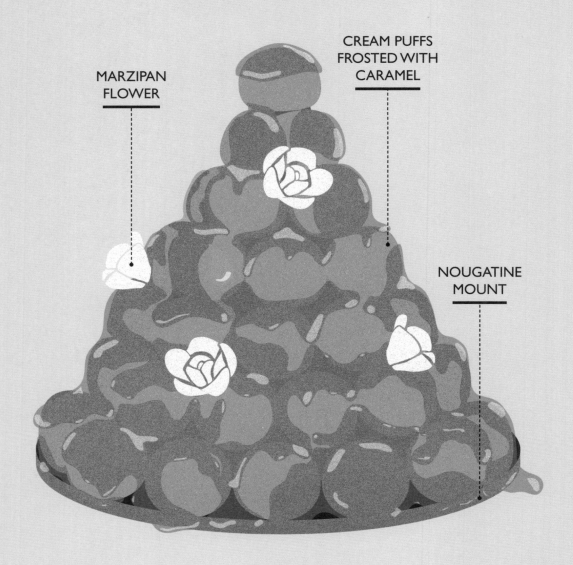

MARZIPAN
FLOWER

CREAM PUFFS
FROSTED WITH
CARAMEL

NOUGATINE
MOUNT

WHAT IS IT?

*Cone of caramelized cream puffs
on a nougatine mount.*

TIME TO MAKE

*Preparation: 3 hours
Cooking: 40 minutes
Refrigeration: 3 hours*

EQUIPMENT

*2 pastry bags
No. 8 plain decorating tip
No. 6 plain decorating tip
7 in dessert ring
2¾ in dessert ring (or nougatine cutter)
Straight rolling pin (or nougatine roller)*

VARIATION

Fondant frosting

TRICKY ASPECTS
Assembly
Cooking the choux pastry (page 282)

TECHNIQUES TO MASTER
Using a pastry bag (page 272)
Glazing (page 270)
Piping choux pastry (page 282)
Making caramel (pages 48 and 278)

ORGANIZATION
Pastry cream – choux pastry – nougatine –
filling and caramelizing the choux puffs –
assembly – decoration

TO MAKE 15

1 CHOUX PASTRY

9 oz (1 cup 2 tbsp) milk
9 oz (1 cup 2 tbsp) water
⅛ oz (1⅓ tsp) salt
⅛ oz (¼ tbsp) sugar
8 oz (1 cup) butter
9¾ oz (about 2¼ cups)
   all-purpose flour
1 lb 2 oz egg (10 eggs)

2 GLAZE

1 egg, beaten

3 CARAMEL

9 oz (1 cup 2 tbsp) water
2 lb 3 oz (5 cups) superfine sugar
7 oz (about ⅔ cup) glucose syrup

4 PASTRY CREAM

5¼ oz egg yolk (about 8 yolks)
6½ oz (about .9 cup) superfine
   sugar
2⅝ oz (about .6 cup) cornstarch
1 lb 11 oz (about 3.4 cups) milk
2 vanilla beans
5¼ oz (⅔ cup) butter

5 ROYAL ICING

5¼ oz (1¼ cups)
   confectioners' sugar
½ oz egg white (about ½ white)
3⁄16 oz (⅓ tbsp) lemon juice

6 NOUGATINE

9 oz (about 2⅓ cups) chopped
   almonds
10½ oz fondant
9 oz (about .8 cup) glucose syrup

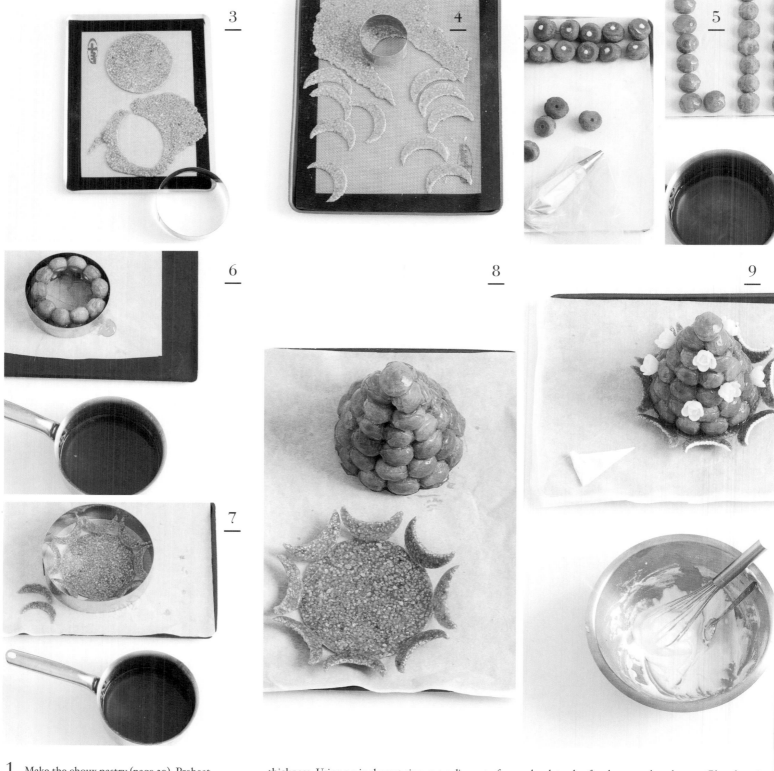

1   Make the choux pastry (page 30). Preheat the oven to 450°F. Fill a pastry bag fitted with a no. 8 plain pastry tip and pipe choux dollops of ¾ in diameter. Glaze with the beaten egg. Reduce the oven temperature to 340°F and bake. At the end of 20 minutes, briefly open the oven door to let out the steam. Cook until the pastry is uniformly colored, about 20 minutes more.

2   Make the pastry cream (page 53), adding the vanilla beans and scraped seeds to the milk. Transfer the pastry cream to a container, cover with plastic wrap touching the surface, and refrigerate.

3   Make the nougatine (page 51). Lightly oil the work surface. Draw the edges of the nougatine toward the center using a frosting spatula, to ensure a uniform temperature. Using a nougatine roller or an oiled straight rolling pin, roll the nougatine to ⅛–³⁄₁₆ in

thickness. Using a 7 in dessert ring, cut a disc out of the nougatine. If the nougatine is too hard, hit the ring with the base of a stainless-steel saucepan.

4   Using a 2¾ in dessert ring, cut half-moons from the remaining nougatine. Cool to room temperature.

5   Whisk the pastry cream to smooth it out. Using the point of a knife, make little holes in the base of the choux puffs. Fill them using a pastry bag fitted with no. 6 plain decorating tip. Make the caramel (page 48), stopping it cooking when it is clear. Allow to cool enough to thicken slightly, then dip the tops of the choux puffs in it. Allow to harden.

6   Oil the 7 in dessert ring, place it on a sheet of baking paper, then assemble the cream puffs: dip them one by one into the caramel (the sides and the base) and glue them to each other, with the rounded side against the ring. Use thirteen choux puffs for the first

level, twelve for the second, and so on. Glue them in staggered rows, gradually adding levels, and gently tilt them toward the middle, to form a cone. Re-melt the caramel if it becomes too hard. Remove the ring.

7   Place the nougatine disc in the center of the ring. Glue the half-moons to the edge of the disc with caramel at an angle, leaning against the ring.

8   Run a ring of caramel around the nougatine disc using a ladle. Glue the assembled choux cone on top.

9   Make the royal icing (page 81), then, using a cone or a pastry bag, decorate the nougatine by making little dots along the inside of the crescents.

DECORATION

Decorate with marzipan flowers (page 82).

BRIOCHE

Understand

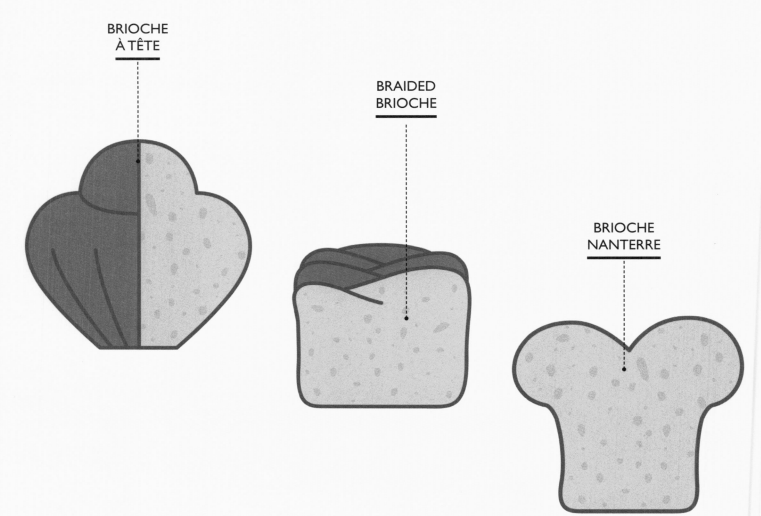

BRIOCHE
À TÊTE

BRAIDED
BRIOCHE

BRIOCHE
NANTERRE

WHAT IS IT?

Very airy Viennese pastry made using a yeast dough.

TIME TO MAKE

Preparation: 1 hour
Proofing: 1 hour 30 minutes to 2 hours
Cooking: 12–45 minutes
Cooling: 12–45 minutes

EQUIPMENT

Brioche Nanterre: rectangular brioche tin or loaf tin
Brioche à tête: fluted round brioche tin

VARIATIONS

Vanilla brioche: add ½ oz (3¼ tsp) vanilla extract to the dough.
Citrus brioche: add the zest of a citrus fruit to the dough.

TECHNIQUES TO MASTER

Forming a ball of dough (page 284)
Knocking back dough (page 284)
Glazing (page 270)

ORGANIZATION

Dough – resting – shaping – resting – baking

TO MAKE 1 BRIOCHE NANTERRE OR 1 BRAIDED BRIOCHE OR 2 BRIOCHES À TÊTE

1 BRIOCHE DOUGH

¾ oz fresh baker's yeast
14 oz (about 3.2 cups) all-purpose flour
⅜ oz (1¼ tbsp) salt
1⅜ oz (about 3 tbsp) superfine sugar
9 oz egg (5 eggs)
7 oz (14 tbsp) butter

2 FINISHING

nib sugar + 1 egg, beaten

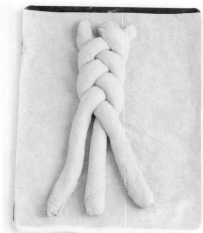

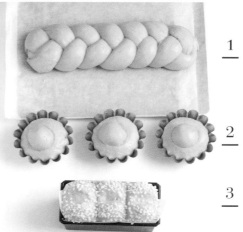

1

2

3

1 BRAIDED BRIOCHE

Make the dough (page 20). Remove the dough from the refrigerator, knock it back (page 284), then divide it into three 10½ oz pieces and form them into balls (page 284). Using your hands, roll each ball into a sausage shape. Make the plait by working from the center toward the base then from the center toward the top. Place on a cookie sheet lined with baking paper. Leave to proof in a 90°F oven or near a source of heat for 1 hour 30 minutes to 2 hours: the brioche should double in volume.

2 BRIOCHES À TÊTE

Make the dough (page 20). Remove the dough from the refrigerator, knock it back (page 284), then divide it into two 1 lb pieces and form them into balls

(page 284), then egg shapes. Using the side of your hand two-thirds of the way along the dough, push on the dough and roll gently to make a head. Put the dough in two fluted brioche tins with the bigger part, the body, downward. Using your index finger, push the dough around the end of the head down into the body. Leave to proof in a 90°F oven or near a source of heat, for 1 hour 30 minutes to 2 hours: the brioche should double in volume.

3 BRIOCHE NANTERRE

Make the dough (page 20). Remove the dough from the refrigerator, knock it back (page 284), then divide it into four 7¾ oz pieces and roll them into balls (page 284) with your hands. Line a rectangular brioche tin with baking paper, then put the four dough balls in the tin,

side by side. Leave to proof in a 90°F oven or near a source of heat, for 1 hour 30 minutes to 2 hours: the brioche should double in volume. Using scissors, slash each ball lengthways, then sprinkle with nib sugar.

BAKING

Preheat the oven to 390°F. Using a pastry brush, glaze the dough with beaten egg. Bake for about 30 minutes. Remove from the oven, remove from the tin/s, and allow to cool on a wire rack for 12–45 minutes, depending on the size and shape.

RUM BABA

Understand

WHAT IS IT?

Gâteau made from a yeast dough, cooked, dried, then soaked in syrup to flavor.

TIME TO MAKE

Preparation: 20 minutes
Kneading: 30–45 minutes
Proofing: 1 hour 30 minutes to 2 hours
Cooking: 30 minutes to 1 hour
Resting: 1 hour to 3 days

EQUIPMENT

8¾ in baba tin (kugelhopf tin)
Pastry bag
Large stainless-steel bowl or saucepan
Round wire rack smaller than the bowl or saucepan
Kitchen twine

VARIATIONS

Classic baba: add 1¾ oz (.3 cup) raisins at the end of kneading and soak the baba in rum syrup.
Classic shapes: little corks (10 babas of 1¾ oz) or cooked in a savarin tin.

TRICKY ASPECTS

Soaking in warm syrup
Pressing on the baba

TECHNIQUES TO MASTER

Making a sugar syrup (page 278)

ORGANIZATION

Dough – syrup – soaking – cream

TIPS

So the baba absorbs more syrup, leave it to dry out for 2–3 days. Soaking technique: fill a tall container with syrup, put the baba/s inside, then put a cookie sheet on top. Turn the baba/s after 15 minutes.

1

3

2

TO SERVE 8

1 BABA

½ oz fresh baker's yeast
9 oz (about 2 cups) all-purpose
  flour
³⁄₁₆ oz (⅔ tbsp) salt
½ oz (3½ tsp) superfine sugar
4½ oz (9 tbsp) milk
3½ oz egg (2 eggs)
2⅝ oz (⅓ cup) butter

2 SYRUP

1 lb 11 oz (about 3⅓ cups) water
12½ oz (about 1.8 cups) superfine
  sugar
3 cardamom pods
1 star anise
½ cinnamon stick
1⅜ oz (2¾ tbsp) rum (optional)

3 CHANTILLY CREAM

9 oz (about 1.1 cups) whipping
  cream (30% fat)
1⅜ oz (⅓ cup) confectioners' sugar
1 vanilla bean

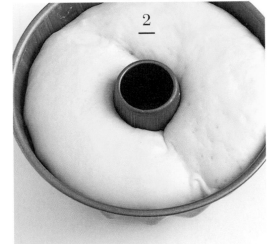

1   Make the baba dough (page 23). Grease the tin with butter and pipe into the tin using a pastry bag with the end cut off to make a large hole.

2   Leave the baba to proof in a 90°F oven or near a source of heat, until it doubles in volume – 1 hour 30 minutes to 2 hours.

3   To make the syrup, put the water, sugar and spices in a saucepan and bring to the boil. Remove from the heat. Add the rum, if using. Cover and set aside to infuse, then allow to cool.

4   Preheat the oven to 320°F. Bake the baba for 30–45 minutes, then remove from the tin. Return to the turned-off oven for 15 minutes to dry out. Allow to cool completely. You can leave it for as long as 3 days.

5   Once the syrup is lukewarm, strain it (page 270) and pour into a large stainless-steel bowl or saucepan. Attach four pieces of kitchen twine to the edge of a round wire rack smaller than the bowl or saucepan so that you can remove the baba from the syrup without spoiling it. The pieces of twine need to be long enough to hang over the edges of the bowl or saucepan. Put the baba on the wire rack, then slide it into the syrup (page 278). Rewarm the syrup slightly if it is cold. The baba should be very moist.

6   Remove the baba from the syrup, pressing on it delicately to avoid tearing it. Leave on the wire rack to drain for 1 hour.

PRESENTATION

Make the chantilly cream (page 63) and flavor it with the seeds scraped from the vanilla bean. Accompany the baba with a rosette of chantilly cream.

TARTE
AU SUCRE

Understand

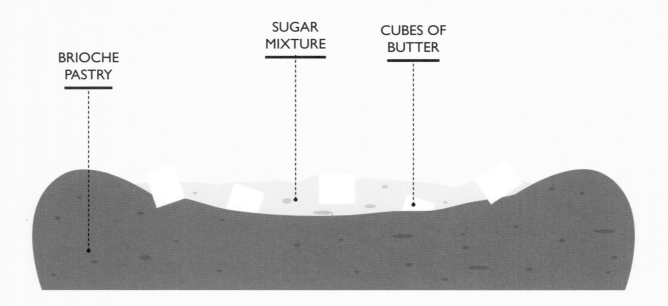

BRIOCHE
PASTRY

SUGAR
MIXTURE

CUBES OF
BUTTER

WHAT IS IT?

A brioche base in the form of a tart or pie onto which a sugar mixture is poured.

TIME TO MAKE

Preparation: 45 minutes
Proofing: 1 hour 30 minutes to 2 hours
Cooking: 20–30 minutes

EQUIPMENT

9½ in springform pan

VARIATION

Flavor the dough with orange flower water or citrus zest.

TRICKY ASPECT
Proofing

ORGANIZATION
Brioche dough – shaping –
proofing – filling – baking

TO SERVE 8

1 BRIOCHE DOUGH

³⁄₁₆ oz fresh baker's yeast
3½ oz (about .8 cup) all-purpose flour
⅛ oz (1¼ tsp) salt
⅜ oz (2½ tsp) superfine sugar
2¼ oz egg (about 1½ eggs)
1¾ oz (3½ tbsp) butter

2 FILLING

2 oz (¼ cup) soft brown sugar
1 oz (2 tbsp) whipping cream (30% fat)
¾ oz egg yolk (about 1 yolk)
2 oz (4 tbsp) butter, cut into small cubes

1 Make the brioche dough (page 20). Take out of the refrigerator and knock it back (page 284). Line a 9½ in springform pan with baking paper, put the dough in the tin and flatten it with the palm of your hand so that it reaches the bottom of the tin. Leave to proof: either in a 90°F oven, or at room temperature. Leave for 1 hour 30 minutes to 2 hours: the brioche should double in volume.

2 Preheat the oven to 360°F. Using a fork, prick the pastry at regular 1¼ in intervals. Sprinkle with the brown sugar. Whisk together the cream and egg yolk, then pour over the dough. Add the butter, then bake for 20–30 minutes. Allow to cool before removing from the tin.

TROPÉZIENNE
TART

Understand

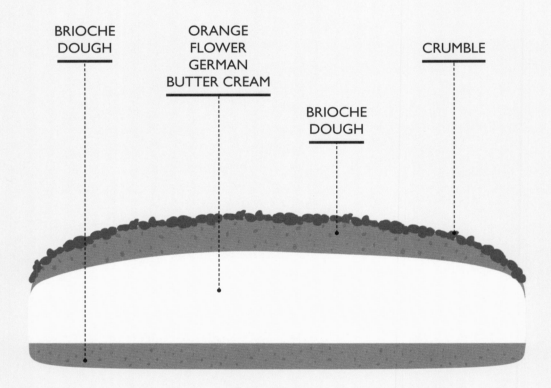

BRIOCHE
DOUGH

ORANGE
FLOWER
GERMAN
BUTTER CREAM

BRIOCHE
DOUGH

CRUMBLE

WHAT IS IT?

Brioche base filled with German butter cream flavored with orange flower water and topped with a brown sugar crumble.

TIME TO MAKE

Preparation: 1 hour
Proofing: 1 hour 30 minutes to 2 hours
Baking: 20 minutes
Refrigeration: 2 hours

EQUIPMENT

9½ in springform pan or tart ring
Pastry bag
No. 14 plain decorating tip
Serrated knife

VARIATION

Vanilla tropézienne tart: replace the orange flower water with the seeds scraped from 1 vanilla bean.

TRICKY ASPECT
Shaping the brioche dough

TECHNIQUES TO MASTER
Using a pastry bag (page 272)
Dusting with flour (page 284)
Knocking back dough (page 284)
Glazing (page 270)

TIP
Let the brioche dough rest well,
to make it easier to shape.

ORGANIZATION
Brioche dough – pastry cream –
brioche – shaping – proofing – baking –
finishing the butter cream – filling

TO SERVE 8

1 BRIOCHE DOUGH

⅜ oz fresh baker's yeast
7 oz (about 1.6 cups) all-purpose flour
³⁄₁₆ oz (2 tsp) salt
¾ oz (1⅔ tbsp) superfine sugar
4⅜ oz egg (about 2½ eggs)
3½ oz (7 tbsp) butter

2 GERMAN BUTTER CREAM

3½ oz egg yolk (about 5½ yolks)
4¼ oz (.6 cup) superfine sugar
1¾ oz (about .4 cup) cornstarch
1 lb 2 oz (2¼ cups) milk
4⅜ oz (8¾ tbsp) butter
4⅜ oz (8¾ tbsp) butter, softened
1 oz (2 tbsp) orange flower water

3 GLAZE

1 egg, beaten

4 CRUMBLE

1⅜ oz (2¾ tbsp) butter
1⅜ oz (about .4 cup) almond meal
1⅜ oz (3 tbsp) soft brown sugar
1⅜ oz (5 tbsp) all-purpose flour

5   Make the brioche dough (page 20). Make the German butter cream (page 56). At the end of cooking, add the orange flower water.

6   To make the crumble, rub the butter into the almond meal, brown sugar and flour with your fingers. Once the mixture resembles breadcrumbs, set aside in the refrigerator.

7   Take the dough out of the refrigerator, knock it back (page 284) and put it in a 9½ in springform pan greased with butter. Push it into shape using the palm of your hand. Leave to proof in a 90°F oven or near a source of heat for 1 hour 30 minutes to 2 hours. The brioche should double in volume.

8   Preheat the oven to 360°F. Glaze the brioche with the beaten egg, wait 10 minutes, then glaze again. Spread over the crumble, then bake for 15–25 minutes. Take out of the oven, remove the tin and leave to cool on a wire rack.

9   To finish the German butter cream (page 56), put it in a pastry bag fitted with a no. 14 plain decorating tip. Using a serrated knife, cut the brioche in two horizontally.

10   On the bottom half of the brioche, pipe a snail shell of cream, starting in the middle (page 273). Smooth it out using a frosting spatula. Replace the top of the brioche and refrigerate for 2 hours. Take out 30 minutes before eating.

PAINS AU CHOCOLAT &
CROISSANTS

Understand

WHAT ARE THEY?

Viennese pastries made from the same base yeast dough folded with butter (croissant dough), but differing in their shapes and fillings.

TIME TO MAKE

Preparation: 1 hour
Proofing: 1 hour 30 minutes to 2 hours
Baking: 12–25 minutes
Resting: 12 hours

EQUIPMENT

Electric mixer with dough hook attachment

TRICKY ASPECTS
Rolling the croissants: roll them carefully; if they are too tightly rolled the layered effect will disappear, and if they are not rolled enough, there is a risk they will unroll during baking.

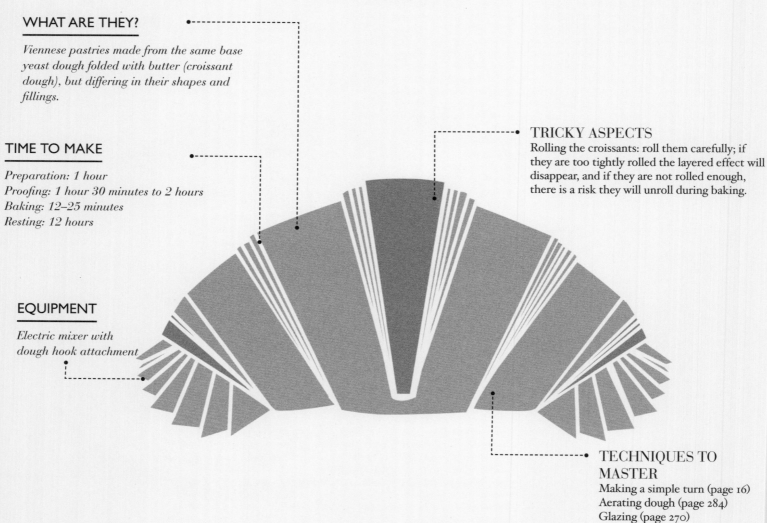

TECHNIQUES TO MASTER
Making a simple turn (page 16)
Aerating dough (page 284)
Glazing (page 270)

VARIATION

Almond croissants: make a syrup with 5¼ oz (⅔ cup) water and 1¾ oz (¼ cup) sugar. Make an almond cream (page 64). Dip the croissants generously in the syrup, cut them in two and fill them with the almond cream. Sprinkle with flaked almonds and bake for a few minutes at 390°F.

ORGANIZATION
Détrempe – turns – shaping – proofing – baking

TO MAKE 15 CROISSANTS OR 15 PAINS AU CHOCOLAT

1 DÉTREMPE

¼ oz fresh baker's yeast
2 oz (¼ cup) water
2 oz (¼ cup) milk
9 oz (about 2 cups) all-purpose flour
⅞ oz egg (about ½ egg)
³⁄₁₆ oz (2 tsp) salt
1 oz (2¼ tbsp) superfine sugar

2 LAYERING

4⅜ oz (8¾ tbsp) dry butter (page 276)

3 FILLING FOR PAINS AU CHOCOLAT

30 chocolate batons for Viennese pastries

4 GLAZE

1 egg, beaten

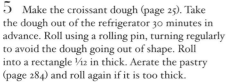

5 Make the croissant dough (page 25). Take the dough out of the refrigerator 30 minutes in advance. Roll using a rolling pin, turning regularly to avoid the dough going out of shape. Roll into a rectangle ½ in thick. Aerate the pastry (page 284) and roll again if it is too thick.

6 To make the croissants, using a knife, cut off bands 6 in wide and in each band cut isosceles triangles with a 4¾ in base. Make a little ⅜ in cut in the middle of the base. Slightly spread the two points on either side of the nick, then roll the croissant without rolling too tightly. At 1¼ in from the point, pull lightly on the tip and then finish rolling.

7 To make the pains au chocolat, using a knife, cut three bands 3¼ in wide and from each band cut rectangles with 4¾ in sides. Put a chocolate baton 1¼ in from the edge, then fold the dough over it. Put the second chocolate baton at the join and fold back over. Slide the join under the pain au chocolat so that the join is on the bottom and in the middle.

8 Line a cookie sheet with baking paper. Put the pastries on it 2 in apart. Leave to proof in a 90°F oven or at room temperature (wait 1 hour 30 minutes to 2 hours). The croissants or pains au chocolat should double in volume.

9 Preheat the oven to 375°F. Using a pastry brush, glaze with the beaten egg a first time. Glaze a second time after 10 minutes. Bake for 12–25 minutes depending on the type and size of the pastries.

FRENCH
APPLE TART

Understand

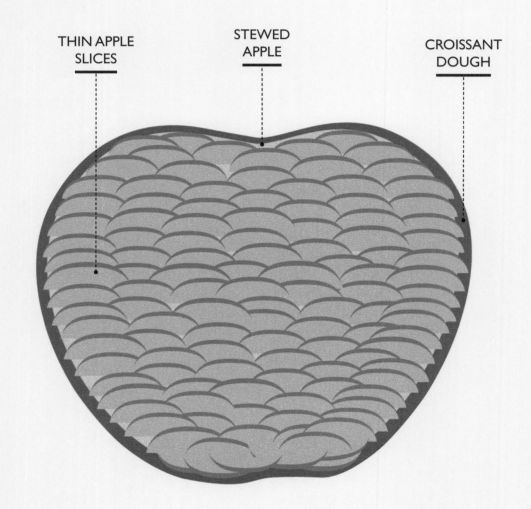

THIN APPLE
SLICES

STEWED
APPLE

CROISSANT
DOUGH

WHAT IS IT?

Tart on a brioche-style base filled with stewed apple and very fine apple slices.

TIME TO MAKE

Preparation: 30 minutes
Proofing: 1 hour
Baking: 30 minutes to 1 hour

EQUIPMENT

Electric mixer with dough hook attachment
12 in × 16 in cookie sheet
Pastry brush

VARIATION

Make a puff pastry base and cook the tart squashed between two cookie sheets. The apple will be soft and shiny.

TRICKY ASPECTS
Shaping the pastry
Arranging the apple slices

TECHNIQUE TO MASTER
Aerating dough (page 284)

ORGANIZATION
Croissant dough – stewed apple – assembly – baking

TO SERVE 15

1 CROISSANT DOUGH

¼ oz fresh baker's yeast
2 oz (¼ cup) water
2 oz (¼ cup) milk
9 oz (about 2 cups) all-purpose flour
⅞ oz egg (about ½ egg)
³⁄₁₆ oz (2 tsp) salt
1 oz (2¼ tbsp) superfine sugar
4⅜ oz (8¾ tbsp) dry butter (page 276)

2 TOPPING

4 lb 6 oz royal gala or pink lady apples
2¾ oz (5½ tbsp) butter
2¾ oz (about .4 cup) superfine sugar
10½ oz (about 1⅓ cups) thick crème fraîche

3 STEWED APPLES

1 lb 2 oz royal gala or pink lady apples
1¾ oz (3½ tbsp) water
3½ oz (½ cup) superfine sugar

1 To make the stewed apples, peel, core and dice the apples, then put them in a saucepan with the water and sugar. Cook over high heat until very dry, almost candied, taking care to stir regularly with a spatula. Blend using a hand-held blender, then set aside to cool.

2 Take the croissant dough (page 24) out of the refrigerator 30 minutes in advance. Roll with a rolling pin, turning regularly to avoid the dough going out of shape. Roll into a ⅛ in thick rectangle, then aerate the pastry (page 284) and roll again if it is still too thick. Place the pastry on a cookie sheet lined with baking paper and spread the stewed apple over it using a frosting spatula or pipe it on in a zigzag using a pastry bag.

3 Peel and core the apples for the topping, then cut in half and cut each apple half in thin slices. Arrange them over the stewed apple; cover it completely in rows of apple slices. Leave to proof for 1 hour at 90°F.

4 Preheat the oven to 360°F. Melt the butter in a saucepan, then, using a pastry brush, cover the tart with butter and sprinkle it with sugar. Bake for at least 30 minutes. Check whether it is cooked by lifting the tart using a frosting spatula to look at the bottom: it should be uniformly golden. At the end of cooking, transfer the tart to a wire rack to cool. Cut and serve with a quenelle of thick crème fraîche.

MILLE-FEUILLES

Understand

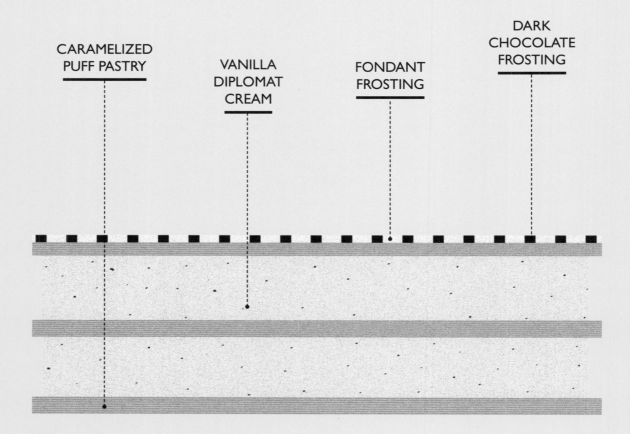

CARAMELIZED
PUFF PASTRY

VANILLA
DIPLOMAT
CREAM

FONDANT
FROSTING

DARK
CHOCOLATE
FROSTING

WHAT ARE THEY?

Stacks of caramelized puff pastry rectangles and layers of vanilla diplomat cream.

TIME TO MAKE

Preparation: 1 hour 30 minutes
Cooking: 20–45 minutes
Refrigeration: 3 hours 30 minutes
Freezing: 15 minutes

EQUIPMENT

Pastry bag
No. 12 decorating tip

VARIATION

Classic mille-feuilles: vanilla pastry cream

TIP
During cooking the pastry will shrink; make the rectangles of puff pastry slightly larger than the size you want. Refrigerate them for 15 minutes before assembling, to ensure a solid structure.

TRICKY ASPECTS
Caramelizing the puff pastry
Assembly
Frosting

TECHNIQUES TO MASTER
Hydrating gelatine (page 270)
Using a pastry bag (page 272)

ORGANIZATION
Puff pastry – diplomat cream – assembly – frosting – decoration

TO MAKE 8–10

1 PUFF PASTRY

détrempe
9 oz (about 2 cups) all-purpose flour
3½ oz (7 tbsp) water
⅜ oz (about 2 tsp) white vinegar
³⁄₁₆ oz (2 tsp) salt
1 oz (2 tbsp) butter, melted

layering
5¼ oz (10½ tbsp) butter
confectioners' sugar

2 DIPLOMAT CREAM

whipped cream
3½ oz (7 tbsp) whipping cream
   (30% fat)

pastry cream
⅛ oz leaf gelatine
1¾ oz egg yolk (about 3 yolks)
2 oz (4½ tbsp) superfine sugar
⅞ oz (3 tbsp) cornstarch
9 oz (1 cup 2 tbsp) milk
1 vanilla bean
⅞ oz (1¾ tbsp) butter

3 FROSTING

9 oz white fondant
1 oz (1½ tbsp) glucose syrup
1⅜ oz dark chocolate

1   Make the puff pastry (page 18). Roll to ¹⁄₁₂ in thickness and the size of a 12 in × 16 in rectangle of baking paper. Cover with baking paper and refrigerate for 30 minutes to let the pastry shrink. Preheat the oven to 360°F. Cut the pastry into three strips 4 in wide. Cut off the margins to give a neat edge. Don't try to detach the pastry strips from the baking paper or they will be stretched out of shape. Put them on a cookie sheet and cover again with baking paper then another cookie sheet, so the layering within the pastry develops uniformly.

2   Put in the oven and after 15 minutes check them every 5 minutes. The pastry and the sides should be evenly golden. Once the cooking is finished, adjust the oven temperature to 410°F. Dust the rectangles with confectioners' sugar and return to the oven for a few

minutes to caramelize them: check every 2 minutes– they burn very quickly. Once the caramelization is uniform, leave them to cool on a wire rack.

3   Make the diplomat cream (page 68), infusing the milk with the vanilla. Set aside in the refrigerator.

4   Use the diplomat cream to fill a pastry bag fitted with a no. 12 decorating tip. Pipe onto two of the puff pastry strips in lengthwise lines. Stack the two rectangles.

5   Heat the white fondant with the glucose syrup in a saucepan. Pour the fondant over the empty strip of puff pastry and smooth it out using a frosting spatula.

6   Melt the dark chocolate in a water bath. Put it in a pastry bag and make a small hole in the end. Pipe parallel lines on the fondant frosting, about ³⁄₈ in apart. Using a utility knife, score the frosting perpendicularly to the chocolate lines, alternating first from top to bottom, then from bottom to top, to create the motif. Put this pastry strip on top of the others and freeze for 15 minutes.

7   Take the mille-feuille out of the freezer. Using a serrated knife, cut the top piece of puff pastry every 1½ in. Using a chef's knife, finish cutting with a single clean cut. Refrigerate for 2 hours before eating.

Mille-feuilles

CHESTNUT & BLACKCURRANT
MILLE-FEUILLES

Understand

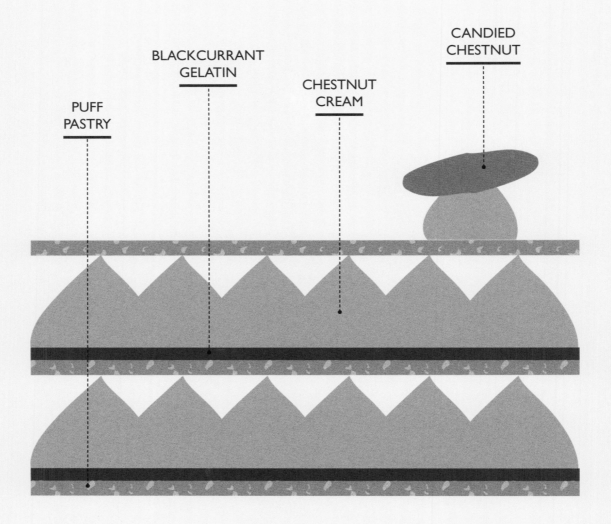

PUFF
PASTRY

BLACKCURRANT
GELATIN

CHESTNUT
CREAM

CANDIED
CHESTNUT

WHAT ARE THEY?

Stacks of caramelized puff pastry, with a chestnut cream and a blackcurrant gelatine.

TIME TO MAKE

Preparation: 1 hour 30 minutes
Cooking: 20–45 minutes
Freezing: 2 hours
Refrigeration: 30 minutes

EQUIPMENT

4¾ in × 9½ in rectangular dessert frame or cake tin
Pastry bag
No. 12 plain decorating tip

TRICKY ASPECTS
Caramelizing the puff pastry
Assembly

TECHNIQUES TO MASTER
Hydrating gelatine (page 270)
Using a pastry bag (page 272)

ORGANIZATION
Puff pastry – blackcurrant gelatine –
chestnut cream – assembly – decoration

1

2

3

4

TO MAKE 6 MILLE-FEUILLES

1 PUFF PASTRY

détrempe
9 oz (about 2 cups) all-purpose flour
4 oz (½ cup) water
⅜ oz (about 2 tsp) white vinegar
³⁄₁₆ oz (2 tsp) salt
1 oz (2 tbsp) butter, melted

layering
5¼ oz (10½ tbsp) butter
  + confectioners' sugar

2 CHESTNUT CREAM

1 lb 2 oz (2¼ cups) chestnut paste
7 oz (14 tbsp) butter, softened

3 BLACKCURRANT GELATINE

³⁄₁₆ oz leaf gelatine
9 oz blackcurrant purée
1 oz (2¼ tbsp) superfine sugar

4 DECORATION

3 candied chestnuts
  (marrons glacés)

<u>1</u>

<u>2</u>

<u>3</u>

<u>4</u>

<u>5</u>

<u>7</u>

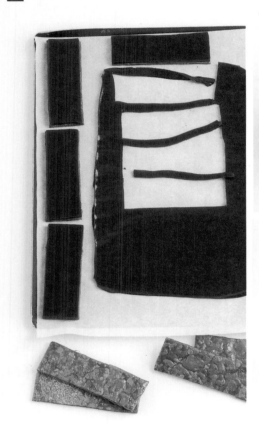

<u>6</u>

1   Make the puff pastry (page 18). To make the blackcurrant gelatine, hydrate the gelatine (page 270). Bring to the boil 3½ oz of the blackcurrant purée with the sugar. Add the drained gelatine. Whisk and incorporate the rest of the blackcurrant purée. Line a 4¾ in × 9½ in dessert frame or cake tin with baking paper or plastic wrap and pour in the gelatine. Freeze for at least 2 hours.

2   Preheat the oven to 360°F. Roll the puff pastry to ¹⁄₁₂ in thickness and the size of a 12 in × 16 in rectangle of baking paper. Cover with baking paper and refrigerate for 30 minutes to let the pastry shrink. Cut the pastry into 1½ in strips, then into eighteen rectangles of 5 in × 1½ in. Don't try to detach the pastry bands from the baking paper or they will be stretched out of shape. Put them on a cookie sheet and cover again with baking paper then another cookie sheet, so the layering

within the pastry develops uniformly. Bake. After 15 minutes, check them every 5 minutes. The pastry and the sides should be evenly golden.

3   Once the cooking is finished, adjust the oven temperature to 410°F. Dust the rectangles with confectioners' sugar and return to the oven for a few minutes to caramelize them: check every 2 minutes – they burn very quickly. Leave them to cool on a wire rack.

4   Take the blackcurrant gelatine out of the freezer. Remove from the frame or tin. Cut into 12 strips of 1¼ in × 4¾ in. Put these on the caramelized side of twelve of the puff pastry strips.

5   To make the chestnut cream, put the chestnut paste in the bowl of an electric mixer and mix using the paddle attachment. Add the softened butter

(page 276) and whip the mixture at high speed. Put the chestnut cream in a pastry bag fitted with a no. 12 plain decorating tip.

6   Pipe domes of chestnut cream (page 275) on the puff pastry rectangles that are covered with gelatine.

7   Stack two pastry strips with filling on top of each other, then finish with an empty pastry strip. Pipe a rosette of chestnut cream on each stack and top with half a candied chestnut.

EPIPHANY
CAKE

Understand

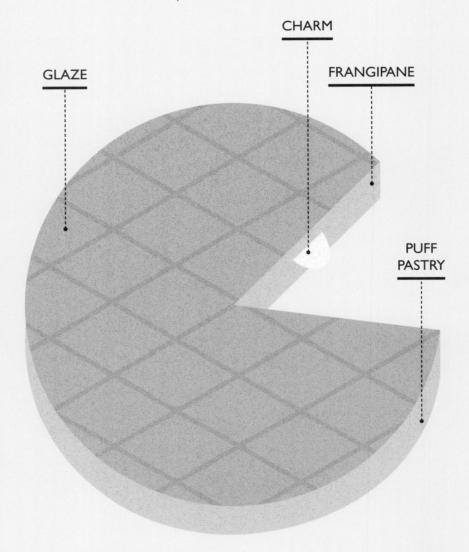

GLAZE

CHARM

FRANGIPANE

PUFF
PASTRY

WHAT IS IT?

Two puff pastry discs filled with a light frangipane cream.

TIME TO MAKE

*Preparation: 1 hour
Cooking: 25–45 minutes
Refrigeration: 1 hour*

EQUIPMENT

*Pastry bag
No. 8 plain decorating tip
Charm*

WHY DOES THE CAKE NEED TO BE REFRIGERATED BEFORE BAKING?

The time in the cold allows the butter in the puff pastry to chill well, which encourages good development of layers during cooking.

VARIATIONS

*Pithiviers: Epiphany cake filled with almond cream. Double the quantity of almond cream.
Rum frangipane: add 1 oz (2 tbsp) rum.*

TRICKY ASPECTS

Creating the pastry layers
Assembly

TECHNIQUES TO MASTER

Pinching the edges of pastry (page 285)
Using a pastry bag (page 272)
Glazing (page 270)

ORGANIZATION

Puff pastry – pastry cream – almond
cream – assembly – decoration

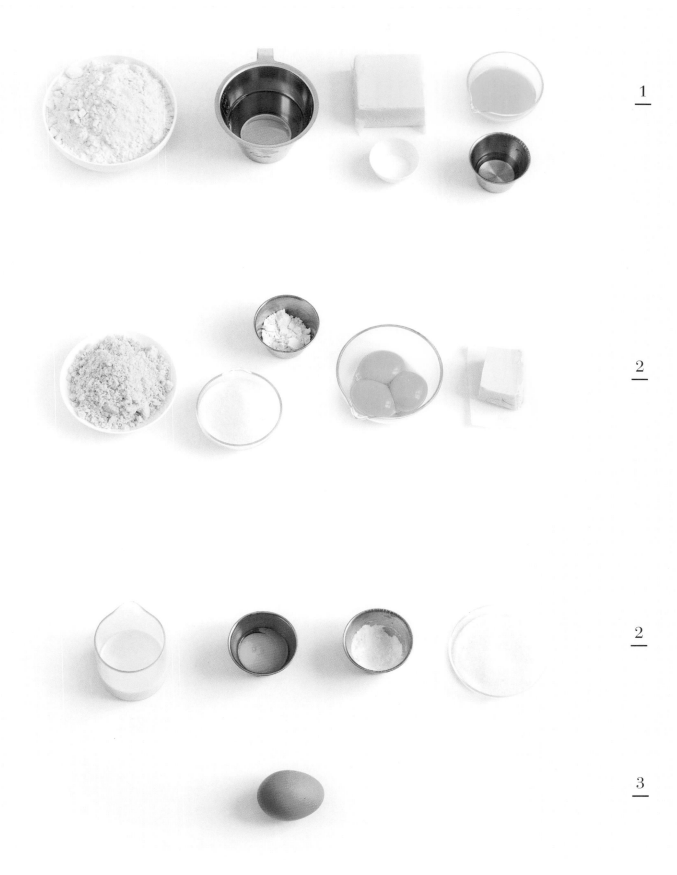

TO SERVE 8

1 PUFF PASTRY

détrempe
9 oz (about 2 cups) all-purpose
    flour
4⅛ oz (about ½ cup) water
1¾ tsp white vinegar

³⁄₁₆ oz (2 tsp) salt
1 oz (2 tbsp) butter, melted
layering
5¼ oz (10½ tbsp) butter

2 FRANGIPANE

almond cream
1¾ oz (3½ tbsp) butter

1¾ oz (¼ cup) superfine sugar
1¾ oz (about ½ cup) almond meal
1¾ oz egg (1 egg)
⅜ oz (4 tsp) all-purpose flour

pastry cream
⅜ oz egg yolk (about ½ yolk)
½ oz (3½ tsp) superfine sugar
³⁄₁₆ oz (2 tsp) cornstarch
1¾ oz (3½ tbsp) milk

3 GLAZE

1 egg, beaten

4 SYRUP

1¾ oz (3½ tbsp) water
1¾ oz (¼ cup) superfine sugar

1 Make the puff pastry (page 18), roll into a rectangle ⅛ in thick, then leave to rest in the refrigerator for 30 minutes. Take out the pastry and cut into two discs of 12 in diameter, using a dessert ring or a large plate.

2 Put one disc on a cookie sheet lined with baking paper. Using a 10¼ in tart ring or a plate slightly smaller than the first, mark the pastry by pushing gently. Glaze outside this mark with beaten egg using a pastry brush.

3 Make the pastry cream (page 53) and the almond cream (page 64), then fold the two creams together, using a spatula to obtain a frangipane cream.

4 Fill a pastry bag fitted with a no. 8 plain decorating tip. Pipe the frangipane on the pastry base in a snail shell from the outside in. Don't pipe on the glazed margin. Push the charm into the cream, on one side of the cake.

5 Cover with the second pastry disc, avoiding air bubbles as much as possible, then press lightly around the edges. Put a sheet of baking paper and a cookie sheet on top of the cake, then turn it over. This will allow the pastry to develop evenly.

6 Using a utility knife and your fingers, pinch the edges of the two pastry discs together to make a neat decorative edge (page 285). Glaze with a pastry brush. Set aside in the refrigerator for 30 minutes.

7 Preheat the oven to 360°F. Take the cake out and glaze it a second time. Using the blunt side of the point of a knife, starting at the middle and working toward the outside, score the pastry in arcs. Be careful not to pierce the pastry. Bake for 25–45 minutes. Using a spatula, lift the cake – it should be uniformly golden.

8 While the cake is baking, put water and superfine sugar in a saucepan, bring to the boil, then remove from the heat. When the cake comes out of the oven, glaze the top straight away with the syrup using a pastry brush.

VANILLA
MACARONS

Understand

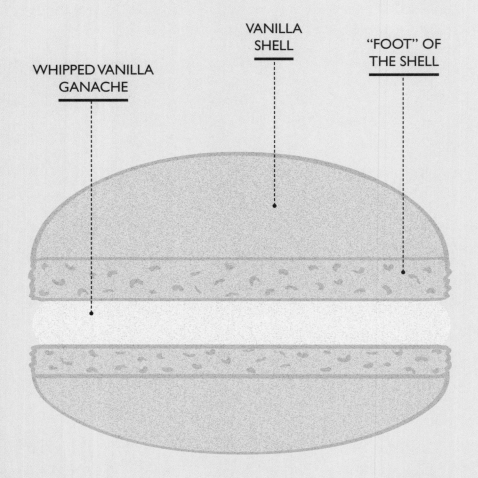

WHIPPED VANILLA
GANACHE

VANILLA
SHELL

"FOOT" OF
THE SHELL

WHAT ARE THEY?

Vanilla macaron shells filled with a whipped white chocolate and vanilla ganache.

TIME TO MAKE

Preparation: 45 minutes
Cooking: 12 minutes
Refrigeration: 24 hours

EQUIPMENT

2 pastry bags
No. 8 and no. 12 plain decorating tips
Candy thermometer

WHY MAKE THE SHELLS WITH ITALIAN MERINGUE?

Italian meringue, which has been cooked in the syrup, is more stable than other meringues and destabilizes the final mixture less.

HOW DOES THE "FOOT" FORM?

During cooking, the expansion of the gases in the macaron mixture brings about the formation of a foot.

TRICKY ASPECTS

"Macaronage" – mixing the dry ingredients into the meringue
Cooking the shells
Whipping the ganache

TECHNIQUES TO MASTER

Using a pastry bag (page 272)
Straining (page 270)
Recognizing ribbon stage (page 279)

TIP

Use fine almond meal to avoid having to sift it.

ORGANIZATION

Ganache, shells – whipped ganache – assembly

2

1

3

TO MAKE 40 MACARONS

1 SHELLS

9 oz (about 2⅔ cups)
   fine almond meal
9 oz (about 2.1 cups)
   confectioners' sugar
1 vanilla bean
3½ oz egg white (about 3 whites)

2 ITALIAN MERINGUE

2¾ oz (⅓ cup) water
9 oz (about 1¼ cup) superfine sugar
3½ oz egg white (about 3 whites)

3 WHIPPED VANILLA
   GANACHE

7 oz (about .9 cup) whipping
   cream (30% fat)
2 vanilla beans
11½ oz white chocolate

1

2

3

4

5

6

7

8

9

1 To make the ganache, infuse the cream with the split vanilla beans and scraped seeds in a saucepan. Bring to the boil. Strain into the white chocolate. Mix and transfer to a container to cool quickly. Cover with plastic wrap with the plastic touching the surface, then leave to set in the refrigerator for at least 3 hours, ideally overnight.

2 To make the shells, preheat the oven to 300°F. Make the Italian meringue (page 45), whisking until it cools.

3 In a stainless-steel bowl, mix the almond meal, confectioners' sugar and the seeds scraped from the vanilla bean. Incorporate the raw egg white using a dough scraper.

4 Fold in one-third of the Italian meringue using the dough scraper.

5 Add the rest of the meringue and continue to mix, crushing the mixture with the scraper. This is called "macaronage" (page 283).

6 Take a large lump of the mixture and check if it is at ribbon stage: it should fall from the scraper in a continuous ribbon. If that is not the case, mix it again.

7 Line a cookie sheet with baking paper. You could possibly use a template (page 283). Hold the paper in place by weighing it down (with a knife, for example). Using a pastry bag fitted with a no. 8 decorating tip, pipe shells of 1¼ in diameter, in staggered rows (page 283). Bake for about 12 minutes (page 283). Remove from the oven and slide the paper off the cookie sheet so the macarons don't dry out. Put pairs of shells side by side.

8 Lightly whisk the ganache until it thickens.

9 Fill a pastry bag (no. 12 plain tip) with vanilla ganache. Pipe the ganache on the bottom shell (foot side up), stopping ³⁄₁₆ in from the edge. Put the hat on and press lightly so the ganache comes just to the edge. Ideally, let the macarons rest in the refrigerator for 24 hours.

220

Vanilla macarons

CHOCOLATE
MACARONS

Understand

CREAMY CHOCOLATE
GANACHE

SHELL WITH
COCOA

"FOOT" OF THE
SHELL

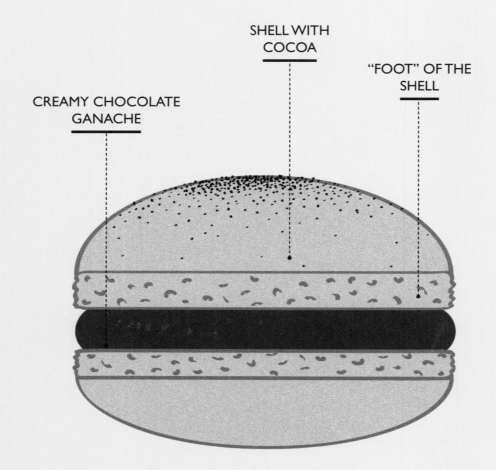

WHAT ARE THEY?

Chocolate macaron shells filled with creamy ganache.

TIME TO MAKE

Preparation: 45 minutes
Cooking: 12 minutes
Refrigeration: 24 hours

EQUIPMENT

Pastry bag
No. 8 plain decorating tip
No. 12 plain decorating tip

VARIATION

Spicy chocolate macarons: infuse the milk for the ganache for 30 minutes with ½ cinnamon stick, 1 star anise and/or 10 cardamom seeds.

TRICKY ASPECT
Cooking the shells

TECHNIQUES TO MASTER
Using a pastry bag (page 272)
Straining (page 270)
Recognizing ribbon stage (page 279)

TIPS
Use fine almond meal to avoid having to sift it.

ORGANIZATION
Ganache – shells – assembly

222

TO MAKE 40 MACARONS

1 ITALIAN MERINGUE

2¾ oz (⅓ cup) water
9 oz (about 1¼ cups) superfine sugar
3½ oz egg white (about 3 whites)

2 SHELLS

9 oz (about 2⅔ cups) fine
   almond meal
9 oz (about 2.1 cups)
   confectioners' sugar
1 oz (⅓ cup) Dutch (unsweetened)
   cocoa powder
3½ oz egg white (about 3 whites)

3 CREAMY CHOCOLATE
GANACHE

3½ oz egg yolk (about 5½ yolks)
3½ oz (½ cup) superfine sugar
1 lb 2 oz (2¼ cups) milk
14 oz dark chocolate

4 DECORATION

1 oz (⅓ cup) Dutch (unsweetened)
   cocoa powder

1 Make the creamy chocolate ganache (page 72). Set aside in the refrigerator.

2 To make the shells, preheat the oven to 300°F. Make the Italian meringue (page 44), whisking until it cools.

3 In a stainless-steel bowl, mix the almond meal, confectioners' sugar and cocoa powder. Incorporate the uncooked egg white using a dough scraper.

4 Incorporate one-third of the Italian meringue using the dough scraper.

5 Add the rest of the meringue and continue to mix, crushing the mixture with the scraper ("macaronage," page 283). Take a large lump of the mixture and check if it is at ribbon stage: it should fall from the scraper in a continuous ribbon. If that is not the case, mix it again.

6 Line a cookie sheet with baking paper. You could possibly use a template (page 283). Hold the paper in place by weighing it down (with a knife, for example). Using a pastry bag fitted with a no. 8 decorating tip, pipe shells of 1¼ in diameter. Pipe them in staggered rows so that the heat circulates correctly, dust them with cocoa powder and bake for about 12 minutes (page 283). The shell shouldn't move when you touch it with a finger. (page 283).

7 Remove from the oven and slide the paper off the cookie sheet so the macarons don't dry out. Put pairs of shells side by side.

8 Take the ganache out of the refrigerator and smooth it out using a spatula. Use it to fill a pastry bag fitted with a no. 12 decorating tip.

9 Pipe the ganache onto the bottom shell (foot side up), stopping ³⁄₁₆ in from the edge, then put the hat on and press lightly so the ganache comes just to the edge. Ideally, let them rest in the refrigerator for 24 hours.

Chocolate macarons

RED PEARL
MACARONS

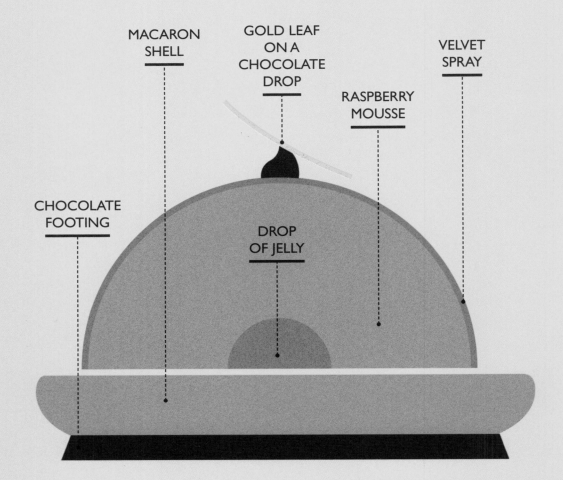

MACARON SHELL

GOLD LEAF ON A CHOCOLATE DROP

VELVET SPRAY

RASPBERRY MOUSSE

CHOCOLATE FOOTING

DROP OF JELLY

WHAT IS IT?

Macaron shell topped with a dome of raspberry mousse.

TIME TO MAKE

Preparation: 1 hour
Cooking: 12 minutes
Freezing: at least 4 hours

EQUIPMENT

2 half-sphere silicone molds (with 20 holes of ¾ in diameter)
Pastry bag
No. 6 plain decorating tip

VARIATION

Tropical macarons: replace the raspberry purée with mango purée.

TRICKY ASPECTS

"Macaronage" – mixing the dry ingredients into the meringue
Cooking the shells
Applying the velvet spray

TECHNIQUES TO MASTER

Using a pastry bag (page 272)
Preparing a water bath (page 270)
Incorporating with a whisk, then a silicone spatula (page 270)

ORGANIZATION

Raspberry domes – shells – assembly – velvet

TO MAKE 40 MACARONS

1 SHELLS

4⅜ oz (about 1⅓ cups)
   fine almond meal
4⅜ oz (about 1 cup)
   confectioners' sugar

1/32 oz red powdered food coloring
1¾ oz egg white (about 2 whites)

2 ITALIAN MERINGUE

1⅜ oz (2¾ tbsp) water
4⅜ oz (about .6 cup) superfine
   sugar
1¾ oz egg white (about 2 whites)

3 RASPBERRY MOUSSE

2¼ oz (4½ tbsp) whipping cream
   (30% fat)
½ oz (3½ tsp) superfine sugar
1/16 oz leaf gelatine
2¼ oz raspberry purée
1¾ oz (2⅓ tbsp) raspberry jelly

4 DECORATION

1¾ oz dark chocolate
red velvet spray in a can
gold leaf

1 To make the raspberry mousse, whip the cream with the sugar as for chantilly cream (page 63), then set aside in the refrigerator. Hydrate the gelatine (page 270).

2 Heat 1¾ oz of the raspberry purée in a saucepan with the sugar. As soon as it boils, remove from the heat, drain the gelatine and whisk it into the purée. Pour into a stainless-steel bowl and add the remaining raspberry purée. Let it cool to room temperature.

3 Whisk in one-third of the whipped cream. Fold in the rest of the whipped cream using a silicone spatula (page 270).

4 Fill a pastry bag with the mousse, cut off the end and pipe into the half-sphere mold. Freeze for at least 3 hours, ideally overnight.

5 Make the macaron shells in the same way as the vanilla shells (page 220), replacing the vanilla with the red coloring.

6 Melt the chocolate in a water bath. Dip the rounded side of each shell in the chocolate. Place on a sheet of baking paper, chocolate side down and let it harden to make a stable footing.

7 Fill a pastry bag (no. 6 plain tip) with the jelly. Pipe a drop of jelly on each shell. Unmold the raspberry mousse domes and place them on top of the jelly, then freeze the lot for 1 hour.

8 Put the red velvet spray can in a bowl of boiling water for about 15 minutes to melt the cocoa butter inside and produce the thermal shock that creates the velvet effect. Take the macarons out of the freezer and spray the cocoa butter over them. Put the remaining melted dark chocolate in a pastry bag, cut off the tip and pipe a little chocolate drop on each dome. End with a piece of gold leaf.

VANILLA & RASPBERRY
MACARON CAKE

Understand

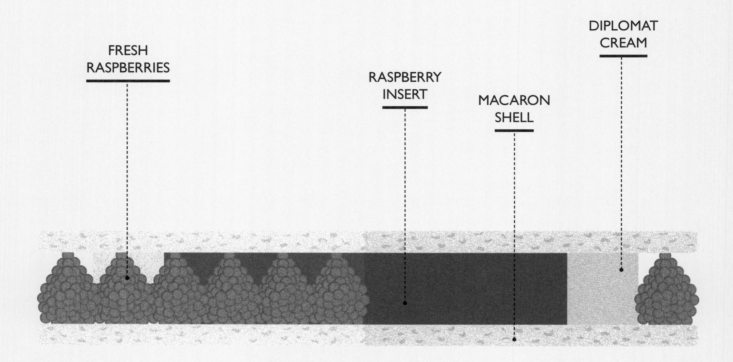

FRESH
RASPBERRIES

RASPBERRY
INSERT

MACARON
SHELL

DIPLOMAT
CREAM

WHAT IS IT?

Large macaron filled with diplomat cream with a raspberry insert and garnished with fresh raspberries.

TIME TO MAKE

Preparation: 1 hour 30 minutes
Cooking: 15 minutes
Freezing: 5 hours
Refrigeration: 2 hours

EQUIPMENT

4 in dessert ring
8¾ in dessert ring
3 pastry bags
No. 12 plain decorating tip
No. 10 plain decorating tip
No. 8 plain decorating tip
Hand-held blender
Candy thermometer

TRICKY ASPECTS
Cooking the large macaron
Assembly

TECHNIQUES TO MASTER
Hydrating gelatine (page 270)
Blanching egg yolks (page 279)
Using a pastry bag (page 272)

ORGANIZATION
Raspberry insert – diplomat
cream – shells – assembly

TO SERVE 8–10

1 SHELLS

9 oz (about 2⅔ cups)
  fine almond meal
9 oz (about 2.1 cups)
  confectioners' sugar
1 vanilla bean
3½ oz egg white (about 3 whites)

2 ITALIAN MERINGUE

2¾ oz (⅓ cup) water
9 oz (about 1¼ cups) superfine
  sugar
3½ oz egg white (about 3 whites)

3 DIPLOMAT CREAM

⅛ oz leaf gelatine
1¾ oz egg yolk (about 3 yolks)
2 oz (4½ tbsp) superfine sugar
⅞ oz (3 tbsp) cornstarch
9 oz (1 cup 2 tbsp) milk
1 vanilla bean
⅞ oz (1¾ tbsp) butter
3½ oz (7 tbsp) whipping cream
  30% fat)

4 RASPBERRY INSERT

¼ oz leaf gelatine
2⅝ oz (about 4 yolks) egg yolk
3½ oz egg (2 eggs)
2⅝ oz (6 tbsp) superfine sugar
9 oz raspberry purée
3½ oz (7 tbsp) butter

5 DECORATION

9 oz raspberries

1 Make the diplomat cream (page 68). Set aside 7 oz for finishing and use the rest to fill a pastry bag fitted with a no. 12 plain decorating tip. Line a cookie sheet with baking paper, put an 8¾ in dessert ring on top and right in the middle a 4 in dessert ring. Pipe the cream between the two rings and smooth over the surface. Freeze for at least 1 hour.

2 To make the raspberry insert, hydrate the gelatine (page 270). Blanch the egg yolk and whole egg with the sugar (page 279). Bring the raspberry purée to the boil. Pour half into the egg mixture and whisk. Once the mixture is smooth, pour it all back into the saucepan. Return to medium heat and cook, stirring constantly, until the mixture coats the back of a spatula (no more than 185°F).

3 Drain the gelatine, then add to the raspberry cream. Add the butter and blend for 2–3 minutes using a hand-held blender. Let it cool to 100°F. Remove the 4 in ring from the circle of diplomat cream and pour the raspberry mixture into the hole in the middle. Freeze for 4 hours.

4 To make the shells, prepare the macaron mixture as for the vanilla macarons (page 220). Using a pastry bag fitted with a no. 8 plain decorating tip, form two shells of 10 in diameter by piping in a snail shell (page 273) on a cookie sheet lined with baking paper. Bake for about 12 minutes. The shell shouldn't move when you touch it with a finger.

5 Remove from the oven and slide the paper off the cookie sheet so the shells don't dry out. Take the insert and cream ring out of the freezer, unmold and place on the bottom macaron (rounded side down).

6 Fill a pastry bag (no. 10 tip) with the reserved diplomat cream. Pipe a ring of cream around the insert and put the fresh raspberries in it. Close with the second macaron shell. Refrigerate for 2 hours to thaw.

Vanilla & raspberry macaron cake

MONT BLANC

Understand

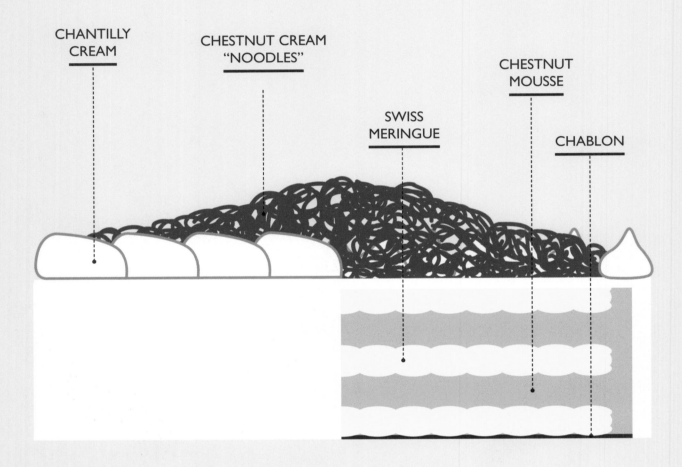

CHANTILLY
CREAM

CHESTNUT CREAM
"NOODLES"

CHESTNUT
MOUSSE

SWISS
MERINGUE

CHABLON

WHAT IS IT?

A dessert composed of three discs of Swiss meringue and chestnut mousse, decorated with chantilly cream and chestnut cream.

TIME TO MAKE

Preparation: 2 hours
Cooking: 2 hours
Refrigeration: 2 hours

EQUIPMENT

8¾ in dessert ring
4 pastry bags
No. 10 plain decorating tip
No. 8 plain decorating tip
Mont-Blanc/grass decorating tip
St Honoré decorating tip
Acetate cake band
Frosting spatula

WHY USE SWISS MERINGUE?

More robust than French or Italian meringue, it is better adapted to assembled desserts.

TRICKY ASPECTS

Drying the meringues
Decoration

TECHNIQUES TO MASTER

Using a pastry bag (page 272)
Hydrating gelatine (page 270)
Creating a chablon layer (page 280)
Preparing a water bath (page 270)
Incorporating with a whisk, then
a silicone spatula (page 270)

TIP

For greater crunch, you can add a chablon
layer (page 280) to each meringue disc with
1 oz melted chocolate.

ORGANIZATION

Meringue – chestnut mousse – chantilly cream
– chestnut cream – assembly – decoration

TO SERVE 8

1 SWISS MERINGUE

3½ oz egg white (about 3 whites)
3½ oz (½ cup) superfine sugar
3½ oz (about .8 cup)
    confectioners' sugar

2 CHESTNUT MOUSSE

¼ oz leaf gelatine
2 oz (¼ cup) + 13¼ oz (1⅔ cups)
    whipping cream (30% fat)
13¼ oz (1⅔ cups) chestnut cream

3 CHANTILLY CREAM

10½ oz (1⅓ cups) whipping
    cream (30% fat)
2 oz (7½ tbsp) confectioners' sugar
1 vanilla bean

4 CHESTNUT CREAM

9 oz (about 1.1 cups) chestnut paste
3½ oz (7 tbsp) butter, softened

5 CHABLON

1 oz chocolate

6 DECORATION

½ oz (2⅔ tbsp) Dutch
    (unsweetened) cocoa powder

1   Make the Swiss meringue (page 47), then leave to cool. Preheat the oven to 195°F. Use the meringue to fill a pastry bag (no. 8 tip) and pipe three discs of 8¾ in diameter on baking paper: pipe in a snail shell from the middle to the outside (page 272). Bake for at least 2 hours: the discs should be dry.

2   To make the chestnut mousse, hydrate the gelatine (page 270). Put the 2 oz (¼ cup) whipping cream in a saucepan to heat up. Once it boils, remove from the heat and whisk in the drained gelatine. Put the chestnut cream in a stainless-steel bowl, add the warm cream and whisk vigorously.

3   Whip the 13¼ oz (1⅔ cups) cream as for chantilly cream (page 63). Whisk one-third of the whipped cream into the chestnut mixture. Fold in the rest of the cream using a silicone spatula (page 270).

4   Line an 8¾ in dessert ring with an acetate cake band and place it on a cookie sheet lined with baking paper. Melt the chocolate in a water bath and add a chablon (page 280) to one of the meringue discs. Place it in the ring, chocolate side down. Fill a pastry bag fitted with a no. 10 plain decorating tip with chestnut mousse and pipe half of it on the meringue.

5   Put a second meringue disc on top and pipe the rest of the chestnut mousse on it. Add the remaining meringue disc on top and press lightly without breaking the meringue. Refrigerate for 2 hours.

6   Make the chantilly cream (page 63), adding the seeds scraped from the vanilla bean. Set aside in the refrigerator. To make the chestnut cream, beat the chestnut paste in an electric mixer using the paddle attachment (or with the plastic blade of a food processor). Add the softened butter and whip together at high speed. Use this cream to fill a pastry bag fitted with a Mont-Blanc/grass decorating tip. Take the dessert out of the refrigerator and remove the ring and the acetate band. Using a frosting spatula, cover the dessert with three-quarters of the chantilly cream (page 274). Cover the top with chestnut cream "noodles." Dust with cocoa powder. Using a pastry bag fitted with a St Honoré decorating tip, pipe quenelles of chantilly cream around the outside of the chestnut cream.

VANILLA
VACHERIN

Understand

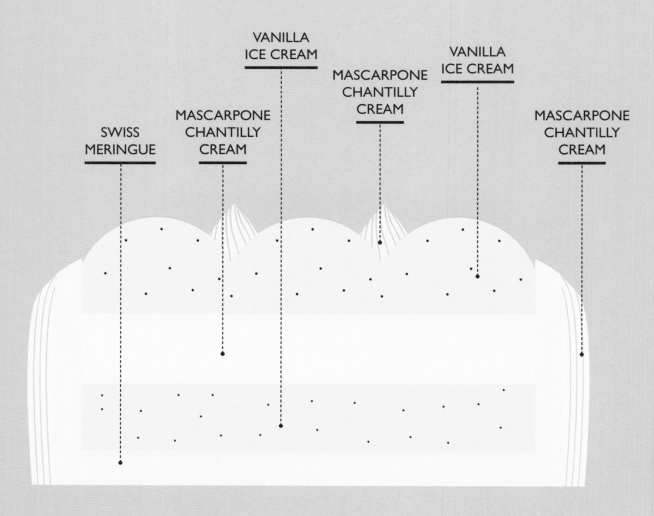

VANILLA
ICE CREAM

MASCARPONE
CHANTILLY
CREAM

VANILLA
ICE CREAM

SWISS
MERINGUE

MASCARPONE
CHANTILLY
CREAM

MASCARPONE
CHANTILLY
CREAM

WHAT IS IT?

Meringue filled with vanilla ice cream and mascarpone chantilly cream.

TIME TO MAKE

Preparation: 1 hour
Cooking: 3–5 hours
Freezing: 3 hours

EQUIPMENT

3 pastry bags
No. 8 plain decorating tip
No. 10 plain decorating tip
Fluted decorating tip
1¾ in ice cream scoop
Electric mixer with paddle and whisk
attachments, or hand mixer

TRICKY ASPECT
Working quickly with the ice cream

TECHNIQUE TO MASTER
Using a pastry bag (page 272)

TIP
To avoid the ice cream melting, prepare the ice cream balls in advance and set them aside in the freezer until you are assembling the dessert.

ORGANIZATION
Meringue – ice cream balls – mascarpone chantilly cream – assembly

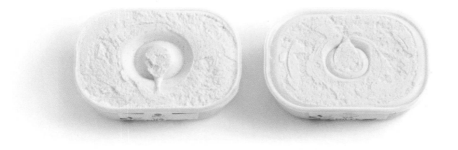

TO SERVE 8

1 SWISS MERINGUE

3½ oz egg white (about 3 whites)
3½ oz (½ cup) superfine sugar
3½ oz (about .8 cup)
   confectioners' sugar

2 MASCARPONE
CHANTILLY CREAM

9 oz mascarpone
2 oz (about ½ cup)
   confectioners' sugar
1 vanilla bean
9 oz (1 cup 2 tbsp) whipping
   cream (30% fat)

3 ICE CREAM

51 fl oz (about 3 pints)
vanilla ice cream

1   Make the Swiss meringue (page 47). Preheat the oven to 195°F. Line a cookie sheet with baking paper. Line a dessert ring of 7 in diameter and at least 2 in height with baking paper and place it on top of the cookie sheet. Using a pastry bag fitted with a no. 8 decorating tip, pipe a snail shell disc of meringue in the ring (page 272). At the edge of the ring, pipe the meringue on top of itself to make a 2 in high border.

2   Bake for at least 3 hours: the meringue should be very dry. Let it cool on a wire rack.

3   Put 17 fl oz (1 pint) ice cream in the bowl of an electric mixer and smooth it out using the paddle attachment, or do it by hand by stirring rapidly with a spatula. Immediately fill the meringue with the ice cream using a pastry bag or a spatula, and smooth the top using a silicone spatula. Freeze.

4   To make the mascarpone chantilly cream, gently beat the mascarpone, confectioners' sugar, the seeds scraped from the vanilla bean and 1¾ oz (3½ tbsp) of the cream in an electric mixer fitted with the whisk attachment. Add the rest of the cream in a thin stream, continuing to whisk. Once the mixture is smooth, increase the speed of the mixer as for chantilly cream (page 63). Take out the vacherin (filled meringue). Using a pastry bag fitted with a no. 10 decorating tip, add three-quarters of the chantilly cream on top of the vanilla ice cream, smooth the top with a silicone spatula and freeze for 1 hour.

5   Using a 1¾ in diameter ice cream scoop, make seven ice cream balls, dipping the scoop in hot water between the balls. Put the balls on top of the mascarpone chantilly cream, then return to the freezer for at least 2 hours. When ready to serve, decorate the surface of the vacherin with the remaining chantilly cream, usinga pastry bag fitted with a fluted decorating tip, then the sides using a pastry bag fitted with a basket-weave decorating tip. Keep in the freezer.

WALNUT
SUCCÈS

Understand

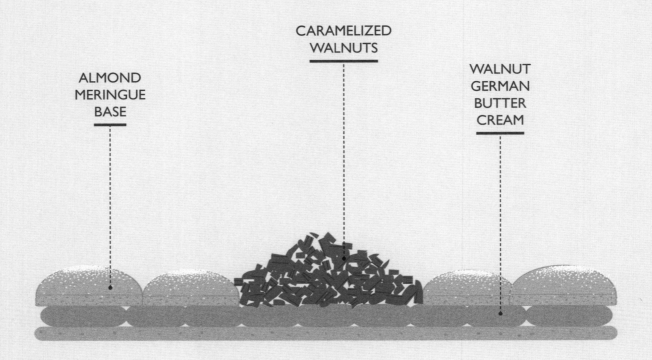

ALMOND
MERINGUE
BASE

CARAMELIZED
WALNUTS

WALNUT
GERMAN
BUTTER
CREAM

WHAT IS IT?

An almond meringue base in a circlet, filled with walnut German butter cream and crunchy caramelized walnuts.

TIME TO MAKE

Preparation: 1 hour
Cooking: 20–50 minutes
Refrigeration: 2 hours

EQUIPMENT

Pastry bag
No. 10 plain decorating tip
No. 12 plain decorating tip
Candy thermometer
Food processor with blade attachment

VARIATION

Replace the walnuts with the same quantity of hazelnuts or almonds.

TRICKY ASPECTS

Piping in a circlet
Caramelizing the nuts

TECHNIQUES TO MASTER

Using a pastry bag (page 272)
Roasting nuts (page 281)

ORGANIZATION

Pastry cream – meringue base – German butter cream – caramelized walnuts – assembly

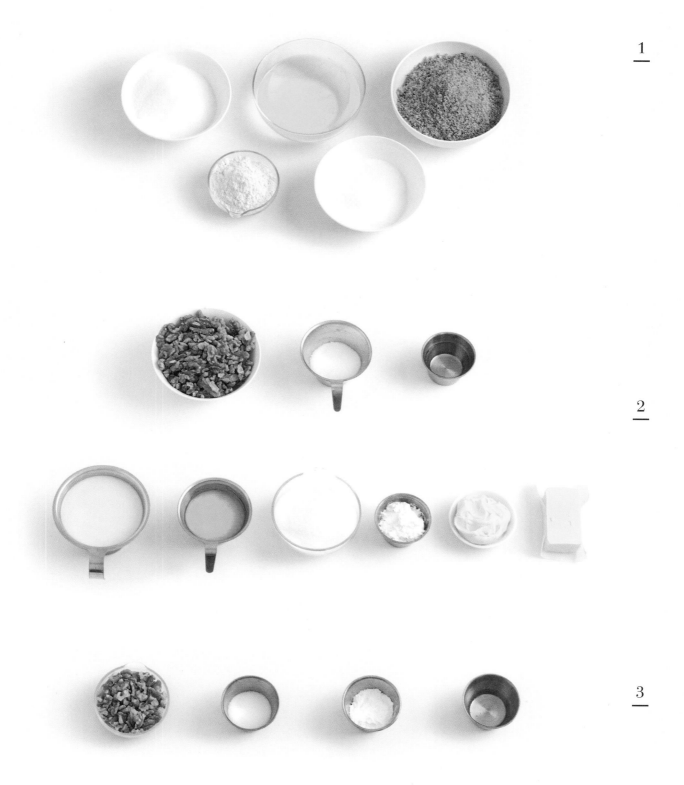

TO SERVE 8

1 ALMOND MERINGUE BASE

6¾ oz egg white (about 6 whites)
2½ oz (about ⅓ cup) superfine sugar
  (for meringue)
1⅜ oz (about ⅓ cup) all-purpose flour
5½ oz (about 1⅔ cup) walnut meal
4½ oz (about ⅔ cup) superfine
  sugar (for nut base)

2 WALNUT GERMAN
BUTTER CREAM

walnut praline
5¼ oz (about 1¼ cup)
  walnuts, roughly chopped
1 oz (2 tbsp) water
4 oz (about .6 cup) superfine
  sugar

pastry cream
1¾ oz egg yolk (about 3 yolks)
2 oz (4½ tbsp) superfine sugar
⅞ oz (3 tbsp) cornstarch
9 oz (1 cup 2 tbsp) milk
2¼ oz (4½ tbsp) butter

butter
2¼ oz (4½ tbsp) butter, softened

3 DECORATION

⅜ oz (¾ tbsp) water
⅜ oz (2½ tsp) superfine sugar
4½ oz (about 1.1 cup)
  walnuts, chopped
1⅜ oz (⅓ cup) confectioners'
  sugar

1   Make the almond meringue base dough (page 38). Put it in a pastry bag fitted with a no. 10 plain decorating tip and pipe an 8¾ in diameter disc on a cookie sheet lined with baking paper. Separately create an 8¾ in circlet by piping 1½ in "pucks" stuck to each other to make an exterior circle, and slightly smaller pucks for an interior circle stuck to the first. Bake as indicated in the base recipe (page 38).

2   For the walnut praline, roast (page 281) the walnuts for 15 minutes in a 360°F oven. Put the water then the sugar in a saucepan and cook to 225°F. Add the roasted nuts and caramelize them by stirring. Let them cool on a sheet of baking paper.

3   Pulse the caramelized nuts in a food processor to make a paste.

4   Make the German butter cream (page 56). At the end of cooking, add the walnut praline.

5   Fill a pastry bag (no. 12 tip) with German butter cream (page 272). Pipe domes around the exterior of the plain disc, then fill the center by piping in a snail shell (page 273). Place the circlet on top and refrigerate for at least 2 hours.

6   To decorate, bring the water and sugar to the boil. Spread the walnuts over a baking sheet lined with baking paper. Pour over the syrup and stir to ensure the nuts are covered. Put in a 360°F oven for about 15 minutes, stirring every 5 minutes with a spatula. The nuts should be well caramelized. Leave to cool. Dust the circlet with confectioners' sugar. Pile the walnuts in the center.

FLAN PÂTISSIER

Understand

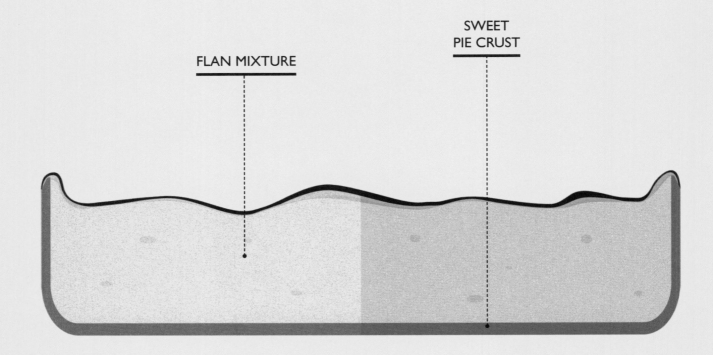

FLAN MIXTURE

SWEET
PIE CRUST

WHAT IS IT?

Sweet pie crust base filled with a cooked cream mixture.

TIME TO MAKE

Preparation: 30 minutes
Cooking: 45 minutes to 1 hour
Refrigeration: 4 hours

EQUIPMENT

9½ in tart ring

VARIATION

Tropical flan: replace 14 oz (1¾ cup) milk with coconut milk. Dust the cooled flan with 1¾ oz desiccated coconut.

TECHNIQUE TO MASTER
Lining a mold with pastry (page 284)

ORGANIZATION
Sweet pie crust – flan mixture – baking

TO SERVE 6–8

1 SWEET PIE CRUST

7 oz (about 1.6 cups) all-purpose flour
3½ oz (7 tbsp) butter
1¾ oz (3½ tbsp) water
1/32 oz (⅓ tsp) salt
⅞ oz (2 tbsp) superfine sugar
½ oz egg yolk (about 1 yolk)

2 FLAN MIXTURE

7 oz egg (4 eggs)
7 oz (1 cup) superfine sugar
2 oz (about ⅓ cup) poudre à flan
   (or potato starch)
1 lb 12 oz (3½ cups) milk
1 vanilla bean

1 Make the sweet pie crust (page 10), preferably the day before. Roll the pastry to 1/12 in thickness and place on a cookie sheet lined with baking paper. Set aside in the refrigerator for at least 30 minutes, ideally overnight.

2 Grease a 9½ in tart ring with butter, place it on a cookie sheet lined with baking paper and line it with the pastry (page 284), then return to the refrigerator for 1 hour. Preheat the oven to 360°F.

3 In a stainless-steel bowl, blanch the egg with the sugar, then incorporate the poudre à flan.

4 Boil the milk with the seeds scraped from the vanilla bean. When it is about to rise to the top of the pan, pour half over the egg mixture to relax it. Whisk.

5 Return the mixture to the saucepan over high heat, whisking vigorously to prevent the mixture sticking. When it starts to boil and pull away from the sides slightly, remove from the heat.

6 Pour into the lined tart ring, then bake for 45 minutes to 1 hour. When it comes out of the oven, let it cool, then refrigerate for at least 3 hours before eating.

CHEESECAKE

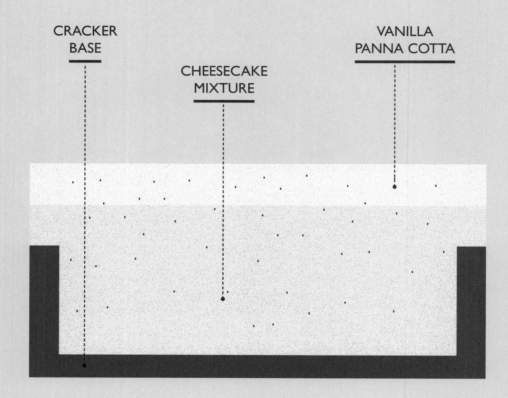

Understand

CRACKER
BASE

CHEESECAKE
MIXTURE

VANILLA
PANNA COTTA

WHAT IS IT?

Creamy gâteau composed of a crumbly base of blended crackers, a vanilla and fromage blanc cream and a silky vanilla panna cotta.

TIME TO MAKE

Preparation: 1 hour
Cooking: 20–40 minutes
Refrigeration: 6–24 hours

EQUIPMENT

4¾ × 9½ × 2¾ in rectangular dessert frame

VARIATION

Citrus cheesecake: replace the vanilla with the zest of 1 lime.

TRICKY ASPECT

Manipulation of the cracker base

TIPS

If the tart ring is adjustable, the cheesecake could slide out during cooking and lose its shape. If this is the case, strengthen the ring by tying ovenproof kitchen twine around it. Work gently with the biscuit base using the paddle attachment of an electric mixer (or the plastic blade of a food processor) to avoid the butter overheating. Otherwise the base will be difficult to use.

ORGANIZATION

Cracker base – cheesecake mixture – assembly – baking – frosting

TO SERVE 6–8

1 BASE

9¼ oz salted crackers
7 oz (14 tbsp) butter
4½ oz (about ⅔ cup) superfine
   sugar
2¼ oz (½ cup) all-purpose flour

2 CHEESECAKE MIXTURE

1 lb 7 oz fromage blanc
1 lb 2 oz (2¼ cups) heavy cream
   (30% fat)
9½ oz (2¼ cups) confectioners'
   sugar
1⅜ oz (5 tbsp) cornstarch
9 oz egg (5 eggs)

seeds of 2 vanilla beans
1¼ oz (2½ tbsp) lemon juice

3 VANILLA PANNA COTTA

⅛ oz leaf gelatine
10½ oz (about 1⅓ cups) whipping
   cream (30% fat)
½ oz (3½ tsp) superfine sugar
1 vanilla bean

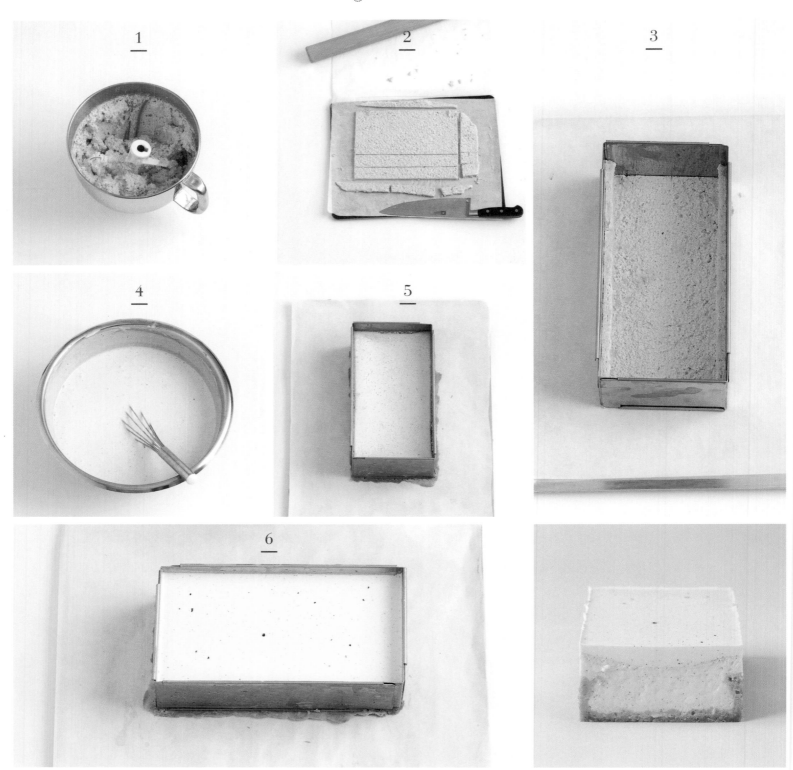

1   To make the base, put the crackers in the bowl of an electric mixer fitted with the paddle attachment or a food processor fitted with the plastic blade. Turn it on gently to obtain a powder. Add the butter, sugar and flour. Keep mixing gently until the mixture has a creamy dough consistency.

2   Using a rolling pin, roll the pastry between two sheets of baking paper to ⅜ in thickness. Refrigerate for 1 hour. Cut out a 4¾ in × 9½ in rectangle (for the base) and two long 9½ in × 1¼ in strips (for the long sides).

3   Place a 4¾ in × 9½ in × 2¾ in rectangular dessert frame on a cookie sheet lined with baking paper. Put the cracker base in the bottom of the frame and the two strips along the long sides. Set aside.

4   To make the cheesecake mixture, preheat the oven to 250°F. In a stainless-steel bowl, whisk the fromage blanc, cream, confectioners' sugar and cornstarch. Whisk in the eg, then the vanilla seeds and lemon juice, until the mixture is smooth.

5   Pour the mixture into the lined frame and bake for 20–40 minutes, making sure you open the oven door for a few seconds every 10 minutes to let the steam out and avoid cracks. When you tap the frame, the cream should be set and wobble only slightly. Allow to cool to room temperature, then refrigerate, ideally overnight.

6   To make the panna cotta, hydrate the gelatine in very cold water. Bring 3½ oz (7 tbsp) of the cream and the sugar to the boil, then remove from the heat. Whisk in the drained gelatine. Add the rest of the cream and the vanilla. Pour over the cheesecake and refrigerate for 2 hours to set. Using a kitchen blowtorch, gently heat the sides to remove the frame, then cut into individual portions.

MADELEINES

Understand

WHAT ARE THEY?

Soft little cakes in the shape of a shell.

TIME TO MAKE

Preparation: 15 minutes
Refrigeration: 3 hours
Cooking: 8–15 minutes

EQUIPMENT

Madeleine tin with 10 holes
Microplane grater

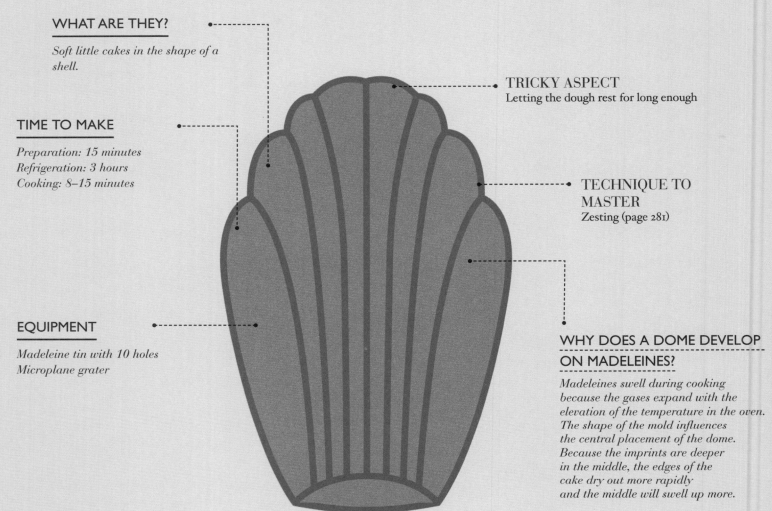

TRICKY ASPECT
Letting the dough rest for long enough

TECHNIQUE TO MASTER
Zesting (page 281)

WHY DOES A DOME DEVELOP ON MADELEINES?

Madeleines swell during cooking because the gases expand with the elevation of the temperature in the oven. The shape of the mold influences the central placement of the dome. Because the imprints are deeper in the middle, the edges of the cake dry out more rapidly and the middle will swell up more.

TO MAKE 10 MADELEINES

1⅞ oz (3¾ tbsp) butter
1¾ oz egg (1 egg)
1¾ oz (¼ cup) superfine sugar
⅜ oz (½ tbsp) honey
1 lemon, zested
1¾ oz (.4 cup) all-purpose flour
1/16 oz (about ⅓ tsp) baking powder

1 Melt the butter, then leave it to cool to room temperature.

2 In a stainless-steel bowl, blanch the egg with the sugar and honey using a whisk.

3 Incorporate the flour, baking powder and lemon zest. Add the flour little by little, to avoid lumps.

4 Add the cooled melted butter. Cover with plastic wrap, with the plastic touching the surface, and set aside to rest in the refrigerator or at least 3 hours, ideally overnight.

5 When ready to bake, preheat the oven to 430°F. Take the madeleine mixture out of the refrigerator 30 minutes before using so that it softens. Using a pastry bag, fill the molds, stopping before the top. Put in the oven, immediately reduce the temperature to 340°F and cook for 8–15 minutes.

6 As soon as they come out of the oven, turn the madeleines out on a wire rack.

FINANCIERS

Understand

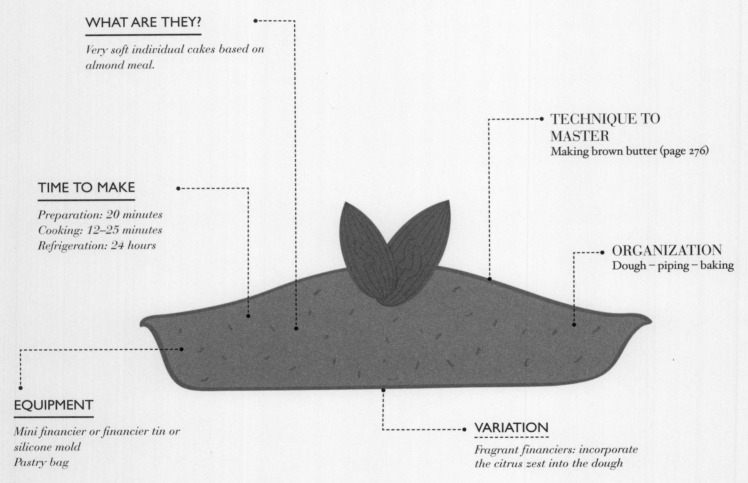

WHAT ARE THEY?

Very soft individual cakes based on almond meal.

TIME TO MAKE

Preparation: 20 minutes
Cooking: 12–25 minutes
Refrigeration: 24 hours

TECHNIQUE TO MASTER
Making brown butter (page 276)

ORGANIZATION
Dough – piping – baking

EQUIPMENT

Mini financier or financier tin or silicone mold
Pastry bag

VARIATION

Fragrant financiers: incorporate the citrus zest into the dough

WHY MUST THE DOUGH BE RESTED CAREFULLY BEFORE BAKING?

The cooling allows the butter to harden, which means that even after 30 minutes at room temperature, the dough will hold together better in the oven and will rise better during baking.

TO MAKE 20 MINI FINANCIERS OR 8 FINANCIERS

1 FINANCIER DOUGH

2 oz (about ½ cup) confectioners' sugar
1 oz (about ⅓ cup) almond meal
¾ oz (about 3 tbsp) all-purpose flour
1¾ oz (3½ tbsp) butter
1⅞ oz egg white (about 2 whites)

2 DECORATION

1¾ oz (about ½ cup) almonds, roughly chopped

1 Combine the confectioners' sugar, almond meal and flour.

2 Make brown butter (page 276) and pour it immediately over the dry ingredients. Whisk, then gradually add the egg white. Cover with plastic film with the plastic touching the surface and refrigerate, ideally overnight.

3 Preheat the oven to 340°F and take out the dough 30 minutes in advance so that it softens. Using a pastry bag, divide the dough between the greased holes in the tin or mold, then sprinkle over the chopped almonds. Bake for 12–25 minutes, depending on the size of the financiers.

255

COOKIES

Understand

WHAT ARE THEY?

Shortbread-style cookies with chocolate nuggets and walnuts.

TIME TO MAKE

Preparation: 15 minutes
Cooking: 10 minutes
Refrigeration: 2 hours

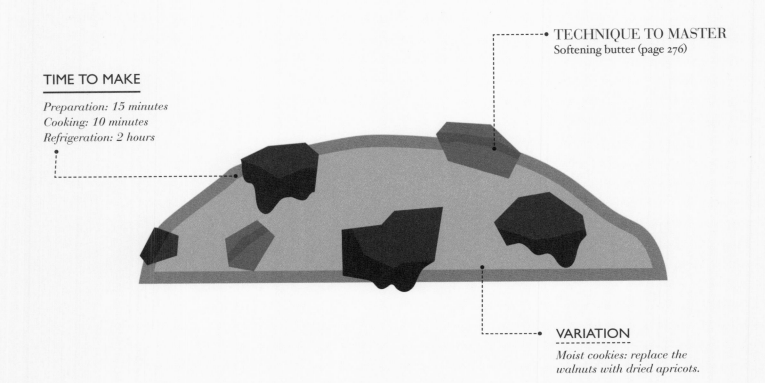

TECHNIQUE TO MASTER
Softening butter (page 276)

VARIATION

Moist cookies: replace the walnuts with dried apricots.

WHAT MAKES A COOKIE DRY OR MOIST?

The texture of the butter in the mixture is an important factor in the final texture. If the butter is soft, the dough will spread more in the oven and the result will be drier.

WHY IS IT NECESSARY TO LET THE DOUGH REST?

For the cookies to be moist, we recommend leaving the dough in the refrigerator to harden before baking.

ORGANIZATION & STORAGE
Dough – cutting – baking
The dough sausage, wrapped in plastic wrap, will keep for 3 months in the freezer.

TO MAKE 12 COOKIES

2 oz (4 tbsp) butter, softened
1 oz (¼ cup) confectioners' sugar
1⅜ oz (3 tbsp) soft brown sugar
1¾ oz egg (1 egg)
3½ oz (about .8 cup) all-purpose flour
1/32 oz (⅓ tsp) salt
⅛ oz (¾ tsp) baking powder
1¾ oz dark chocolate, roughly chopped
1⅜ oz (⅓ cup) walnuts, roughly chopped

1 Put the softened butter (page 276) in a stainless-steel bowl with the confectioners' sugar and the brown sugar, and mix. Add the egg, flour, salt and baking powder, then mix. Add the chocolate and walnuts and mix again.

2 Roll the dough into a sausage of about 2½ in diameter and wrap in plastic wrap. Refrigerate for 2 hours to harden.

3 Preheat the oven to 320°F. Take out the dough sausage and cut it into ⅜ in thick slices. Place them on a cookie sheet lined with baking paper. Bake for about 10 minutes. When you touch them with a finger, the edges should be hard and the middle soft. Remove the cookie sheet from the oven and slide the baking paper with the cookies onto the benchtop to stop them cooking.

SELF-SAUCING CHOCOLATE
DESSERTS

Understand

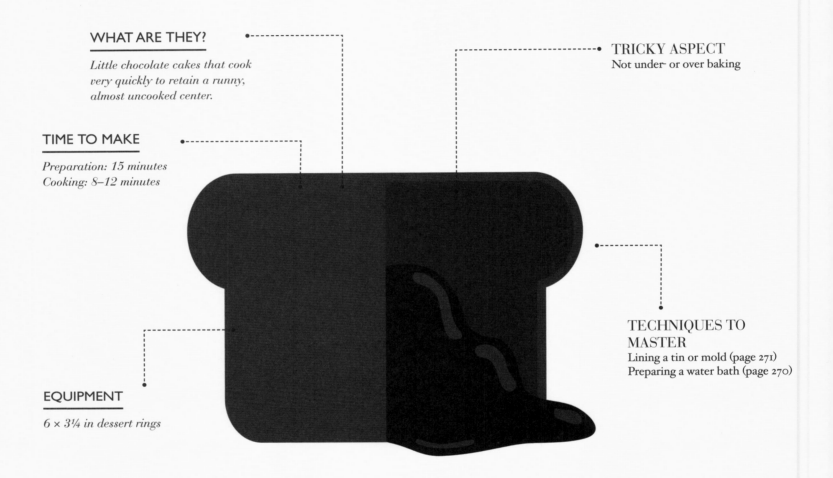

WHAT ARE THEY?

Little chocolate cakes that cook very quickly to retain a runny, almost uncooked center.

TIME TO MAKE

Preparation: 15 minutes
Cooking: 8–12 minutes

EQUIPMENT

6 × 3¼ in dessert rings

TRICKY ASPECT

Not under- or over baking

TECHNIQUES TO MASTER

Lining a tin or mold (page 271)
Preparing a water bath (page 270)

TO MAKE 6 DESSERTS

5¼ oz dark chocolate
5¼ oz (10½ tbsp) butter
¾ oz (about 2¾ tbsp) all-purpose flour
3½ oz (about. 8 cup) confectioners' sugar
5¼ oz egg (3 eggs)

1   Preheat the oven to 360°F. Line six 3¼ in dessert rings with baking paper, with the paper sticking out above the ring (page 271). Put them on a cookie sheet lined with baking paper.

2   Melt the chocolate with the butter in a water bath. In another stainless-steel bowl, mix the flour and the confectioners' sugar. Gradually add the egg, using a whisk to avoid lumps. Add the melted butter and chocolate.

3   Pour the mixture into the prepared rings. Bake for at least 8 minutes. The middle should be darker, like an "eye," as the edges should be cooked and the center runny.

VARIATION

White chocolate center: push a square of white chocolate into the middle of the dough before baking.

TIPS

Use aluminum dessert rings because they transmit the heat faster, which makes cooking and unmolding easier. Continue baking for a few minutes if the edges don't seem cooked enough.

RUSSIAN
CIGARETTES

Understand

WHAT ARE THEY?

Dry rolled cookies used to accompany desserts.

TIME TO MAKE

Preparation: 20 minutes
Cooking: 8–10 minutes
Refrigeration: 3–24 hours

TRICKY ASPECT
Judging the coloration of the cigarettes

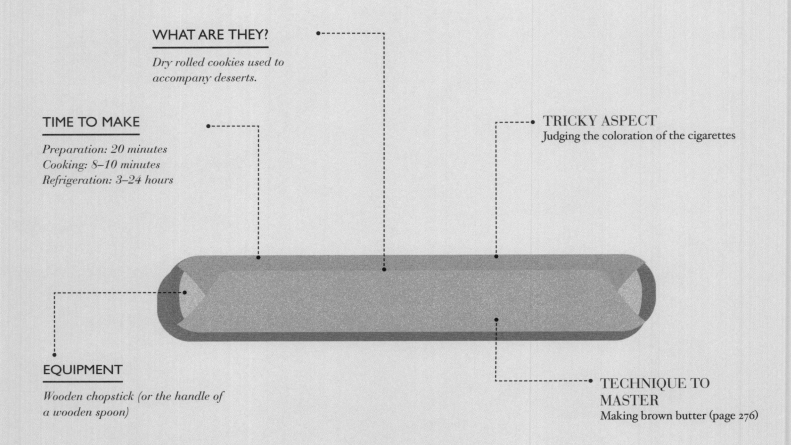

EQUIPMENT

Wooden chopstick (or the handle of a wooden spoon)

TECHNIQUE TO MASTER
Making brown butter (page 276)

CLASSIC USES

Decoration, accompaniment to creamy desserts, ice creams and sorbets

VARIATION

Filled version: fill the cigarettes with creamy ganache (page 72). Eat them straight away because the cookies soften very quickly.

WHY LET THE DOUGH REST BEFORE BAKING?

Thanks to the cooling stage, the dough will spread out less during cooking and the discs will be easier to roll when they come out of the oven because they will be softer.

TIP
Using chopsticks makes it much easier to roll the cookies into cylinders.

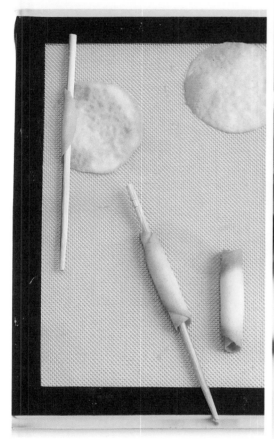

TO MAKE 20 CIGARETTES

1¾ oz (about .4 cups) confectioners' sugar
1¾ oz (.4 cup) all-purpose flour
1¾ oz (3½ tbsp) butter
1¾ oz egg white (about 1½ whites)

1 Combine the confectioners' sugar and flour in a stainless-steel bowl. Make a brown butter (page 276). Pour it into the bowl straight away and mix using a spatula.

2 Gradually add the egg white, then cover with plastic wrap, with the plastic touching the surface, and leave to rest in the refrigerator, ideally overnight.

3 Preheat the oven to 390°F. Line a cookie sheet with baking paper, put dollops of dough on it, then, using a frosting spatul, form them into quite thin discs of about 3¼ in diameter (you could even use a stencil). Put a maximum of 4–6 discs on each cookie sheet to avoid them running into each other. Bake for 8–10 minutes; the edges should be well colored and the middle blond.

4 Remove from the oven and immediately roll the cookies up using a chopstick.

261

LANGUES DE CHAT

Understand

WHAT ARE THEY?

Dry, crispy cookies based on egg whites.

TIME TO MAKE

Preparation: 10 minutes
Cooking: 10–15 minutes

EQUIPMENT

Pastry bag
No. 8 plain decorating tip

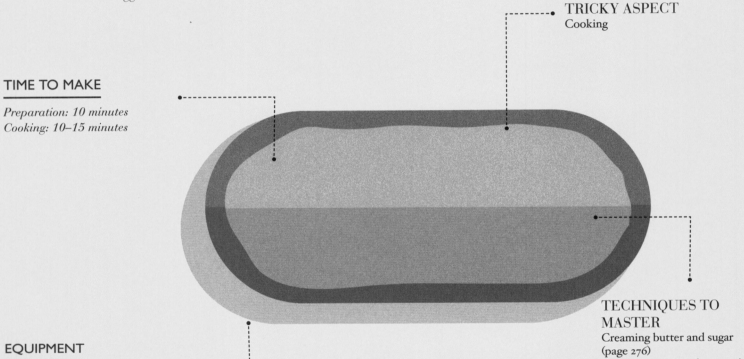

TRICKY ASPECT
Cooking

TECHNIQUES TO MASTER
Creaming butter and sugar
(page 276)
Using a pastry bag (page 272)

TO MAKE 30 LANGUES DE CHAT

2 oz (4 tbsp) butter, softened
1 oz (2¼ tbsp) superfine sugar
1¾ oz egg (1 egg)
2 oz (.45 cup) all-purpose flour

1 Preheat the oven to 375°F. In a stainless-steel bowl, cream (page 276) the butter with the sugar using a spatula.

2 Incorporate the egg, then the flour. Mix until just smooth.

3 Line a cookie sheet with baking paper. Fill a pastry bag and pipe well-spaced sausages 2 in long on the sheet (page 272). Bake for about 10 minutes; the edges should be brown and the middle golden. Detach them quickly then leave them on a wire rack to cool.

VARIATIONS

Almond langues de chat: before baking, sprinkle the dough sausages with flaked almonds. Vanilla langues de chat: add ³⁄₁₆ oz (1¼ tsp) vanilla extract to the dough.

ALMOND PRALINE CHOCOLATE
ROCHERS

Understand

CHOCOLATE
COATING

ROASTED
ALMONDS

PRALINE

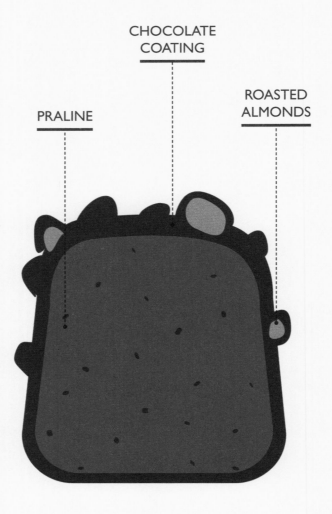

WHAT ARE THEY?

A praline center coated in chocolate and roasted chopped almonds.

TIME TO MAKE

Preparation: 30 minutes
Refrigeration: 30 minutes
Cooking: 15–25 minutes

EQUIPMENT

Candy thermometer
Pastry bag
No. 8 plain decorating tip

WHY IS IT NECESSARY TO TEMPER THE CHOCOLATE?

Tempering is important to avoid the whitening of the chocolate and to make the rochers crisp and shiny.

TECHNIQUE TO MASTER
Tempering chocolate (page 86)

ORGANIZATION
Ganache – balls – roasted almonds – tempering – dipping

TO MAKE 12 ROCHERS

1 ROCHER CENTER

4½ oz dark chocolate
3½ oz praline (ground caramelized almonds)
confectioners' sugar, for dusting

2 COATING

⅜ oz (¾ tbsp) water
⅜ oz (2½ tsp) superfine sugar
5¼ oz (about 1 cup) almonds, chopped
3½ oz dark chocolate

1 Melt the chocolate for the center in a water bath. Put the praline in a stainless-steel bowl and pour the melted chocolate over it. Mix using a spatula.

2 Line a cookie sheet with baking paper. Fill a pastry bag with the rocher mixture and pipe 12 "pucks" of about ¾ oz each. Refrigerate for 30 minutes. Take them out, dust your hands with confectioners' sugar, and fashion each chocolate disc into a ball. The confectioners' sugar stops the chocolate sticking to your fingers. Set aside at room temperature or in the refrigerator.

3 For the roasted almonds, preheat the oven to 320°F. Put the water and sugar in a saucepan, bring to the boil and remove from the heat. Allow to cool, then pour over the chopped almonds and mix together. Spread the almonds over a cookie sheet lined with baking paper. Bake for 15–25 minutes, stirring regularly until they are golden. Remove from the oven and allow to cool.

4 Temper the chocolate (page 86). Plunge the rochers one at a time into the chocolate, retrieve them with a chocolate dipping fork and roll them in the roasted almonds. Allow to cool and set.

CHAPTER 3
GLOSSARY

UTENSILS

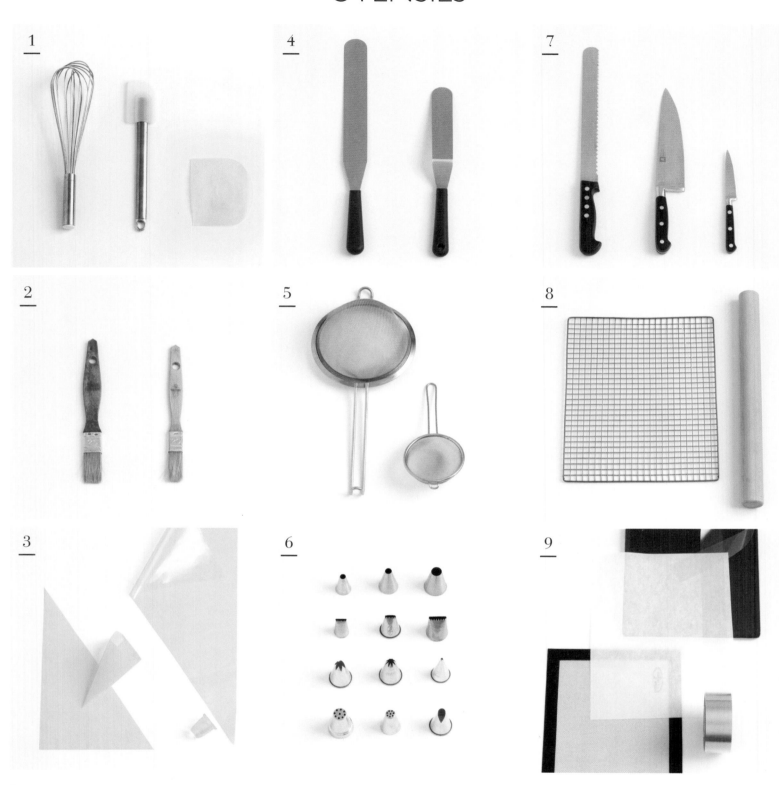

1 Whisk, silicone spatula, dough scraper

2 Pastry brushes

3 Disposable pastry bags

4 Frosting spatula and bent frosting spatula

5 Strainer and sieve

6 Decorating tips

7 Serrated knife, chef's knife, utility knife

8 Wire rack, straight rolling pin

9 Nonstick cookie sheet, silicone mat (Silpat brand), acetate cake ring, baking paper

UTENSILS

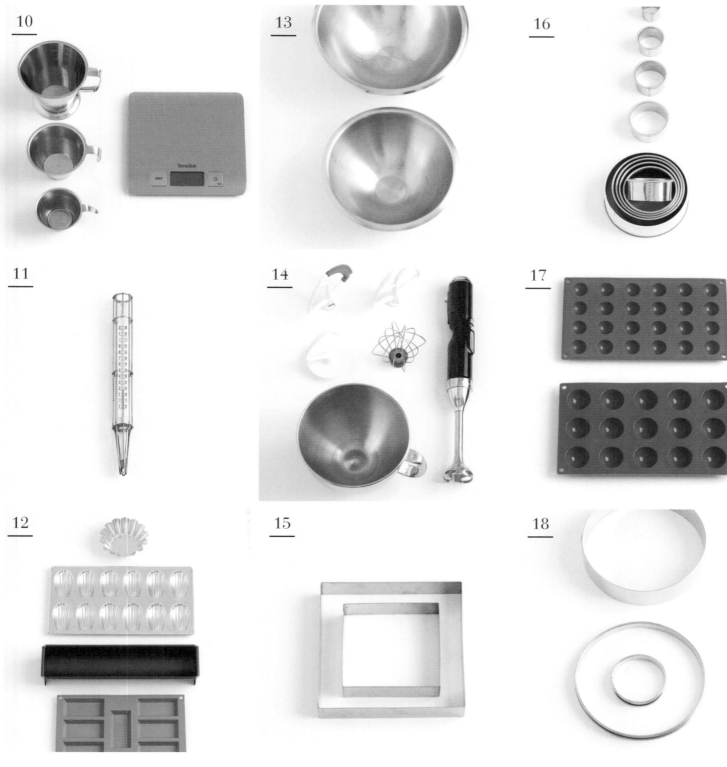

10 Measuring cups, electronic kitchen scale

11 Candy thermometer

12 Fluted round brioche tin, madeleine tin, yule log tin (guttered cake tin), silicone financier mold

13 Stainless-steel bowls

14 Electric mixer attachments (beater, paddle, dough hook, whisk), hand-held blender

15 Square dessert frames

16 Cookie cutters

17 Half-sphere silicone molds

18 Dessert ring, tart ring, tartlet ring

BASICS

1 COMBINING TWO MIXTURES

Work in two steps to suit the textures. Incorporate the first third using a whisk and mixing vigorously to loosen the thickest mixture, then fold in the remaining two-thirds more delicately, using a silicone spatula, to retain the lightness. It is possible to whisk in the remaining two-thirds using the whisk like a silicone spatula; the mixing will occur more rapidly. Use the silicone spatula to check if the mixture is smooth.

2 HYDRATING GELATINE

Leaf gelatine has been dehydrated and must be rehydrated in order to melt it into a mixture. If it isn't hydrated well, it will absorb any missing water from the mixture itself, causing it to shrink.

Immerse the gelatine in a bowl of very cold water (it melts at low temperatures). Let it soak for at least 15 minutes, then drain it and squeeze it between your hands before adding it to the mixture.

Gelatine "glues" mixtures together; in other words, it gives them their structure. The setting time is quite quick. Use the mixture straight away, so that the jelling power kicks in as soon as the mixture is put in place, or set it aside and whisk it before using to restore its consistency.

3 PREPARING A WATER BATH

A water bath (bain-marie) heats ingredients with steam rather than direct contact with a heat source. The heat on the mixtures is less intense, which means it heats them gently. This prevents chocolate from burning or eggs from coagulating.

Take a large saucepan and a stainless-steel bowl that will rest on the edge without being in contact with the water. Put water in the saucepan and heat it (it must be simmering). Put the ingredient/s in the bowl and the bowl on the saucepan, double-checking it does not touch the water.

4 STRAINING OR SIFTING

Pass an ingredient or mixture through a pretty fine strainer or sieve to eliminate any solid residues. This is the case for vanilla beans in a crème anglaise or for a powder you wish to make finer (such as almond meal). It also helps make a liquid preparation, such as a frosting, more fluid.

5 GLAZING

Beat an egg or egg yolk. Dip in a pastry brush and drain off any surplus before brushing choux pastry, a pie or brioche.

PREPARING A TIN OR MOLD

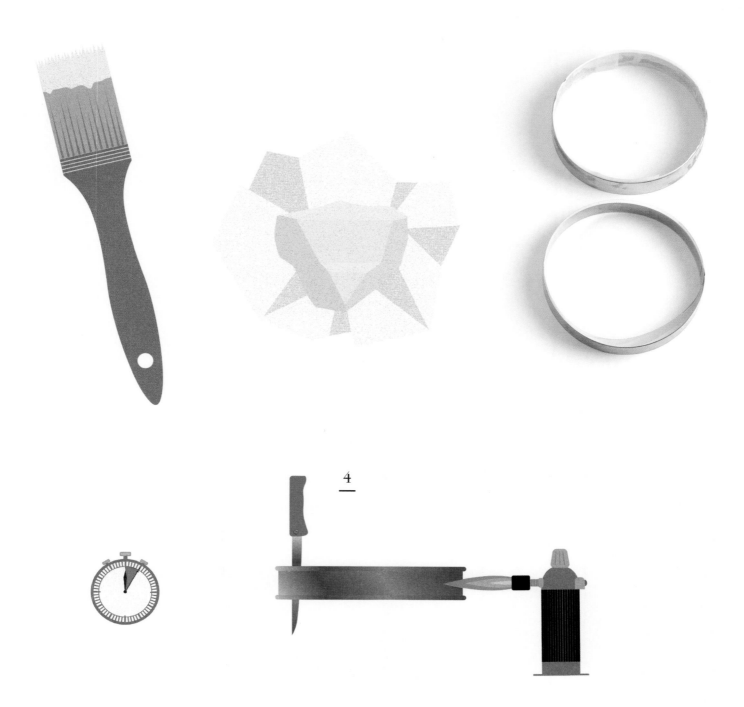

1 GREASING A TIN OR MOLD

This is necessary for unmolding after cooking. For tarts, greasing the ring with butter also helps stick the pastry to the ring, which prevents it subsiding during baking.

Grease a tart ring with soft butter using a pastry brush or paper towel. Use melted butter for a moist preparation.

2 LINING A TIN OR MOLD

Lining a tin or mold is indispensable for some desserts, to avoid the preparation sticking to the sides. Use acetate cake band (quite rigid plastic) or baking paper. Acetate cake band is better for mousse-based desserts because it doesn't wrinkle. Cut it ¾ in longer than the circumference of the mold. Use 1½ in or 2½ in wide cake band depending on the dessert. If you use baking paper, grease the mold lightly so that the paper sticks. The cake band will stick by itself.

3 LINING A COOKIE SHEET

There are nonstick cookie sheets, but the majority need to be lined with a nonstick surface: either a silicone baking mat or baking paper. A silicone baking mat is perfect for baking macarons but isn't suited to choux pastry. Guitar sheets or acetate sheets are used for working with chocolate. Baking paper is very practical but less stable.

Hold down the corners using clothes pegs or by putting weights on them (a knife or a glass). Pipe the dough in question, then remove the weights or pegs when the weight of the piped dough is great enough to hold the paper in place.

4 UNMOLDING OR REMOVING A FRAME

Acetate cake band or baking paper guarantee immediate unmolding. If the mold isn't lined, there are several possibilities:

Using a kitchen blowtorch: freeze the dessert. When you wish to unmold it, aim the blowtorch at each side for 5 seconds. Don't heat it too much, as mousse-base desserts melt quickly and could taste burnt. It is sometimes necessary to return the dessert to the freezer after unmolding so that it regains its structure. This technique is not suited to a fraisier cake, because the strawberries cannot be frozen.

Using a knife: for all desserts, pass a hot knife between the dessert and the mold.

In a water bath: when the mold can be dipped, such as with a log cake.

USING A PASTRY BAG

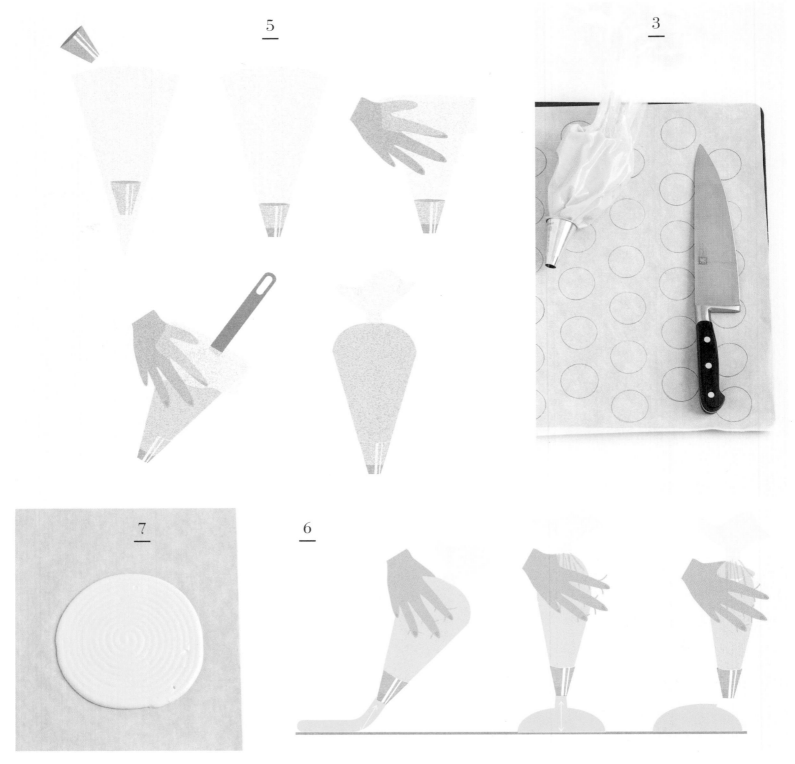

5

3

7

6

1 PASTRY BAGS

Disposable pastry bags are ideal because they pose no hygiene problems. You can use a pastry bag without a decorating tip to fill a tart case cleanly, pass from one small piece to another or pipe fine lines with frosting. Cut the end of the bag to the desired size, fill it, then pinch the end between your thumb and index finger to control the flow.

2 DECORATING TIPS

There are several types of tip (plastic or stainless steel) for decorating and filling neatly: Mont Blanc or grass tip, St Honoré tip (slit on one side) and so on. The shapes obtained depend on how the bag is held, upright or on a slope. The tips are named according to the diameter of their opening in millimeters: a no. 10 tip has a ⅜ in opening.

3 COOKIE SHEETS

Pipe onto a metal cookie sheet lined with baking paper, directly onto a nonstick metal cookie sheet or onto a silicone mat (such as Silpat brand) – except for choux pastry.

4 TEMPLATES

To obtain evenness with piping, use a template. Trace circles in staggered rows on a large piece of paper using a drinking glass or a cookie cutter. Place the template on the cookie sheet and cover it with a sheet of baking paper (that way you can reuse the template, but you could also trace the circles directly onto baking paper, then turn it over before piping). To keep the paper on the sheet, put some weights (knife, glass) on it, then gradually move them as you pipe.

5 FILLING A PASTRY BAG

Put the chosen tip in the bag. Mark or nick the end of the bag where the tip sits correctly. Lift the tip and cut along the mark. Put the tip in place, twist the bag just above it and push the twisted part into the bottom of the nozzle so the mixture doesn't run out before you start piping. Fold the top of the bag back over your hand (left hand if you are right-handed). Take the mixture with a silicone spatula and put it in the bag, scraping the spatula against the hand holding the bag. Fill to two-thirds maximum to avoid the bag overflowing. Put the top of the bag back up and give it a quarter turn while pushing the mixture toward the tip. Pull on the tip to remove the "cork" and turn the bag to make the mixture move down.

DECORATING WITH A PASTRY BAG

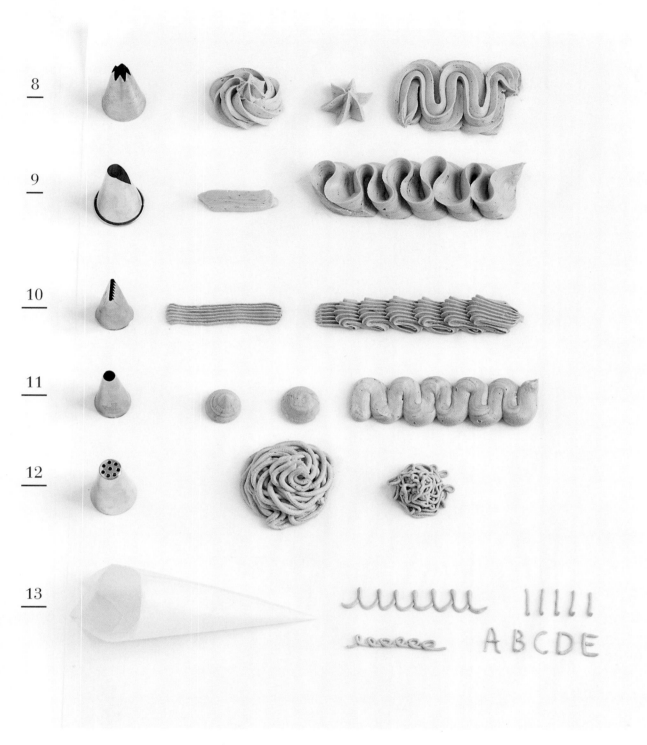

6 PIPING

Hold the bag straight up to pipe discs or domes, on an angle to form éclairs. Press with one hand, while stabilizing and guiding the bag with the other. When there is not enough of the mixture in your hand, push it down and twist the bag a quarter turn again.

7 PIPING IN A SNAIL SHELL

To make large round bases, or to fill a dessert with cream, piping the mixture ensures an even thickness over the entire surface. This is done by piping in a snail shell.

Pipe by starting in the middle and pressing as evenly as possible, to obtain "sausages" of a constant thickness. Each row must be stuck to the last without overlapping. Pipe quickly.

8 FLUTED TIP

Make a simple star, a rosette by turning the bag or a wave by piping the sausages close together.

9 ST HONORÉ TIP

Make a simple line or a wave by piping rapidly without lifting the bag.

10 BASKET-WEAVE TIP

Draw a waved line or a garland by regularly bringing the tip back over the piped line in a quick movement.

11 PLAIN TIP

Make a drop or a dome by holding the bag completely perpendicular to the surface. Do the same to pipe a wave.

12 MONT-BLANC OR GRASS TIP

Simply pipe in swirls until the surface is covered.

13 USING A CONE

Cut a right-angled triangle out of baking paper. Roll the cone with the point in the center of the long edge. Tighten to make a cone with a closed tip. Fold the points sticking out back into the cone.

Half-fill with royal icing or fondant frosting and fold over the end to close. Push the content toward the tip and cut off the end with scissors.

Sliding method: if you can lean on the surface, write as if you were using a pen.

Dropping method: if you cannot lean on the surface, write while holding the cone above the surface.

DECORATING A CAKE OR DESSERT

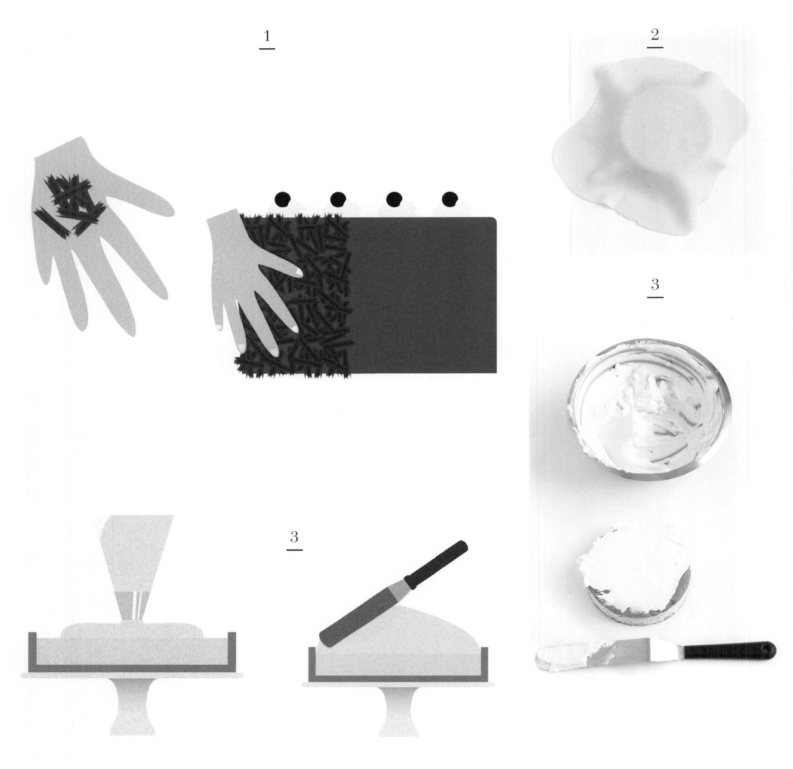

1 COVERING WITH CHOCOLATE SHAVINGS

The dessert must be glazed or covered with cream: the surface must be sticky so the shavings adhere. Manipulate the shavings quickly to avoid them melting. Sprinkle them uniformly over the top of the dessert. To cover the sides, take a handful and press them against the dessert.

2 COVERING WITH MARZIPAN OR SUGAR PASTE

Working on a work surface lightly dusted with potato starch, roll the marzipan out to $\frac{1}{12}$ in thickness using a rolling pin. Place it over the cake and gently smooth the sides with your hand, working from top to bottom, carefully lifting the base from time to time to avoid folds. Cut off the surplus using a utility knife. Use marzipan that is 22 percent almonds – any higher and it will be difficult to roll. Work in the same way with sugar paste. This generally contains margarine and has a less natural taste.

3 COVERING WITH CREAM

Put the cream on the dessert. Smooth it out on top using a frosting spatula, then on the sides, being careful to maintain an even thickness. Use a firm cream (chantilly cream, butter cream or ganache).

DECORATING A CAKE OR DESSERT

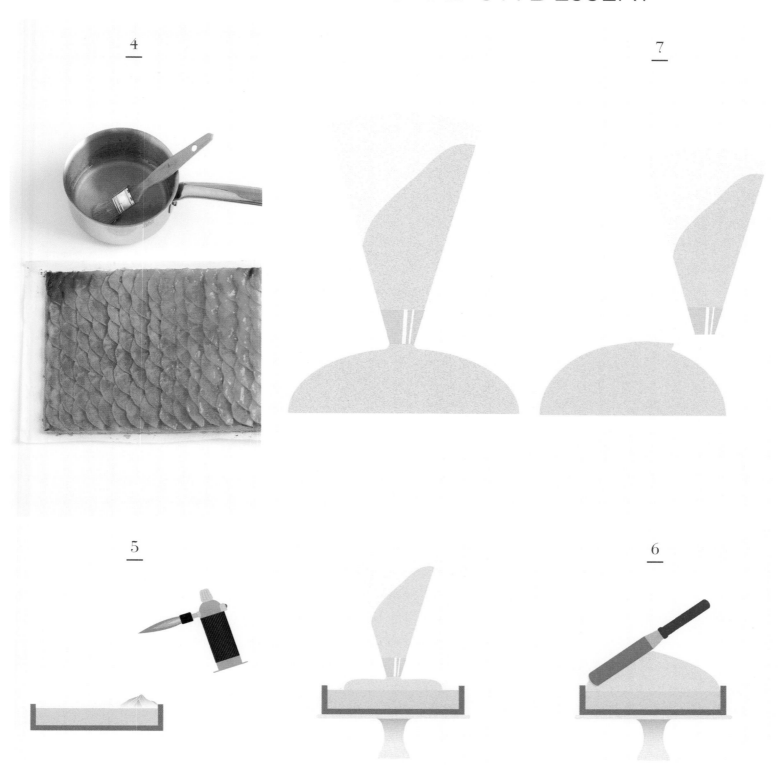

4 GLAZING

Apply a layer of glaze over fruits to make a tart or mousse cake shine.

Boil the glaze and apply it quickly using a pastry brush. Generally we use apricot glaze, which you will find in specialty stores. It is possible to use jelly or well-blended gelatine.

5 COLORING WITH A KITCHEN BLOWTORCH

The kitchen blowtorch allows us to color the surface of a dessert without cooking the inside: e.g. chiboust cream, Italian meringue. It also lets us caramelize a sugared surface, as on a crème brûlée. Keep it about 8 in from the dessert and take care to move the flame regularly to avoid burning the dessert.

6 MAKING A DOME WITH A FROSTING SPATULA

Pipe the cream from a pastry bag fitted with a large plain decorating tip. Smooth from the top to the bottom using a frosting spatula to make a dome, either rounded or pointed. The frosting spatula must be held completely flat to avoid dislodging the cream with each stroke.

7 MAKING A DOME WITH A PASTRY BAG

Pipe the cream from a pastry bag fitted with a large plain decorating tip. Press without moving, keeping the flow as smooth as possible. Once the dome forms, stop pressing and move the tip to one side, to avoid creating a point.

BUTTER

2

4

6

1 THE PRODUCT

Use unpasteurized butter (made from cream that has not undergone any treatment) – if it is available – or pure pasteurized butter. It contains about 82 percent fat. Butter provides taste, creaminess and crumbliness to mixtures. For mixtures that will be salted (generally to enhance the flavors), use unsalted butter so that you can control the salt content more precisely.

2 COLD BUTTER

In certain mixtures, such as sugar crust pastry, the butter must be very cold when it is incorporated into the other ingredients. It must not be completely mixed into the flour. The little pieces of butter that remain in the pastry will form air pockets during baking, giving the pastry its crumbly texture.

3 DRY BUTTER

The melting point of butter varies according to the season it is produced and the food the cows eat. The butter produced in winter is hard and its melting point is elevated (above 90°F); this butter is called "dry." It is used for pastries, in particular those involving turning and folding (people also call it "turning butter"), because it can be worked for longer. You will find it in specialty pastry supply stores.

4 CREAMING BUTTER & SUGAR

This operation consists of rendering butter or a mixture of butter and sugar airy and creamy by whisking it vigorously. We usually start with softened butter.

5 SOFTENING BUTTER

This is butter softened and worked until it takes on the consistency of a cream before being incorporated into a mixture. It helps avoid lumps and provides creaminess.

Cut the butter in pieces, let it soften at room temperature or soften it by applying gentle heat (without letting it melt, or it will lose its creaminess), then work it into a smooth cream using a spatula or whisk.

6 MAKING BROWN BUTTER

This is gently heated butter, from which the water evaporates and which takes on a hazelnut color (which is why the French call it "beurre noisette"). It is the casein (the protein in butter) that colors the brown butter and gives it its taste.

CREAM

1 THE PRODUCT

There are different types of cream: unpasteurized (with no treatment), pasteurized (treated at 196°F) or sterilized (treated at a very high temperature). We define cream as the product coming from cows and containing at least 10½ oz fat per 2 lb 3 oz cream (30 percent fat). Crème fraîche is unpasteurized or pasteurized cream. It can be runny or thickened by adding lactic fermentation agents. In pâtisserie, we use runny cream with 30 per cent fat, because fat allows the cream to be whipped and provides taste.

Crème fleurette: this name is given to a runny cream with 30 percent fat.

2 COLD CREAM

Cold is obligatory for the formation of fat crystals, without which whipped cream could not be stabilized. As well as the cream, it is preferable to maintain a cold environment by putting the whipping utensils (bowl, whisk) in the refrigerator before use. Use stainless steel in preference, as it transmits temperatures better.

3 WHIPPING CREAM

We often add whipped or "expanded" cream to lighten mixtures.

Whisk the cream vigorously until it doubles in volume. It is simultaneously aerated and held together by its fat content, which crystallizes around the air bubbles. Use an electric mixer fitted with the whisk attachment, a food processor with the blade fitted or a hand mixer.

4 WHIPPING CREAM TO STIFF PEAKS

At the end of whipping, whisk the cream in large movements to render it even more dense and smooth. Stop whipping when it holds together well, otherwise you risk making butter. The cream will take on a matte appearance when it is done.

5 MAKING A MOUSSE

In pâtisserie, when we say mousse, we mean a mixture to which whipped cream has been added. It is this aerated cream that gives the mousse its foamy texture.

SUGAR

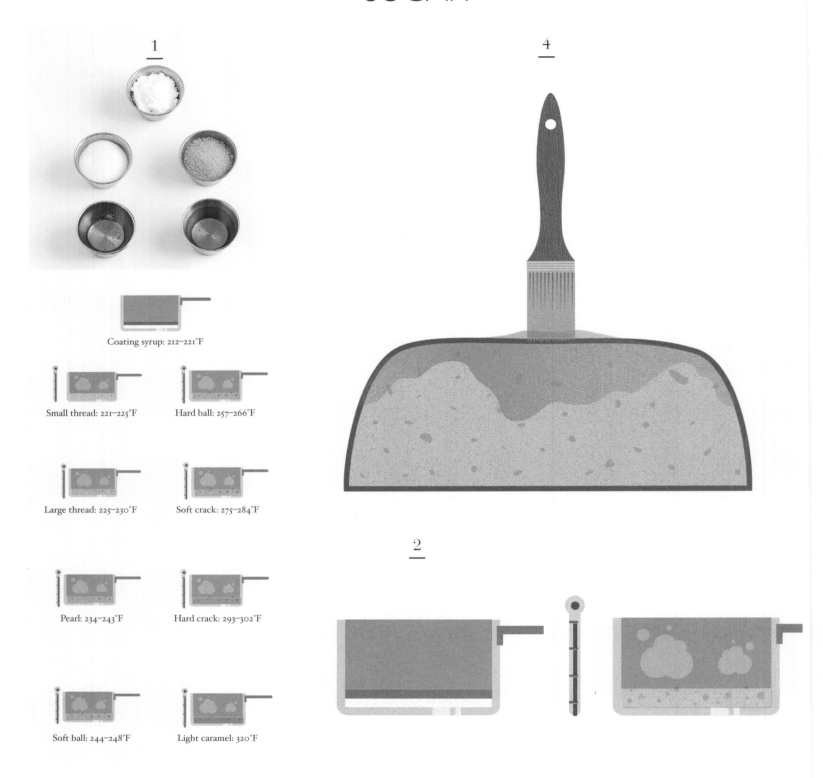

Coating syrup: 212–221°F

Small thread: 221–225°F

Hard ball: 257–266°F

Large thread: 225–230°F

Soft crack: 275–284°F

Pearl: 234–243°F

Hard crack: 293–302°F

Soft ball: 244–248°F

Light caramel: 320°F

1 THE PRODUCT

Sugar brings out flavours, gives crunchiness, nourishes the yeast in leavened doughs, colors cakes during baking and allows them to be doused in syrup.

Superfine sugar: refined granulated sugar traditionally used in pâtisserie.

Confectioners' sugar: white powdered sugar finely ground and enriched with starch (to prevent caking).

Soft brown sugar: unrefined granulated sugar extracted directly from the sugarcane.

Glucose syrup: thick colorless syrup made from corn starch or potato starch. It prevents the crystallization of sugar during cooking. We use it in frostings and nougatine.

Invert sugar: an equal mixture of glucose and fructose. It replaces sugar in certain recipes because it stays moist and smooth (it absorbs humidity and does

not crystallize). We use it in frostings. It can be replaced with some honeys.

Nib sugar: sugar in large grains used to decorate pastries such as chouquettes.

2 CARAMELS

There are different ways of making caramel, depending on its intended use (sauce, mousse, frosting, decoration).

Classic caramel (based on sugar and water), for sugar decorations and frosting choux puffs.

Dry caramel (made without water) used in making caramel flavors (for example for caramel mousse). Its taste is more pronounced.

We add **glucose syrup** to sugar when we need to cook the caramel longer and at higher heats; it prevents the sugar from sticking together (it does not crystallize).

3 MAKING A SUGAR SYRUP

Use clean and dry utensils. Weigh the water then the sugar and pour them gently, without mixing. Clean any crystals from the side of the pan using a wet pastry brush. Heat over medium heat.

4 DOUSING DESSERTS IN SYRUP

Dousing a cake in alcohol syrup: dip a pastry brush in the syrup and tap on the cake to moisten it. It must be completely moistened without being soaked. To test: press on the cake with a finger; syrup should appear.

5 DUSTING WITH SUGAR

Dust two fine layers of confectioners' sugar over a mixture using a sieve, waiting 3 minutes between the two layers. During cooking, the second layer will form little pearls of crunchy sugar.

EGGS

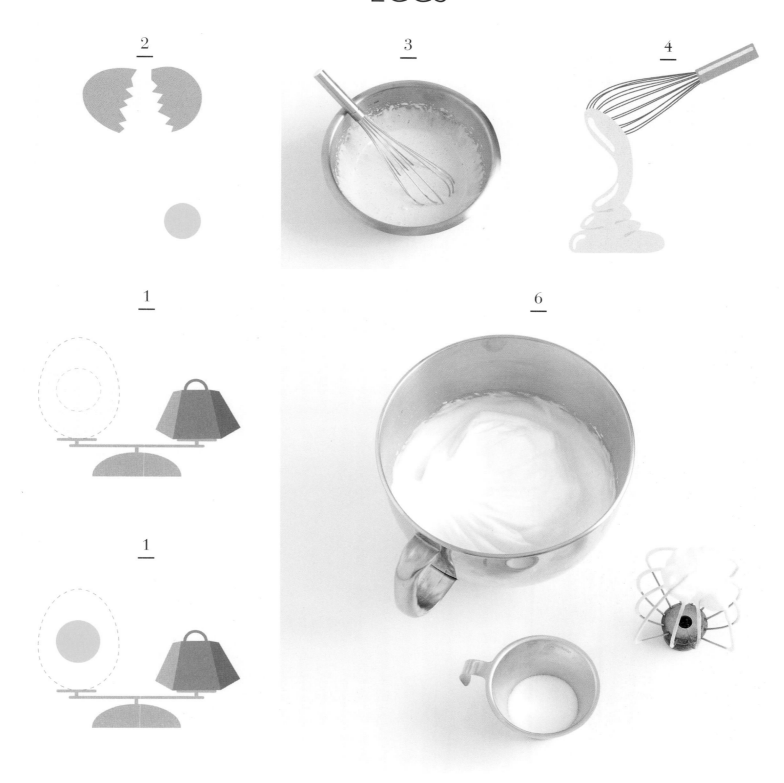

1 THE PRODUCT

Fresh egg: 1¾ oz

White: 1–1¼ oz

Yolk: ½–¾ oz

For some recipes, notably macarons, it is preferable to weigh the eggs.

Storage of yolks: they will keep for 24 hours at the most in refrigerator. Storage of whites: they will keep for 1 week at the most in the refrigerator.

Egg products: eggs (whites, yolks or whole eggs) are sold out of the shell in various forms (liquid, frozen, powdered). These allow very precise weighing, while respecting hygiene standards and saving time. They are sold in specialty pastry supply stores.

2 SEPARATING (CLARIFYING)

The French call separating the white from the yolk "clarifying" an egg.

3 BLANCHING EGG YOLKS

Whisk the egg yolks with sugar to obtain a foamy mixture. It will double in volume. The process of homogenization will take several minutes and is achieved faster with an electric whisk.

4 RECOGNIZING RIBBON STAGE

For yolks: whisk the yolks and the sugar. The consistency should be silky and smooth for it to tumble from the spatula in a continuous band. The mixture will fall like a ribbon folding back on itself.

For whites: when a macaron base is well mixed, you will obtain a ribbon.

5 PREPARING EGG WHITES

To achieve the best result, use egg whites that have been separated for several days, kept in the refrigerator then taken out 1 hour in advance. By this time they will be liquefied: the albumin they contain acts like a spring, imprisoning the air during whisking.

6 WHIPPING EGG WHITES TO STIFF PEAKS

To whisk the whites to stiff peaks, use an electric mixer fitted with the whisk attachment. At the end of beating, whisk vigorously with a large and fast movement to make the whites smooth, shiny and coherent. You can also add a little superfine sugar.

CHOCOLATE

1 THE PRODUCT

Chocolate is composed of cocoa butter, cocoa solids and sugar, in varying proportions. The taste of chocolate, its strength and its melting point depend on the balance between these components. A chocolate with 70 percent cacao contains at least 30 percent sugar for 35 percent cocoa butter and 35 percent cocoa solids.

Couverture chocolate: this is chocolate in which the cocoa butter content is higher than in a classic cooking chocolate. It can be worked more easily because it reacts better to cooking and is more fluid. It can often be replaced by classic cooking chocolate, but is indispensable for decorations and chocolate pieces (which necessitate tempering the chocolate, page 86). It is available in specialty stores, online or from professional wholesalers.

2 CREATING A CHABLON LAYER

A chablon is a thin layer of chocolate applied on a sponge or cake base, which hardens as it dries and stops the cake sticking.

Use classic cooking chocolate. Don't temper it. Melt it in a water bath, pour it over the cake and spread it out as thinly as possible using a frosting spatula. Leave to harden. During assembly, put the chocolate side down on a sheet of baking paper.

3 FROSTING A DESSERT

Heat the frosting to 104°F, pour it over the frozen dessert and immediately spread it in a single movement using a frosting spatula to spread the frosting in a thin layer.

4 PURCHASED CHOCOLATE FROSTING PASTE

A mixture typically consisting of cocoa, sugar and vegetable oil. It can be used for chablons and in some frostings such as the frosting for an opera cake.

5 CHOCOLATE-BASED MIXTURES

Chocolate is the base of numerous pâtisserie mixtures, of varying texture: sponge, mousse (chocolate + whipped cream), creamy ganache (chocolate + crème anglaise + cream), dark chocolate frosting (cocoa powder), chocolate pastry cream, dark chocolate sauce, milk chocolate sauce and chocolate decorations.

COLORINGS, FLAVORS & NUTS

1 COLORINGS

There are fat-soluble colorings, which dissolve in the fat content (chocolate, butter cream), and water-soluble colorings, which dissolve in mixtures where fat is not a major component (macaron shells, sugar decorations).

Powdered colorings are very strong but they don't destabilize mixtures. Add using the tip of a knife or using accurate electronic scales. Liquid colorings are added drop by drop. In all cases, add them gradually (the strength varies from one coloring to another).

Chocolate: use a fat-soluble coloring.

Macaron shells: add a water-soluble coloring to the base mixture.

Fondant frosting: add a water-soluble coloring to the warm frosting.

Titanium dioxide: this food coloring molecule is a pigment that allows mixtures to be whitened (macarons, white chocolate icing). Mix it well.

2 FLAVORS, SPIRITS, ESSENCES & EXTRACTS

Vanilla, cinnamon, star anise, mint, walnut, coffee, pistachio . . . Add them in a paste or powder, or infuse them in fatty mixtures that fix the taste.

Kirsch, rum, Cointreau, Grand Marnier, Kahlua . . . Their flavor remains after cooking, even though the alcohol has evaporated. When they are added to a dousing syrup, the alcohol remains.

Essences are obtained by pressing, distillation or solvent extraction. Add a few drops at the end of mixing. Add carefully; the flavor is very strong. Extracts are obtained through concentration (coffee, vanilla). Add them at the end of mixing. Advantages: no infusion time, immediate use, lower cost (most notably for vanilla).

3 ZEST

The visible colored skin of citrus fruit, with an intense, slightly acidic flavor. The pith is the bitter white part between the zest and the pulp; don't use it.

Zester: to produce fine threads of zest (without pith).

Knife: take off the whole citrus peel, cut it into bands then into 1/12 in strips; remove the pith.

Microplane grater: for very fine zest with a powdered and coloring effect.

4 CANDYING ZEST

Blanch for 30 seconds in boiling water. Drain on paper towel. Make a sugar syrup, bring to the boil and remove from the heat. Add the zest and let it candy until use.

5 ROASTING NUTS

Spread them on a cookie sheet lined with baking paper. Put in a 340°F oven for 15–25 minutes, depending on their size. This develops their flavors.

CHOUX PASTRY TIPS

1 MAKING A PANADE & DRYING OUT

The first step in making choux pastry: mix water + salt + sugar + butter + flour away from heat.

Cook this "panade" to prepare it for the addition of the eggs: when the mixture is smooth, flatten it in the bottom of a saucepan and heat it without mixing. Leave it attached to the bottom of the saucepan, then, when you hear crackling, shake the saucepan to see the bottom: if a uniform thin film catches on the bottom, the pastry is dried.

2 CRAQUELIN

This "crumble" guarantees round, even and crispy choux puffs. Roll the mixture between two sheets of baking paper, then harden it in the refrigerator. Cut out discs, then place them on top of the choux balls before baking.

3 PIPING

Use cookie sheet lined with baking paper or a nonstick cookie sheet (but not a silicone mat).

Choux puffs: use a no. 8 plain decorating tip. Hold it perpendicular to the surface, ⅜ in above. Squeeze the pastry to obtain a disc of 1¼ in diameter. Never lift the pastry bag gradually. Cut off the flow of pastry by making a small, quick quarter turn, remaining at the height of the choux puff.

Éclairs: use a no. 14 plain decorating tip. Hold the pastry at a 45 degree angle to the surface. Squeeze the pastry evenly and move the bag quickly. Cut off as for the choux puffs or using a knife.

Circlet or long stick of choux: pipe choux puffs next to each other, so that they are just touching; they will swell and stick together during baking.

4 BAKING CHOUX PASTRY

Well-cooked choux pastry is golden, even brown. The cracks in the pastry must be colored. Open the oven after 20 minutes to let out any excess steam. Continue cooking while watching until the pastry colors (10–20 minutes more).

If the choux pastry is not dry enough, it will soften due to the moisture of the filling and of the refrigerator; indeed, it will collapse. A well-cooked choux pastry stays soft on the inside. It is possible to bake two sheets at once in a convection oven.

5 FILLING CHOUX PUFFS

Using the point of a knife, make a little hole in the puff. Take it in one hand, and fill it using a no. 6 plain decorating tip in constant contact with the puff and pressing on it. The filled puff should become heavy.

MACARON TIPS

1

2

3

1 MACARONAGE

This stage consists of mixing the Italian meringue with the almond paste using a dough scraper or a silicone spatula. Incorporate one-third of the meringue into the almond paste vigorously to loosen it. Incorporate the rest more delicately, crushing the mixture regularly to smooth it out. Scrape every part of the bowl to combine the two mixtures perfectly.

The dough should have a silky, smooth and slightly runny texture. If it is too liquid, the macarons will be flat; if is it not worked enough, they will be dented or cracked.

Check your macaronage with the ribbon test: take a large piece of mixture with the scraper or spatula and let it drop; the mixture should run continuously, in the form of a ribbon.

2 TEMPLATES & PIPING

Make a template by drawing staggered rows of circles of 1¼ in diameter on baking paper (see page 272). Hold the pastry bag vertical and squeeze to form discs within the circles. Don't lift the bag; keep the decorating tip ⅜ in from the surface. Make a quarter turn with the bag to cut off the dough. The point will smooth down on its own if the dough is well mixed.

3 BAKING

The shells cook rapidly (in about 12 minutes) at low temperature (300°F). It is possible to bake two sheets at once in a convection oven.

If the vanilla shells color too quickly, cover them with a sheet of baking paper.

Check the cooking after 10 minutes. Touch the shells with a finger: they should not move. If you don't cook them enough, the shells won't detach from the baking paper. If they are overcooked, they will be dry.

At the end of cooking, slide the baking paper off the sheet onto a wet work surface to make detaching them easier.

4 STORAGE

We recommend letting filled macarons mature in the refrigerator for 24 hours to allow osmosis: the ganache gives flavor to the shell and makes it more melt-in-the-mouth.

The cooked unfilled shells can be frozen for 3 months in an airtight container wrapped in plastic wrap. Filled macarons can be frozen if they are filled with ganache or jelly, but not pastry cream (which defrosts badly).

PASTRY TIPS

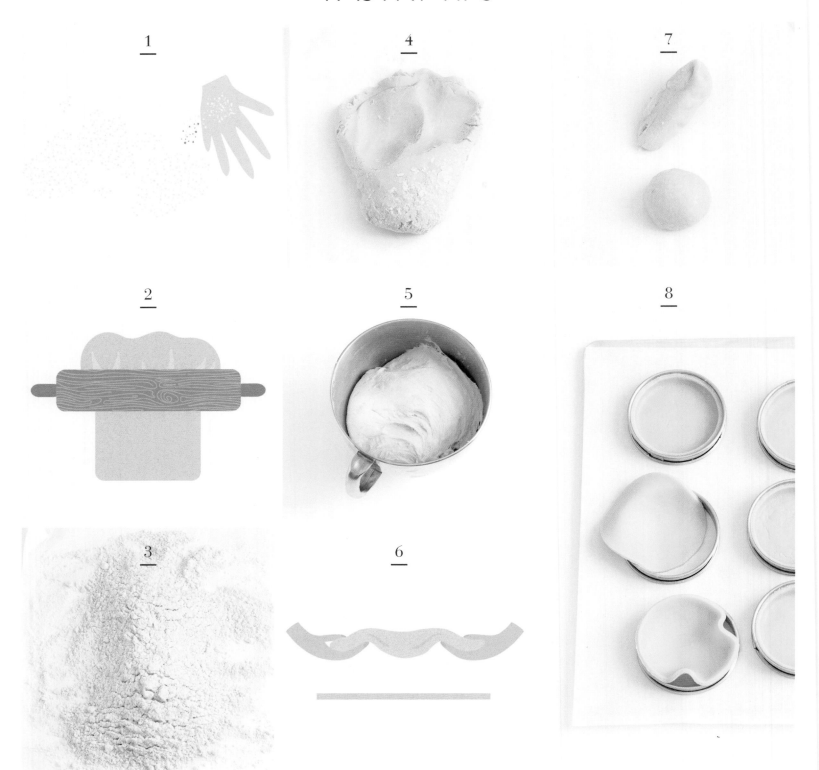

1 DUSTING WITH FLOUR

Spread a fine film of flour over the work surface so the dough doesn't stick. Don't use too much or it will modify the composition of the dough.

2 ROLLING THINLY

Using a rolling pin, roll the dough to the desired thickness on a floured work surface. Press on the rolling pin as evenly as possible and regularly turn the dough
a quarter turn as you go.

3 RUBBING IN BUTTER

Add butter cut into small cubes to the flour. Rub with the ends of your fingers and then between your hands, without crushing, until the mixture is sandy or resembles breadcrumbs.

4 LIGHT KNEADING

Crush the dough with the palm of your hand to check its smoothness. Do this once or twice.

5 KNOCKING BACK DOUGH

Punch or crush the dough after proofing to release the carbon dioxide gas.

6 AERATING DOUGH

Pass air under the dough by lifting it slightly. This prevents it from shrinking during baking.

7 FORMING A BALL OF DOUGH

Form the dough into a ball to allow even proofing. After dividing the dough, roll it between your palm and an unfloured work surface, so it holds a ball shape.

8 LINING A MOLD WITH PASTRY

A tart ring allows immediate unmolding, and resting it directly on a cookie sheet prevents the formation of air bubbles.

To line a tart ring, start by greasing it with butter. Roll the pastry onto the rolling pin to transport it without tearing it, then place it on the ring, taking care not to tear it. With one hand, lift the edges, with the other push it down to create a right angle. Push gently with your thumb, without leaving a mark. The pastry must stick well. You can also cut out a disc of rolled-out pastry (measure the diameter of the ring + twice the height of the sides).

PASTRY TIPS

9 FINISHING: PINCHING OR TRIMMING

Pinching the edges: nick the edges of the pastry before cooking to provide a neater finish. Use pastry pinchers or a small knife and make diagonal nicks. For a galette, such as an Epiphany cake, hold your fingers ³⁄₁₆ in from the edge of the pastry, pushing lightly. With the blunt side of the point of a knife, pull the pastry toward your fingers with the knife on an angle.

Trimming: cut off the surplus pastry with a utility knife or by running the rolling pin over the top of the ring.

10 BAKING PASTRY

A tart shell can be cooked unfilled or with its filling (such as for an apple tart). The majority of tart shells are cooked unfilled. The fillings are added warm (pastry cream) or uncooked. They are poured into the precooked tart shell then set in the refrigerator. There are several techniques for cooking unfilled pastry:

Sweet crust pastry and sugar crust pastry

If the pastry is used to line a tart ring on a cookie sheet and the lining is well done, the pastry can be cooked as is, without swelling up. For greater security, you can prick it with a fork or bake it blind.

If the pastry is used to line a tin with a bottom, such as a springform tin, and the lining is not perfect, bubbles of air could form and the pastry swell up. It is better to prick it with a fork or bake it blind.

Pie crust and puff pastry

These will swell up easily because of their water content. It is better to prick them with a fork or bake them blind.

Pricking with a fork: be careful not to create holes too big, particularly if you will be adding a liquid filling.

Baking blind: cut a disc of baking paper. Place it on the pastry and add cooking weights or dried beans.

11 CHECKING IF THE PASTRY IS COOKED

For unfilled pastry, lift the bottom using a frosting spatula: it should be uniformly golden.

For brioche, prick it with a knife: the blade should come out clean.

For sponges and cakes, touch it; your fingerprint should disappear and the cake should spring back.

For cookies (such as ladyfingers), look under the baking paper: the cookie should look very spongy and airy.

RECIPE LIST

INDEX OF INGREDIENTS

PÂTISSERIE AT HOME

Copyright © 2016 by Hachette Livre (Marabout).

All rights reserved. No part of this book may be used or reproduced in any manner whatsoever without written permission except in the case of brief quotations embodied in critical articles and reviews. For information address Harper Design, 195 Broadway, New York, New York 10007.

HarperCollins books may be purchased for educational, business, or sales promotional use. For information please email the Special Markets Department at SPsales@harpercollins.com.

Published in 2016 by
Harper Design
An Imprint of HarperCollins*Publishers*
195 Broadway
New York, NY 10007
Tel: (212) 207-7000
Fax: (855) 746-6023
harperdesign@harpercollins.com
www.hc.com

Distributed throughout North America by
HarperCollins *Publishers*
195 Broadway
New York, NY 10007

ISBN 978-0-06-244531-5
Library of Congress Control Number 2015954934

Printed in China

First Printing, 2016

Graphic design: Yannis Varoutsikos
Styling: Orathay Souksisavanh
Editing: Aurélie Legay and Natacha Kotchetkova
Translation: Nicola Young

First published by Hachette Livre (Marabout) 2014